PS 1517 .Z5 P42 1996

Pfaelzer,

Parlor radical

W9-DAE-330

NEW ENGLAND INSTITUTE
OF TECHNOLOGY
LEARNING RESOURCES CENTER

Parlor Radical

Parlor Radical

Rebecca Harding Davis and the
Origins of American Social Realism

Jean Pfaelzer

University of Pittsburgh Press

NEW ENGLAND INSTITUTE
OF TECHNOLOGY
LEARNING RESOURCES CENTER

3/97

3441764

Published by the University of Pittsburgh Press, Pittsburgh, Pa., 15260
Copyright © 1996, University of Pittsburgh Press
All rights reserved
Manufactured in the United States of America
Printed on acid-free paper
10 9 8 7 6 5 4 3 2 1

Library of Congress Cataloging-in-Publication Data

Pfaelzer, Jean.
    Parlor radical : Rebecca Harding Davis and the origins of American
social realism / by Jean Pfaelzer.
      p. cm.
    Includes index.
    ISBN 0-8229-3950-9 (alk. paper). — ISBN 0-8229-5607-1 (pbk. : alk. paper)
    1. Davis, Rebecca Harding, 1831–1910—Criticism and interpretation. 2. Literature
and society—United States—History—19th century. 3. Women and literature—
United States—History—19th century. 4. Radicalism—United States—History—
19th century. 5. Social problems in literature. 6. Social realism in literature.
7. Radicalism in literature. I. Title.
PS1517.Z5P48 1996
813'.4—dc20   96-12742
                                                       CIP

A CIP catalog record for this book is available from the British Library.

To my daughters
Johanna Justine Pfaelzer
and
Sophia Meira Panuthos

It always seemed to me that each human being, before going out into the silence, should leave behind him, not the story of his own life, but of the time in which he lived,—as he saw it,—its creed, its purpose, its queer habits, and the work which it did or left undone in the world. Taken singly, these accounts might be weak and trivial, but together, they would make history live and breathe.

Rebecca Harding Davis

Contents

Acknowledgments

ALONG THE WAY, many have listened and read, questioned and commented. I am particularly grateful to Carolyn Karcher, Andrea Kerr, Edwin Fussell, Violet Lippett, and Thorell Tsomondo who carefully read many versions, and to Amy Ott, Gwen Girvin, Johanna Pfaelzer, Jen Johnson, Shari Jacobson, Sue Serra, and Sandy Hawke who persevered in the archival and manuscript aspects of this project and of its sister, *A Rebecca Harding Davis Reader*, and to the members of the Nineteenth-Century American Women Writers Study Group, who continue to jostle my thinking about this difficult era. I am deeply indebted to the skillful librarians at the University of Virginia, the Huntington Library, the West Virginia Historical Society, and the Library of Congress. Jane Flanders of the University of Pittsburgh Press monitors my work with astute observations and graceful persistence. Peter Panuthos has graciously welcomed Rebecca Harding Davis to our table and travels for several years, and I have relied on his wisdom and love throughout this project.

My writing on Rebecca Harding Davis is made possible by the provision of a research office at the Library of Congress and by financial support from the National Endowment for the Humanities, the American Philosophical Society, and the University of Delaware.

I am very grateful indeed.

Parlor Radical

1 ❦ Introduction

History, Narrative, and Subjectivity

In "MARCIA" (1876) by Rebecca Harding Davis, a young woman comes to Philadelphia from her family's decaying plantation in Mississippi, explaining, "'I think I have something to say, if people only would hear it.'" "Vowing herself to literature," resolved to use her writing to "assist in the Progress of humanity, Marcia has chosen the "business" of authorship over the "business" of marriage.[1] But although her tales "remained in [his] mind strong and vivid as a desert by Gérôme or a moor by Broughton," a prominent publisher believes that the literary world is unprepared for Marcia's stories about Mississippi swamps, tired women, and slave quarters, "with all their dirt and dreary monotony." He rejects them all. Marcia still refuses to produce marketable stories about countesses, larks, or romance, "of which she knows nothing," and takes a job stitching socks for three dollars a week. After she nearly dies of starvation, she gives in to her father's plan to marry her to his brutal overseer and returns to Mississippi. In this story of a destitute woman who fails as a realist writer, Davis conflates Marcia's choices with the situation of American literature.

Rebecca Harding Davis shared Marcia's literary choices but not her literary destiny. During a long career (1861–1910), Davis produced over 275 stories,

12 novels (most published serially), 125 juvenile stories, over 200 essays that can be identified as hers, and perhaps an equal number of unsigned essays.[2] Her work was published in such prestigious journals as the *Atlantic Monthly*, *Harper's New Monthly*, *Scribner's Monthly*, as well as in more widely circulated magazines like the *Independent*, the *Saturday Evening Post*, *Lippincott's*, and *Peterson's*. In 1891, a decade past her peak as a writer of fiction, Davis wrote,

> I have a hope that this body of women who have the habit of broad and accurate thought will not always be content to expend their force in society, or even in charitable work. They will be stirred by the ambition to leave something more permanent behind them than reports of Sanitary or Archeological clubs, and will paint as they only can do, for the next generation, the inner life and history of their time with a power which shall make that time alive for future ages.[3]

For Davis, "the inner life and history of their time" were indivisible topics; portraits of women's economic, social, and political suffering would prompt the "echo [of] pathos" and stimulate a sympathetic reaction in her characters and, in turn, in her reader.

The emotive route to reform was not unique to Davis—the list of social and economic demands of the first American women's rights convention at Seneca Falls in 1848 was entitled the "Declaration of Sentiments," and expressions of grief, rage, and loss shape exhortations in abolitionist stories and poetry. In rooting the objective in the subjective, Davis appeals to feelings as well as to details from "life in the commonplace" to criticize systems that sanction child prostitution, abusive husbands, involuntary institutionalization, the rape of slaves, the isolation of housework and child rearing, the loneliness of single or unmarried women, the muteness of poverty, and the abandonment of wives as husbands flee impoverished rural communities in search of work and adventure.

Davis's stories of mill girls, child prostitutes, female journalists, utopians, opera singers, and circus performers call into question the very existence of a world untouched by the marketplace. The distinction between public and private breaks down with her working women who inhabit both worlds. Davis's wives and mothers understand that romance and the protective covenant of marriage are threatened by a disorderly public world in which businesses collapse, husbands are fired, and mortgages foreclosed. The family—the sentimental metaphor for desire and the image of material respite—emerges as an analogue of economic and gender tensions, rather than as an alternative social geography.

Davis's realistic depictions are frequently filtered, mediated by a narrator who frames, explicates, and evaluates the activities of working-class figures, lonely mothers, slaves, prostitutes, and alcoholics. As Jackson Lears observes, in the nineteenth century "reality itself began to seem problematic, something to be sought rather than merely lived."[4] According to Amy Kaplan, realistic narratives "enact this search not by fleeing into the imagination or into nostalgia for a lost past but by actively constructing the coherent social world they represent; and they do this not in a vacuum of fictionality but in direct confrontation with the elusive process of social change."[5] Because Rebecca Harding Davis was the voice of David decrying the Goliaths of slavery, industrialism, and patriarchy from the safe confines of a bourgeois home, activity appears to be an exhibition produced and staged for her readers' and her own consumption and observation. Davis's fiction bears out Kaplan's view of realism "as the staging of spectacles for the enforcement of power,"[6] but on this stage, Davis struggled to represent reality against competing and contradictory traditions of representation. Paradoxically, it is in her most bitter stories that she succumbs to literary stereotypes and sentimental visions of social stasis.

A moment in Charlotte Perkins Gilman's "The Yellow Wallpaper" (1891) helps me understand Davis's conflicts in representation as well as her muted legacy to her critics and biographers. In Gilman's searing portrait of repression, the distraught narrator, forbidden to write, recalls,

> I did write for a while in spite of them; but it does exhaust me a good deal—having to be so sly about it, or else meet with heavy opposition. . . . John says the very worst thing I can do is think about my condition, and I confess it always makes me feel bad. So I will let it alone and talk about the house.[7]

I find in Gilman's sly discursive shift an explanation for the ambivalent postures and contradictory forms of Davis's writing. Similarly discouraged by a repressive ideology from talking about "her condition," Davis also "let it alone" and talked about something else—the condition of other women. In

January 1863, she wrote Annie Fields that soon she was to be married and would move to Philadelphia: "It isn't easy for me to tell you this. I don't know why. I would rather tell other women's stories than my own."[8] To some degree, these stories would become one and the same.

As she told other women's stories, which inevitably fold back upon themselves, Davis withheld her own. Her journal is cut into hundreds of snippets, kept in a big envelope at the University of Virginia (and still catalogued with the papers of her son Richard Harding Davis). We do not know who cut her journal up, or why.[9] Aping William Burroughs, I have rearranged the snippets many times and created many Rebeccas. But these postmodernist Rebeccas have more to do with me and my moment in history than with hers. Her only extensive correspondence is with Annie Fields, at the time the wife of James Fields, Davis's literary mentor and editor of the *Atlantic Monthly*. She wrote to Annie Fields frequently, sometimes daily, between 1861 following the publication of "Life in the Iron-Mills" through the early period of Reconstruction, when her relationship with the magazine foundered. Yet in these hundred letters from Rebecca to Annie I find few allusions to the world of love and ritual, although there is an atypical comment in a letter to Annie Fields dated 6 December 1862:

> The other day a lady in Philadelphia wrote to me that a lady whom I dont [*sic*] know who had been in Boston told *her* that 'dear Mrs. Fields was quite in love with Miss Harding.' Why think Annie of that previous bit of heartbreak to your 'Jamie' [James Fields] travelling long away out here by such circuitous routes! I send Mrs. Slander back to you to strangle at your leisure —but send a kiss along with it meaning to make it *true* if I can some day.[10]

For the most part, Davis's letters to Annie contain comments like "I am doing the kind of knitting I've never done before." This is the only way Rebecca tells Annie that she is pregnant. Only in a period of intense despair—a time when, like Charlotte Perkins Gilman, she was treated for depression by S. Weir Mitchell and forbidden to write fiction—was she forthcoming.

Davis did reveal her feelings—her sense of injustice, her compassion, and her rage—in her work as a writer of political fiction, which is always, regardless of her historical topic, about female subjectivity. Clearly, the notion that feelings are expressed only in personal life is a fallacy. To understand Davis, we must read through the public issues that she forcefully inscribes in her fiction: slavery, industrialism, divorce, the lives of the new working women. My best route to Davis is through literary hermeneutics. When I get nervous about the inevitable distortions of this sort of biographical inquiry—from transference, identification, and projection (hers and mine)—I keep in mind Patricia Williams's observation that withholding is an ideological act; denial of one's self is "not the same as elimination of oneself; it is ruse, not reality. And the object of such ruse is to empower beyond the self, by appealing to shared understandings."[11]

To account for Davis's radical voice in stories about the Civil War, Reconstruction, factory life, and women's sexual fantasies, I turn to the stories themselves (and I acknowledge at the outset the tautology of what I have done). I believe it makes sense to read her fiction in order to interpret the facts of her biography because her fiction is about women's personal reactions to their very public social dislocations—the frustration of a woman struggling to gain admission to medical school; the confusion of a small-town woman who contemplates a divorce from her abusive husband; the quiet bravery of a mountain woman who leads runaway Confederate soldiers across icy gorges of the Appalachians; the rage of a slave who murders his master. Within the safe confines of public topics, Davis wrote with great bitterness about the private miseries of the female condition—the muteness of female poverty, the false utopia of family, and the isolation of housework and child rearing—even as she approached her own wedding.

From documents, letters, clippings, county records, biographies of Rebecca and of her son Richard Harding Davis, and from her own memoirs—a loose collection of self-reflexive essays modestly titled *Bits of Gossip*—we can reconstruct the facts of Davis's life. She was raised in Wheeling, an industrial and slave town just across the river from the free state of Ohio; she apparently wrote for the *Wheeling Intelligencer*; she witnessed West Virginia split from Virginia over secession; she watched Union troops loot her neighbor's house; and she knew about the discovery of knives hidden in a neighbor's barn in anticipation of John Brown's uprising.

To reconstruct Davis's understanding of history, however, I turn to her best fiction, written in the 1860s and 1870s, and explore the way she couples social realism to the ideology of sentimentalism—the available vocabulary for feelings. As Davis develops a mimetic aesthetic to represent the historic changes of her era—early industrialism, abolition, Reconstruction, urbanization, utopianism, manifest destiny, and the profound transformations in the lives of both working and middle-class women—she identifies with slaves, mill workers, impoverished women writers, destitute fishermen who scavenge in the wrecks along the Jersey shore, lonely women in coastal villages compelled to take rude tourists into their homes as boarders, and Tennessee mountain women who rescue runaway slaves. Not simply appropriating their outcast status, Davis posits a reciprocal discourse of repression and liberation among those whose creative and sexual passions are stymied by circumstance, gender, and race. These figures do not become ventriloquists' dummies.[12] Rather, her characters—prostitutes, mill workers, or fugitive slaves—grant Davis access to political discourse. Ironically, Davis's outcasts produce her basic freedom, the freedom of expression.[13] At the same time, this freedom of expression is intertextually bound—by the cultural traditions of sentimentalism, romanticism, and transcendentalism, and by the cultural stereotypes of women, slaves, and European immigrants, within which and against which she writes. Thus, my analysis of Davis is a study of history, literary traditions, and projection itself.

In the mid-nineteenth century, fiction had few conventions to represent a woman's public identity, a woman involved in what Mary Wollstonecraft called "the duties of life." Sentimentalism in particular suggested that a woman's dreams were at best egoistic and frequently aberrant. It is not then surprising, as Suzanne Clark observes, that the superiority of the rational over the sensible became fundamental to the history of liberal feminism.[14] Profoundly conflicted, Davis represents both aspects of this divisible psyche. Further, her narrative forms in themselves challenge the split between public and private, and thus attack the solipsistic self that hovers at the edge of transcendentalism. Davis's characters locate themselves both in the world and in the matrix of feelings and then explore the painful tensions of these ever competing demands. Davis makes the private space public in order to show that emotional life cannot transcend history. Her female doctors, "mill girls," slaves, and authors inherit and interrogate sentimental assumptions about domestic confinement in order to raise public and, thus, political questions.

During the time when American literary women such as Lydia Maria Child, Harriet Beecher Stowe, and Charlotte Perkins Gilman emerge as activists in abolition, suffrage, and property law reform, Davis remains an ambivalent literary historian—somewhat like her narrating figure from "Life in the Iron-Mills" who invites us to "come right down" and hear her story of factory life. Davis writes of isolated, abandoned, and uneducated women who search for an empathic community (often in their family) only to be disappointed by alcoholic husbands and indifferent children. Davis's astute depiction of female ambivalence confirms those theories that question the possibility of psychological coherence. Her characters are themselves what Theresa de Lauretis terms the "site of differences" that are racial, sexual, economic, cultural, and often at odds with each other.[15] They remain mired in conflicts as Davis resists the nineteenth-century novel's paradigm of the unified self.

Like Davis, I cannot presume to tell another woman's story with constancy, objectivity, or even the comfort of a reliable critical genre. Although her personal sensibility remains elusive and her public voice frightened at its own insurgency, we do know that Rebecca Blaine Harding was born in 1830, lived first in the cotton plantation country of Big Spring (now Huntsville) Alabama, where her father, Richard Harding, a British emigré, a quixotic, displaced, and unsuccessful businessman, had taken his young bride, Rachel Leet Wilson.[16] Rebecca's father was stern and distant—a man, she recalled, of "no energy or business ability whatever."[17] Still, she said that he bestowed on her his social conscience, his hatred for "vulgar American life," and his love of telling stories. A rather unsettled but whimsical man, Richard Harding took his children on fanciful flights into the Middle Ages with Monsieur Jean Crapeaud, an imaginary twelve-inch knight who lived in a locked closet cut into the dining room chimney. Released only by her father, M. Crapeaud would carry a drawn sword and a banner, blazoned with the lilies of France, into dungeons, high towers, and gilded salons. In Davis's many stories that center on a father-daughter relationship, the father is generally a kind if ineffectual man who often misunderstands his daughter's intelligence and independence and is "savagely" jealous of her lovers.

By contrast, she admired her mother, "the most accurate historian and grammarian" she had ever known, who had "enough knowledge to fit out half a dozen modern college bred women."[18] It was Rachel Harding who gave Rebecca a sense of history and a love of literary style and precision. Unlike Richard, Rachel rooted her tales in regionalism and realism, early correctives to the myths of pastoralism, southern romanticism, and the prevailing fascination with transcendentalism. Rachel's stories were often of southern women who did not lead the picturesque idle life which their northern sisters imagined and envied: "Much of the day was spent in weighing provisions or cutting out clothes for field hands. They had few books— an odd volume of poems and their Bibles, which they read devoutly—and no amusements but an occasional hot supper to which they went in faded gowns of ancient cut."[19]

When Rebecca was five, the family moved to Wheeling (then in Virginia) where she lived until her marriage at age thirty-one. Like Big Springs, Wheeling was a village: "The world that we lived in when I was a child would seem silent and empty to this generation. There were no railways in it, no automobiles or trolleys, no telegraphs, no sky-scraping houses. . . . There was not, from sea to sea, a trust or a labor union. Even the names of those things had not yet been invented."[20] The town of Wheeling and the surrounding mountains of the Alleghenies would become compelling influences on Davis's writing.

During Rebecca's childhood, Wheeling would grow before her eyes into a booming industrial town. As the site for much of Davis's fiction, it also remained a border town. Built at the crossroads of the Ohio River and the National Road, Wheeling stood at a line between West and East, South and North, Confederacy and Union, plantation and mill—tense contrasts that would impel Davis's best fiction. As a young girl she would gaze down at steamships bound for St. Louis or New Orleans and watch as huge vans, laden with bales of cotton, trundled from the slave plantations of the South toward the northern industrial towns. As she saw the white-topped Conestoga wagons carrying emigrants from Norway, Poland, and Germany to "the Ohio" (which, as she observed, the whole West was then vaguely called), real history became more exciting than her father's fables: "These wagons were full of romance to us children. They came up with these strange people out of far-off lands of mystery, and took them into the wilderness, full of raging bears and panthers and painted warriors, all to be fought in turn. We used to look after the children peeping out at us with bitter envy for . . . we never left home."[21] As an adult, however, she would find this border conflicted and emotionally dangerous and its complexities misunderstood by New England intellectuals.

Wheeling gave Davis a closer knowledge of slavery and the Civil War than most northern writers. The industrial mountain town flanked the North and South; it had an active slave trade, yet, located across the river from the free state of Ohio, it also had become a station on the underground railroad, and Davis believed it was picked by John Brown as a site for his insurrection. In 1861, after a painful debate over the issues of slavery and union, Wheeling also became the political center of the split from Virginia. Just a few blocks from Rebecca's house, a citizens' convention voted to nullify Virginia's Ordinance of Secession and to pass a new constitution granting gradual emancipation to slaves. By 1862, General Rosecrans had headquartered the Mountain Garrison across the street from the Harding house, and Davis spent the early war years under martial law, living on the edge of a battleground.

At her mother's insistence, Rebecca received considerably more education than most girls of her time. Rachel Harding was her daughter's first and perhaps most influential teacher. She urged Rebecca to read Shakespeare's *Julius Caesar* and *The Tempest* when she was eight years old. As a young girl, Rebecca also read "Bunyan and Miss Edgeworth and Sir Walter."[22] One day she climbed into her tree house with a cheap collection of stories that included two or three pirated from Nathaniel Hawthorne's *Twice-Told Tales*: in these tales she first discovered that the "commonplace" belonged in literature:

> Among them were two or three unsigned stories which I read over so often that I almost know every line of them by heart now. . . . There was no talk of enchantment in them. But in these papers the commonplace folk and things which I saw every day took on a sudden mystery and charm, and, for the first time, I found that they, too, belonged to the magic world of knights and pilgrims and fiends.[23]

As Rebecca grew older, the Hardings hired tutors for Rebecca and her brother, Wilse. Finally, for three years, 1845–1848, she attended the Female Seminary in her mother's home town of Washington, Pennsylvania. Although Rebecca was valedictorian, her graduation (at the head of her class) marked the end of her formal education, which thereafter depended on that of Wilse, who was able to attend Washington College in Pennsylvania. In his summer vacations he would pass along to Rebecca his recent knowledge of the German language and his growing fascination with German romanticism, in particular the works of Johann von Goethe and Johann Gottlieb Fichte. Rebecca would later reject the German romantics as obsessive and egotistical, but Rachel Harding's and Nathaniel Hawthorne's interest in "commonplace folk" would most profoundly influence the course of her writings.

Davis's literary apprenticeship began some time in the late 1850s, when she met Archibald W. Campbell, editor of the local Wheeling *Intelligencer*,[24] a daily paper with the largest circulation in western Virginia. During these antebellum years, the *Intelligencer* reprinted national news, reported secessionist proceedings, covered local events and trade reports, reprinted best-selling fiction, and twice a week published poetry.[25] In the late 1850s Rebecca apparently sent *The Intelligencer* reviews, poems, and, of greatest pleasure to herself, editorials because, as she wrote to Campbell, "I have the most insane ambition that way." (Davis later dismissed these early journalistic pieces. In discussing her development as a writer, she wrote to James Fields, "Whatever I wrote before the Iron Mill story I would not care to see again—chiefly verses and reviews written under circumstances that made them unhealthful. I would rather they were forgotten.")[26] Nonetheless, like her other ambitions, writing editorials was not an "insane" idea on Davis's part for by this time Margaret Fuller had already edited the *Dial* and Child had edited the *National Anti-Slavery Standard*. In any case, since none of Davis's early pieces has been identified, there is nothing really to prepare us for "Life in the Iron-Mills," a novella accepted for publication in the *Atlantic Monthly* in 1861 when Rebecca was thirty-one years old.

That same year she met and quickly planned to marry a young attorney, L. Clarke Davis, who had written her a fan letter after reading "Life in the Iron-Mills." With her career taking shape during a moment of great political upheaval, painfully felt at the most local level, and with her marriage to Clarke, an abolitionist, a few months away, Davis wrote a series of stories that focus on the psychological brutalities of slavery and the divisive and traumatic experiences of rural life in a border state during the Civil War.

Anticipating career and children, Davis never believed that marriage would mark the end of her writing. Late in January she wrote to Annie, "I must have leave to say my word in the Atlantic as before, when the spirit moves me. It is necessary for me to write—well or ill—you know every animal has speech and that is mine."[27] Within six months of the wedding, despite her contentment with Clarke and her pleasure at her research desk at the Philadelphia Free Library, Rebecca suffered an acute attack of nervous exhaustion that stemmed, it seems, from a difficult pregnancy, from sharing a small house with Clarke's family, and from tending to Clarke and his sister, who were both ill. During this breakdown, Rebecca was treated by Dr. S. Weir Mitchell who prescribed for her the same rest cure that Charlotte Perkins Gilman so formidably describes in "The Yellow Wallpaper." Davis's impressions of this frightening year appear in "The Wife's Story," written during a time of despondency at middle-class poverty, her concern that her talent was unauthentic, and her terror that her delayed marriage and imminent childbirth would destroy her new literary reputation. Despite recurrent images in Davis's fiction of husbands thwarting women's creative ambitions, there seems to be no evidence, however, that Clarke Davis tried to impede Rebecca's career, although he did encourage her to write for popular journals. In fact, he frequently acted as an agent, as a broker, and at least once as a collaborator; never, according to their son, Richard Harding Davis, did Clarke edit Rebecca's writing.

The publication of her first story, "Life in the Iron-Mills," in the *Atlantic* immediately gained her the attention of the coterie of transcendentalists surrounding James and Annie Fields, who invited her to Boston. There, in 1862, she met Louisa and Bronson Alcott, Hawthorne, Holmes, and Emerson, whom she called "memorable ghosts": "While they thought they were guiding the real world, they stood quite outside of it, and never would see it as it was."[28] Scorning the visionaries who talked in "strained high notes of exaltation"[29] of a Civil War they had never seen, and who analyzed the spiritual influence of fruit, she traced the political inertia within romanticism to the narcissism of its philosophers.

Transcendentalism, she held, was a philosophy that lacked the backbone of fact; its theories were like bubbles blown from a child's pipe, "queer reflections on them of sky and earth and human beings . . . all a little distorted."[30] In particular, Davis satirized Bronson Alcott as a man who had covered miles with paper while his home was bleak and his children hungry, and, along similar lines, Emerson, who studied souls as "a philologist does words or an entomologist beetles," only to forget that "the negro or I were in the world—having taken from each what he wanted."[31] Such self-absorption, marked as insensitivity to "the Negro or I," led Davis to distrust the transcendentalists' faith in their discovery of the "new god" within themselves.[32] For Davis, the disengaged and mythologizing literary practices of romanticism were inseparable from the male egotism of its authors. Her impressions of Bronson Alcott and Emerson in particular shaped her first novel, *Margret Howth*, in which efforts toward social change are informed by what Davis took to be the egoistic and solipsistic tendencies of transcendentalism.

By 1862, as the issues of abolition and the Civil War swept through Wheeling, Davis began to write about slavery and the war. "John Lamar," "Blind Tom," and "David Gaunt" are uncommon explorations of the rage and repression of slavery and its powerful impact on white identity. With "Promise of the Dawn" (1863), "Paul Blecker" (1863), and "The Wife's Story" (1864), Davis launched a series of short stories that focus on women's isolated and frustrated lives. In the early 1860s she invoked and portrayed fervent emotions as appropriate reactions to women's plight, splicing the political and the sentimental through her understanding of misogyny and female inequality. These tales explore women's uncomfortable discovery that despite their changed roles during and after the Civil War and their new role in an emerging industrial society, they were still illiterate, unemployed, impoverished, and frequently dependent on cruel or inept men. During the sixties Davis appropriated the subversive elements within sentimentalism to expose the pain of an ethos that repressed women's independence, individuality, and creativity,[33] even as her female characters embark on its conservative path from independence to subservience, from initiative to stasis. During the seventies these victimized female characters reemerge in Davis's fiction as New Women whose professional, sexual, and political energies are seen as serious threats to bourgeois culture.

The only alternative Davis sees to the culture of domestic restriction and northern industrialism is found in stories of rural life that polarize city and country, civilization and wilderness, mind and body. In "Out of the Sea"

(1865), *Dallas Galbraith* (1868), "A Faded Leaf of History" (1873), and "The Yares of Black Mountain" (1875), Davis describes how literary tradition has delimited nature, and she exposes cultural conventions that suggest that rural life, like marriage, is simple, static, and continuous. She portrays the ways in which assumptions about nature have become inescapably bound to commerce, slavery, post–Civil War nationalism, and patriarchy, and concludes that nature in itself offers no utopian telos for women.

The late 1870s was an era marked by a series of economic depressions, increased hostility to European and Chinese immigrants, brutal wars against Native Americans, the collapse of Reconstruction, and the rise of movements and organizations that expressed the radical energy and political engagement of women. Paradoxically, this era also marks the last period of Davis's creative engagement of fiction and history. The power and pain of her female figures had undercut her own plots, giving the lie to her endings of masculine superiority and control. Davis's fiction in these years describes the professional and psychological dilemmas of work, suffrage, and divorce as it reveals her struggle to find a literary form to represent women's public activities. Ultimately, she was unable to heal the disjunctions between the literary marriage plot and the new realities of women's lives. The failure to find a usable form, closely tied to Davis's own rage about the female condition and her ambivalence about the New Woman, resulted in years of literary silence. Davis never rediscovered the powerful literary voice of the decades of the 1860s and 1870s.

Unable to preserve that voice in her historical fiction, Davis began to write numerous articles, essays, and editorials that soon established her as a serious commentator and social historian. During the seventies Davis began her long affiliation with the *New York Daily Tribune* and the *Independent*, although so far I have been unable to assign authorship to most editorials in the *Tribune* written in these years. During the 1880s and 1890s, in the topical and journalistic essay Davis would revisit issues she had been unable to resolve in her earlier fiction. Between 1870 and 1910, her concerns about alcohol addiction, political corruption, the condition of mental institutions, the premature demise of Reconstruction, the treatment of Native Americans, the restricted job opportunities for women, and the role of women in utopian communities appear in her journalistic essays.

During these decades, Davis also published travel narratives based on extended vacation visits and thorough research of rural life and local history. These pieces stress the cultural differences between North and South, England and the United States, as well as among African-Americans, Native Americans, and European immigrants. "By-Paths in the Mountains" (1880), her long study of the mountain people of Virginia, West Virginia, and Maryland, mingles narrative, adventure, character sketches, botany, and social analysis. "In the Gray Cabins of New England" (1895), Davis suggests that single women and widows who live in lonely New England villages, taking opium or compulsively cleaning house, should find industrial training or emigrate to the West. In "The Newly Discovered Woman" (1893) she describes her intimidation at the "shrill feminine hurly-burly"[34] and decries the new "sex-consciousness" of modern woman, exultant in her guilds, Chautauquan circles, colleges, and charities but unaware of the contribution of pre-industrial women.[35] Davis is however consistently concerned about female aging. The subject of "The Middle-Aged Woman" (1875) has "crows' feet at either temple, and yellowish blotches on the flesh below the soggy under-jaw," yet survives "the prison house of nature,"[36] while the mountain woman feeds her family on corn cakes, fried opossum, and rye coffee.

Around the turn of the century, Davis wrote a series of essays on the failed legacy of Reconstruction. Revisiting the themes of "John Lamar," "Blind Tom," and *Waiting for the Verdict*, she analyzes racism's enduring role in limiting economic equality for northern blacks and concludes that political rights without industrial training and financial security are irrelevant. Anticipating the views of Booker T. Washington, in "Some Testimony in the Case" (1885) Davis argues that freedmen need training in mechanics and carpentry rather than in Latin and metaphysics, and she questions the utility of higher education for African Americans. In "Two Points of View" (1897), "Two Methods With the Negro" (1898), and "The Black North" (1902), she enters the debate between Booker T. Washington and W. E. B. Du Bois on the side of Washington, concluding that "the negro to live must find work"— preferably in the South.[37] Although her conclusions are perhaps consistent with her southern background, throughout these essays Davis also points to the economic and psychological damage of demeaning racial stereotypes. While claiming to understand Du Bois's rage at the social and economic failure of Reconstruction, she argues that blacks must cease striving for white recognition and should instead establish schools such as the Hampton Industrial School where they could train to become carpenters, plumbers, and mill hands for the new industries in the South. At the same time, she speaks forcibly against the "puerile prejudice" of southern apologists who support convict labor, which she calls another species of slavery, and she denounces northern trade unions that refuse to admit blacks.

With the rise of American imperialism in the 1890s, Davis revisits the issue of "David Gaunt"—the romanticization of war—as she speaks to the dangers of American and British military interventions overseas. Written in reaction to the massacre at Khartoum, "The Work Before Us" (1899) describes British plans to establish an African university that will teach only in English, insist on Western dress and British manners, and in general, "force [Africans] into our mold of life."[38] Davis sardonically observes that Lord Kitchener, backed by the enthusiastic applause of Queen Victoria and the English people, "thinks that the Sudanese can be as easily turned into an Englishman as into a corpse,"[39] and she goes on to compare his attitude to America's treatment of Native Americans. In "The Mean Face of War" (1899) Davis again describes the dangers of militarism as she watches Americans eagerly support the invasion of Cuba and "policing" actions in the Philippines. She predicts that politicians—"captives" of monopolies and trusts—will make war a "regular business" and, in lieu of jobs, will offer "the flag" to the high numbers of unemployed and bored young men. Davis returns to the theme of pacifism in "Lord Kitchener's Methods" (1901), where she denounces the hypocrisies of Englishmen who loudly protest the slaughter of albatrosses by British fishermen but remain silent when British soldiers massacre peasants in Ireland or India or are ordered to starve Boer farmers into surrender by burning their homes and crops and driving families into the barren veldt. Recalling General Sherman's march through Georgia, she warns that Americans too should be aware of the long hatred that follows brutal suppression—in Ireland, India, or the American South.

These astute essays that mark the end of Davis's fifty-year career as a writer suggest to me that Davis had failed to find a mimetic aesthetic to embody her political animus. During these years as a literary journalist and essayist, Davis traveled extensively in the Northeast and South and raised her three children. Of her daughter, Nora, her attendant and companion, she says virtually nothing. Her middle child, Charles Belmont, she calls a "sequel to the story—an after piece—an every-day matter,"[40] although it was Charles who managed her financial matters and, in his own writing, carried on her interest in "underdogs." From the time of his birth in 1864, Davis showered an overwhelming and obsessive attention to the whims, needs, education, and writing of her eldest son, Richard Harding Davis. It is hard not to conclude that in this lifelong concern with Richard, Rebecca deflected attention from her own career. She died in 1910 and is buried in Philadelphia with her husband in the same grave, under a headstone marked "L. Clarke Davis and his wife."

LOCATED AT THE intersection of subjectivity and history, this study investigates the politics of Davis's literary forms. During her most prolific years as a writer of fiction, powerful forces—the antislavery movement, the Civil War, and industrialization—were exploding the myth that women do not inhabit public life. Although Davis began writing just at the time that Nancy Armstrong suggests "writing invaded, revised and contained the household by means of strategies that distinguished private from social life, and thus detached sexuality from political history,"[41] Davis thrusts her creative, erotic, and competent female characters into the world. As her female characters participate in the destruction of an outdated concept of the household, they suddenly find themselves vulnerable in a world they did not make. Searching for an aesthetic to tell their stories, Davis repudiated the sentimental ethos that values a woman for her virtues while it restricts the implementation of those virtues in society; she could not, however, fully repudiate the sentimental form. In stories about women written in the 1860s, Davis first attacks sentiment's notion that a separate female sphere offers women a zone of refuge, community, culture, and circumscribed freedom. Frequently, an ironic narrator lets us know that the punishment and self-doubt women endure when they pursue autonomous lives is unearned and unmerited.

Davis returned subjectivity to its place in history. But how to inscribe history in female narrative? Davis needed to invent a form to depict the many kinds of activities and behavior of mid-nineteenth-century American women other than home, heart, and courtship. In sentimentalism Davis found ways to use domestic and sexual relationships as metaphors for other kinds of power relationships; her female characters typify many forms of social subjugation—racial, economic, and ecological. In the 1860s, she began to experiment with the domestic language of sexual relations to depict political relations in an enslaving and industrializing society. At the same time, she found that marriage itself was no longer self-contained and had come to embody the vocabulary of the marketplace. In Davis's stories about divorce, inheritance, or parental authority, the family subsumes rather than abandons political necessity. She frequently writes about married women whose creativity atrophies inside the house; once outside the house, their authority no longer derives from their husbands. Meanwhile, as Davis's literary households succumb to economic strain, her literary husbands lose status, control, and agency.

Davis drew from sentimental fiction and the domestic novel portraits of daily life and domestic power often credited to realism. In many of her stories, she included signs of what Elaine Showalter terms female "covert rebellion"; to undercut images of stoic womanly suffering and to record acts of female resistance, Davis pictures sexual solidarity among women, the plight of unmarried women, feminized male heroes, and engaging female rebels.[42] Her tales of the sixties and seventies typify Claudia Tate's suggestion that nineteenth-century women's texts appropriate sentimental conventions "to mask the heroine's growing self-consciousness, rationality, and ultimately her desire to redefine feminine propriety . . . and participate in emergent nineteenth century bourgeois society."[43] What is unique to Davis is that she locates her strong, tired, and homely women in mills, fields, publishing houses, or stops along the underground railroad, where they are subject to inexorable economic, sexual, and geographic pressures. If in Davis we find impotent characters we also find characters who can conceptualize their situation and who survive.

Thus, Davis blurs the public-private distinction from which the very notion of gender derives. She astutely pictures confusion and at times, unbearable pain, in midcentury women's conflicted identities. As the walls of domesticity tumble down, her female characters redefine their relationship to the world outside—sometimes tormented by guilt, as in "The Wife's Story," or subject to abuse, as in "The Story of Christine" (1866), yet still unwilling to live in partitioned female space, as in "The Harmonists" (1866). Frequently, as in "Blind Tom," "Berrytown" (1873), and "Dolly" (1874), Davis invokes the sentimental image of a restricted body to oppose the notion that the soul of the female or slave thrives in constriction, violation, or humiliation. Throughout her writings, Davis questions the sentimental tenet that the home is a refuge from the tensions of the workplace and that capitalism offers a protective covenant for women.

Nonetheless, even as images of emotional and intellectual hunger undo the domestic promise, at the end of her stories Davis restores the angel to the house. Yet her portraits of marriage suggest that neither the redemptive power of love nor the selfless joy of motherhood will endure for her female characters. Women's unfilled needs for creativity and self-definition persist beyond the ending. Davis's stories expose her profound ambivalence about the domestic contract whereby women gain authority by redeeming men, rather than by pursuing their own lives and power. Thus she follows the pattern of earlier sentimental tales, in which Joanne Dobson finds "a strong emotional undertow that pulls the reader in the opposite direction."[44]

In stories of slavery, prostitution, and "the marriage market," Davis returns to the sentimental figure of the body, first ironized in the powerful, demanding korl woman of "Life in the Iron-Mills." Her representation of slavery and prostitution clearly indicate the limits of the sentimental ideology of sacrifice and passive submission, which, as Nancy Bentley observes, is "naturalized" in the female body. Bentley further notes that sentimentalism "coexists with another principle—also expressed in the language of the body —that 'vindicates' liberty through the masculine pleasures of inflicting righteous violence."[45] In Davis's representation of the female body, the spirit of revolt coexists with the spirit of subservience and each implicates the other.

Even though Davis locates her domestic crises in authentic historical contexts, her plots work themselves out on the psychological plane and hence, they reinforce the notion that resolution lies in subjectivity and empathy. Traditionally, sympathy rather than "righteous violence" was the intended effect of literary suffering. Particularly in Davis's stories that are mediated by an ironic narrator, however, sympathy slides into visions of hierarchy, pity, and difference. In reading her tales about women, slavery, and poverty, it is useful to keep in mind Philip Fisher's admonition to distinguish the successful politics of sentimental representation from the representation itself.

Sentimentalism, he suggests, extends "normal states of primary feeling to people from whom they have been previously withheld . . . [who] earn the right to human regard by means of the reality of their suffering."[46]

Because Davis believed that female suffering promoted an understanding of other sorts of oppression, the politicization of sympathy and the feminization of public life became her fundamental literary strategy. In particular, the repression and exile of domesticity positioned women to understand slavery. Like many abolitionists, Davis believed that women's moral superiority, which originated in child rearing and domestic work, gave them an understanding of the best needs of a community as a whole. In "John Lamar," "Blind Tom," and her Reconstruction novel, *Waiting for the Verdict* (1867), she shows how slavery erases the border between private life and economic life. In Davis's narratives, women and blacks endure parallel forms of control—physical abuse, psychological intimidation, economic deprivation, unrealizable goals, and painful limits on their aspirations. For the slave, however, neither the home nor the plantation offers refuge. If the endings of Davis's stories about white women repudiate traditional sentimental gestures of survival such as deceit, madness, and creativity, she invokes these same gestures as understandable forms of slave resistance. Rejecting the sentimental view that suffering was a form of martyrdom, she challenges the era's mutually enforcing romanticization of domesticity and slavery.

Davis's representation of African Americans further complicates sentimentalism by frustrating its promise that virtue will earn material reward. In sentimental fiction, powerlessness eventually earns self-worth, romantic justice, and sometimes personal revenge. In Davis's vision, however, slavery externalizes sentimental suffering; the pain of slavery is historical, political, institutional and public, and hence, cannot be resolved by sentimental closures. Her descriptions of the tortured and overworked bodies of slaves also subvert the sentimental notion that the body offers a stable grammar of social and psychological signs. Hence, the representation of slavery impelled Davis toward realism, a form in which powerlessness requires and receives public and secular responses.

Yet while Davis, raised in slaveholding Virginia, clearly exposes the brutality of slavery, her portraits of slaves themselves are tinged with ambivalence. The representation of black characters becomes the site of her contested understanding and loyalties. In these stories two discursive traditions collide: rhetorics from abolition, Quakerism, transcendentalism, and the social gospel conflict with rhetorics of early eugenics, southern romanticism, and proslavery apologetics. Davis's troubling images of African Americans as lazy, subservient, and at times bestial confront images of blacks that reveal her belief in human rationality, conscience and growth. At the same time, Davis rejects facile and romanticized images of the Civil War itself. She was haunted by the suffering she saw on both sides. With the publication of "David Gaunt" in the *Atlantic* in 1862, early in the war, Davis sent north a portrait of a West Virginia village painfully divided in its loyalties over union, religion, and the role of women.

Davis found it impossible to reconcile the politics of sympathy with romantic notions of liberal individualism. While true femininity represents social commitment, martyrdom, and life in the commonplace, romanticism, she thought, promises self-indulgence and solipsism. "Life in the Iron-Mills" anticipates her later stories of marriage, slavery, and women's employment by raising the question that haunted Emerson and Thoreau: the conflict between duties to the self and duties to the world, between solipsism and commitment. If indeed, as Davis reiterates about industrial poverty, "there is no hope that it will ever end,"[47] the fault lies in part in the romantic self-absorption of the reader, who, like the visitors to the iron mill, has gone out slumming in her story: "You, Egoist, or Pantheist, or Arminian, busy in making straight paths for your feet on the hills . . . do not see it clearly."[48]

In *Margret Howth* and "The Harmonists" Davis shows her mistrust of any formula whereby the dreams of a single man would shape a community. Yet the tension between transcendentalism and sentimentalism in her fiction exposes her conflicted stance about American womanhood. For example, in "The Wife's Story" she equates women's desire for autonomy with romantic egoism at the same time that she suggests that motherhood, female sexuality, and marriage represent the death of the unique self and the end of women's links to social community. Writing from 1870 on in a row house which the family called the "centre of the Universe," Davis seeks philosophies forged through dependence, conflicted though it may be, and she calls into question masculine ideas of identity based on autonomy or repudiation of domestic connections and honors feminine ideas of identity forged within relationships.[49] Nonetheless, the image of a mother, the traditional source of female intimacy, is rare in Davis's fiction. Like many female authors of her time, Davis usually repressed the figure of the mother who is often absent, silenced, or dead,[50] even as she seems to have heartily enjoyed mothering her three children.

From within these critiques of sentimentalism and transcendentalism, Davis founded a prototypical realist discourse. She believed that she could represent material reality by depicting working-class and ordinary middle-class people, by inscribing vernacular language (which was usually quite accurate), by representing characters in relations to institutions, geography, and class struggles, by embedding her plots in historical contingency, and finally by questioning symbols that signify human universals.[51] Davis's realist perspective, style, and vocabulary derive from her belief in human agency and her faith in the capacity of language to connote, if not denote, material reality. Through travels, library research, extensive reading, and rigorous editing, she strove for mimetic accuracy and disdained universal truisms. I believe that Davis presumed on the ability of her language to refer, to typify, to depict. This reading of the fictional writings of Rebecca Harding Davis confirms Amy Kaplan's observation that "realists do more than passively record the world outside; they actively create and criticize the meanings, representations, and ideologies of their own changing culture."[52]

Davis was a founder of American realism, in the forefront of the tradition promoted by a series of editors of the *Atlantic*—James Russell Lowell, James Fields, William Dean Howells, Thomas Bailey Aldrich, and Horace Scudder—who sought an aesthetic that could depict authentic regional details. Influenced by T. W. Higginson, they wanted a form to debunk the over-generalized descriptions, essentialist characterizations, and pastoral nostalgia of sentimentalism. With her focus on the daily lives of women, Davis launched a school of feminist realism that would include the grim antipatriarchal stories of Rose Terry Cooke, the ironic tales of rural matriarchies of Mary E. Wilkins Freeman, the fictional studies of early class consciousness of Elizabeth Stuart Phelps.

Davis also anticipated the close observation of southern botany, geology, and language of such later regional writers as Mary Murphy and Constance Fenimore Woolson. As early as the 1860s, Davis began to explore an alternative vision to the culture of northern industrialism. In "Life in the Iron-Mills" the narrator remarks that the "dream of green fields and sunshine is a very old dream—almost worn out, I think."[53] But it was not worn out for Davis. Rooted in her childhood in the mountains of West Virginia and in her frequent trips to a farm in Manasquan on the barren New Jersey coast are tales of rural life that depict the tensions between the ideology of Jeffersonian agrarianism, the conventions of pastoralism, the popularity in fiction and drama of comic folk figures, and the economic realities of rural life.

Because political, economic, and cultural relationships between city and country signify relationships between men and women, nature and woman appear mutually available and vulnerable to human intervention, control, or even definition. Based on years of trips to Point Pleasant on the New Jersey coast, to Lewes on the Delaware coast, and frequent travels through the rural South, Davis saw rural life as a site of work and politics. Nature was neither the "innocent amusement of a garden's narrow space," by which some women authors tried to tame or erase the primal wilderness nor the masculine site of a brutal exodus to an unpromising land, an eroticized site of violent conquest, or provocative reminder of civilized destruction.[54] In "Earthen Pitchers" Davis sees the wildness in nature as a dangerous and layered symbol of a woman's unconscious that she must control and domesticate; in "A Faded Leaf of History" she sees nature as a conflated site of inexorable nationalism and interracial female empathy; and in "The Yares of Black Mountain" she views the wilderness as a complex metaphor for female community, maternal power, and political resistance. Her stories of rural life challenge the analogy between woman and nature in which both are seen as mutually backward, ignorant, and fertile. Neither woman nor nature is innocent. Even rural women cannot transcend the artificiality of society; a life close to nature provides neither nurture, abundance, nor unalienated labor. Even so, at times Davis's characters succumb to fantasies of a harmonious natural place where they will find a maternal presence, an enclosing receptive environment that offers painless satisfaction.[55] Her stories that picture the rise of civilization through domination of nature represent the triumph of masculine values.[56]

Davis repopulates Arcadia with intelligent and sturdy women who fish with harpoons, rescue tourists trapped in bogs of quicksand, track a horse, build a log cabin in a blizzard, find a wounded lover in a blinding snow-storm, and row out to sea in a gale to save a shipwrecked son. Abandoning the "heroine's text" of seduction, betrayal, and marriage, she describes the realities of rural relationships—at times comfortable, caring, and mutually involved in the projects of agrarian work and rural survival, at other times lonely, repressive, and intellectually barren. In her regional stories, Davis recasts the rhetorics of romanticism in order to portray rural life and nature itself as a female community. Nature emerges as an image of dependence rather than autonomy, intimacy rather than isolation, speech rather than silent awe. In a feminist sense of transcendence, when Davis's characters submit to nature or find friendship with a rural woman, they discover images of unity that allow the ego to dissolve.

THIS STUDY OF Rebecca Harding Davis began as a biography. As I came to understand the limits of the data of her life and the vast literary and topical range of her fiction, this study evolved from cultural biography to historiography to this offering: a literary analysis that engages political, legal, historical, literary, and psychoanalytic studies. As the process developed, a complicated conversation arose between me and my subject. I doubt that I am autonomous from the topic I have chosen to narrate and interpret. Like Davis, I find myself writing at the intersection of subjectivity and history—hers and mine. Because she remains so elusive, she has become a character, a character who is to determine the significance of another character. How ironic that Davis, whose characters are enraged when others attempt to confer an identity upon them, is here constructed by my interpretation. However, she will change in the future, for much Davis work needs to be done. In particular, I look forward to investigations of her mystery stories and her essays—both beyond the scope of this project.

In "Life in the Iron-Mills" the writer confesses, "I dare not put this secret into words. I told you it was dumb" (5). This book investigates Davis's attempt to put the secrets of her era into words, to find a voice to tell those secrets, to create a form to embody them, and to listen herself to the unspeakable history she has uttered.

2 ❦ The Terrible Question of "Life in the Iron-Mills"

EARLY IN "Life in the Iron-Mills" the narrator addresses the reader: "you . . . my friend, who study psychology in a lazy, *dilettante* way," and then she insists,

> This is what I want you to do. I want you to hide your disgust, take no heed to your clean clothes, and come right down with me,—here, into the thickest of the fog and mud and foul effluvia. I want you to hear this story. There is a secret down here, in this nightmare fog, that has lain dumb for centuries: I want to make it a real thing to you. You, Egoist, or Pantheist, or Arminian, busy in making straight paths for your feet on the hills, do not see it clearly,— this terrible question which men here have gone mad and died trying to answer.[1]

From the outset, however, this hostile narrator (who continues to insult her reader throughout the story) announces that in fact she cannot answer the "terrible question"—not merely because her reader is a self-indulgent transcendental dilettante. The narrator confesses that she too "dare[s] not put this secret into words," and hence she colludes in its repression, adding, "I told you it was dumb" (4). "Life in the Iron-Mills" is about Rebecca Harding Davis's attempt to tell the secret—that is, it is about her struggle to find an aesthetic language to express the ineffable nature of industrial reality.

Why was it secret, why would the readers of the *Atlantic Monthly* in 1861 want to ignore it, and why couldn't the narrator put it into words? And why was "this terrible dumb question . . . its own reply"?

In 1861, Rebecca Harding Davis, a heretofore unpublished author, sought to write her way out of this trap by devising a literary form that could make the foul mud "a real thing." Transcendentalism, she believed, was a philosophy of masculine egotism and imploded spiritualism that floated literature above the commonplace. Even so, Davis found in transcendentalism motifs that expressed a woman's plight: anxiety about aggression and violence, suspicion of authority, a critique of hierarchical ways of knowing, commitment to the cognitive validity of feeling, identification with a victim, fascination with the social function of suffering, and an interest in the construction of subjectivity. As a woman raised in the wild mountains of West Virginia, Davis also found in American romanticism a respect for the relevance of place and atmosphere; in "Life in the Iron-Mills" and *Margret Howth,* Davis pictures the dialectic between a female subject and an industrial space alien to her romantic projections.

Despite her pessimistic prediction about the capacity of narrative, in "Life in the Iron-Mills" Davis did in fact reveal the victory of industrial labor and industrial consciousness over a craft-based, farm-based, and slave-based economy; she showed how the new urban factory life dehumanized the immigrant working class, and she exposed the effects of mill work on women. Written when the domestic novel reigned over the literary marketplace, in her unsigned story of the Wolfes, a Welsh family employed in the iron and cotton mills of Wheeling, she found an innovative way to describe the physical and psychological impact of this disruptive transition. Building on the available traditions of transcendentalism, sentimentalism, and vernacular fiction, Davis forged a new rhetoric to portray the dependent relationship between subjectivity and social economics, and hence, between sentimental representation and industrialism. In her early industrial fiction, "Life in the Iron-Mills" and *Margret Howth,* Davis used transcendentalism, a discourse of the self, against itself to create a discourse of the "commonplace." Here, in the commonplace, she fused the imaginative and the economic, the private and the public.

The question becomes "its own reply" because even to utter it shatters literary convention. Like the factories and mills, Davis found the literary discourse of the time to be veiled in its own "fog" and hidden in its own "foul vapor." But unlike her frustrated narrator and her reluctant reader, Davis sensed that the new industrial reality was turning against its own repression, trying to undermine the poetics of its solipsistic self. The literary career of Rebecca Harding Davis involves her attempts to invent a language that could show the impact of industrial reality on subjective life.

The narrative tension in Davis's first story thus stems from a fundamental epistemological and political tension within transcendentalism—the problem of knowing and responding to the needs of another. "Life in the Iron-Mills" explores how industrial culture—and, to some degree, slave culture—locks characters into cognitive isolation. To explore alternative discourses and to structure analogous portraits of emotional and artistic confinement, the narrator uses the voices of the frame tale or tall tale; to transcend the barriers of class and race, the narrator uses a romantic vocabulary of gender. Unlike the typical tall tale, a formative genre in American realism in which a gentleman narrator distances himself from the local characters he describes in order to enhance their humor and contain their plebeian energy, the narrator of "Life in the Iron-Mills" is not a man, and the "folk" are not comic rural yokels. Davis's narrating figure is an ironic female persona who introduces and concludes the story of the mill workers, "framing" the action, attempting to empathize with the characters, but ultimately failing to interpret them correctly. Like the dilettante reader, she too is "idle"—confined in and by her class. Like the "true woman," she is confined to her room—a common symbol of gender.

Davis had no source in American literature for the plot of a frustrated woman artist who attempts to tell the story of Deborah and Hugh Wolfe, two Welsh immigrants, cousins, who work in the textile and iron mills in a booming raw industrial town. The genteel narrator's story begins late one Saturday night when a group of Welsh and free black women leave the cotton mill, drunk and half-naked after a twelve-hour shift standing at the "spools." The women, who have helped each other to finish their work, invite Deborah, a hunchbacked "picker," to go out dancing and drinking.[2]

Instead, cold, wet, and tired, Deb dutifully returns to the basement hovel that she shares with Hugh, Hugh's father, and a young girl, Janey. Deborah's only escape is her love for Hugh, who does not return her feelings. When she discovers that Hugh is working the night shift, she fills a dinner pail with bread and "flitch" (rank salt pork) and includes her own portion of ale. Going back out into the dirty rain, she trudges through the muddy town to the mill, where Hugh is stoking a coal furnace. After he condescendingly accepts her meager meal, Deb lies down on a pile of warm ashes to await the end of his shift.

Late in the night, unexpected visitors come to the furnace where Wolfe is at work. The mill overseer is leading a journalist, a doctor, and a wealthy friend on a tour of the works. As they turn to leave, the visitors suddenly come upon "the white figure of a woman . . . of giant proportions, crouching on the ground, her arms flung out in some wild gesture of warning" (14). This ominous and prognostic female form is a statue that Hugh has carved from korl, a "light, porous substance . . . refuse from the ore after the pig-metal is run" (10)—like himself, the refuse of the mill. Deb quietly listens as the visitors debate the meaning of this desperate figure, discuss Hugh's surprising artistic talent, and then quickly conclude that any reform efforts on behalf of the industrial poor are futile. When Deb overhears the visitors agree that money is the "answer to the riddle," she steals a wallet from one of them, gives the funds to Hugh to build a home for Janey and himself, and offers to disappear. Although he at first resolves to return the wallet, Hugh spends the next day struggling with temptation about what to do with the stolen money. He wanders through alleys and into the churches of the factory town, dreaming of the freedom that might be his. Arrested for the theft and quickly sentenced to nineteen years in prison, he commits suicide. After serving a three-year term as an accomplice, Deb is rescued by a Quaker woman who takes her to live in a Friends' community in the nearby hills, where she spends her remaining years in the restorative countryside, meek, quiet, and enduring.

The female narrator is closely aligned with and situated in the story. She opens:

> A cloudy day: do you know what that is in a town of iron-works? The sky sank down before dawn, muddy, flat, immovable. The air is thick, clammy with the breath of crowded human beings. It stifles me. I open the window, and, looking out, can scarcely see through the rain the grocer's shop opposite, where a crowd of drunken Irishmen are puffing Lynchburg tobacco in their pipes. (3)

Although the narrator resembles the women in the illustrated magazines of the time, pictured alone and removed from the action, idly watching the world of work and activity through a window, she is in the very tenement that the Wolfes shared with five other families thirty years ago. As she sits by herself in a domestic world that is equally defined and enclosed, she identifies with the oppression of the "stifling" atmosphere of the life outside, frequently mumbling, "I know." She also sees that industrial pollution and poverty have rendered the mill town "pregnant with death," a image that conflates gender, industry, and place. The narrator thereby sympathizes with the emotional suffocation and the creative rebellion of the working poor. Indeed, female sympathy, imported from sentimentalism, is the structuring device of "Life in the Iron-Mills." Nonetheless, the narrator's fantasy of female commonality is thwarted by the cultural expectations of class. Davis's reference to the pollution of the city becomes a way to vilify the people who inhabit it.[3]

What can the narrator really "know," since she never leaves her room? Settings of physical confinement—whether the narrator's room, the Wolfes' hovel, the iron mill, or the town jail—are never protected domestic spaces in "Life in the Iron-Mills." Rather like the confined spaces in the writings of Catherine Beecher, Davis's enclosed sites signify the culture's violence against the totality of female identity.[4] Unlike a roaming male narrator, this woman is physically constrained by her gender; her femaleness itself calls into question her epistemological autonomy. Hence, although the narrator boasts that her "eyes are free . . . to look deeper" (5), Davis surrounds her with images of containment and repression. Psychically damaged, the narrator is like the "little broken figure of an angel pointing upward" (3) that sits on her mantel, mocking the sentimental imperative to turn away from temporal life. The clay statue, a wounded angel in the house, mocks the possibility of spiritual escape. Echoing the narrator's description of the sky as "immovable" and the sunshine as "thwarted" (5), she reiterates the futility expressed in the story's epigraph, from Tennyson's "In Memoriam": "Is this the end? / O Life, as futile, then, as frail! / What hope of answer, or redress?"[5] These opening images—both domestic and environmental—shape the sense of inexorable social defeat and align the narrator with the maligned reader.

"Life in the Iron-Mills" is structured by a series of narrative paradoxes:

the frame tale encourages identification across class lines, invoking sympathy while at the same time distancing the reader from the story's black and Welsh working-class characters through the use of dialect, foreign phrases, and elevated vocabularies, through a series of spectators who guide us "downward" and interpret for us, and through the stereotypical feminizing of working-class men. The frame, however, not only mediates conflicting class values and gender identities; it also mediates the tensions between realism and romanticism. In romanticism characters are often envisioned as projections of desire, and hence they appear to overlap, merge with, and reflect each other. In "Life in the Iron-Mills" the narrator assumes a rather fluid subjectivity that flows between her and the other residents of the town. They all become fictively as well as socially interdependent.[6] For Davis, this interdependence universalizes experiences across gender and class, encouraging the reader to envision working-class life as a species of common suffering. Through this flowing projection, she generalizes subjectivity into a transcendent and unified experience. Humanistic essentialism, however, contradicts the narrator's description of the particularities of the Wolfes' class position. The sentimental language of suffering also intertextualizes images of factory life, locating Davis's portrait of frustration, isolation, and degradation in the context of popular novels that define suffering as working-class and female,[7] such as Susan Warner's *Wide, Wide World* (1850) and Maria Cummins's *The Lamplighter* (1854).

In "Life in the Iron-Mills," Davis envisions the capacity for sympathy, and thus the capacity for a politics of interdependence, as female. Images of womanly compassion undercut images of class isolation and confinement. The narrator comments, "I know: only the outline of a dull life, that long since, with thousands of dull lives like its own, was vainly lived and lost: thousands of them,—massed, vile, slimy lives, like those of the torpid lizards in yonder stagnant water-butt" (4). The confusing elision of empathy, contempt, and self-contempt also appears in the imagistic convention of the female/house, the female/space/body: the narrator explains that she has chosen this story to tell "because there is a secret underlying sympathy between that story and this day with its impure fog and thwarted sunshine,—or perhaps simply for the reason that this house is the one where the Wolfes lived" (5).

In "Life in the Iron-Mills" Davis explores female compassion as a political motif. Compassion, it is important to remember, was a feature of transcendental epistemology as well as of sentimental moralism. In "The American Scholar," for example, Emerson announces,

> The world,—this shadow of the soul, or *other* me, lies wide around. Its attraction are the keys that unlock my thoughts and make me acquainted with myself. I run eagerly into this resounding tumult. I grasp the hands of those next me, and take my place in the ring to suffer and to work, taught by an instinct, that so shall the dumb abyss be vocal with speech. I pierce its order; I dissipate its fear.[8]

Because Davis's narrator similarly claims to see the industrial poor as the "other me," she believes that she too can "pierce the order" and dissipate the fear of the "dumb abyss." In "Life in the Iron-Mills" emotions are the basis of both transcendental and feminine consciousness. Like much of women's public rhetoric that emerged in the 1830s, which appealed for social change and the abolition of slavery through personal descriptions of religious and emotional experiences,[9] the narrator's use of the romantic vocabulary of feeling mobilizes democratic sentiments even while it implicates her as a highbrow.[10] As Suzanne Clark observes, sentimental hyperbole frequently "locates moral values in the (feminized) heart and denies the importance of external differences."[11] Thus the narrator typifies the sensible and the rational, the unconscious feminine and the empiricist masculine rhetoric. Through images of suffering and victimization, she speaks in the new public language of sociological types, neutrally casting herself outside her stereotyped characterizations yet posing herself as a participant. Driven by her own desire, the narrator's pain helps make the other characters real.[12]

Frequently interfering in the tale, the narrator continues to taunt the reader as self-absorbed. Her comments, judgments, soliloquies, and asides mark not only the fictionality but, more important, the referentiality of the story. By reiterating the sentimental appeal to compassion, she establishes a sympathetic actual reader to repudiate her putative egotistical reader who, she assumes, will not want to read her "tiresome story, as foggy as the day" (4). Unlike the "engaging" narrators in Gaskell's *Mary Barton* (1848), Stowe's *Uncle Tom's Cabin* (1852), and Eliot's *Adam Bede* (1859), who appeal to their readers through their friendly interventions and empathetic addresses to "you,"[13] Davis's narrator attacks the reader as insensitive and distanced—indeed, like the visitors to the mill, "another order of being" (12). Looking out her back window at brickyards, idly tapping her windowpane, Davis's narrator challenges the reader: "What do you make of a case like that, amateur psychologist? You call it an altogether serious thing to be alive: to these men it is a drunken jest, a joke,—horrible to angels perhaps, to them commonplace enough" (4). Thus the narrator claims a higher authority as she distinguishes her ability to understand character from that of the reader who studies psychology "in a lazy, dilettante way" (4). Such attacks define the two readers; a putative reader who suffers from romantic pretensions, class blindness, and ultimately, misogyny, ironically encourages the actual readers of the *Atlantic Monthly* to view themselves as sympathetic.

At the same time, Davis makes it clear that her narrator is as trapped in her class as the reader she taunts. Romantic fogs and vapors obstruct middle-class perception of female and working-class life and build toward Davis's critique of nineteenth-century ways of knowing. Veils, curtains, prison bars, and secrets mark Davis as an "epistemological nihilist," Ronald Martin's term for writers who are concerned not only with exploding the "canon of knowledge" but also the midcentury "canon of credibility . . . the *means* of knowing and representing."[14] In attacking the new middle class's self-protective assumptions about truth and language, Davis participates in the "infrapolitical" democratization of access to reality. By questioning the egoist, pantheist, and Arminian view that knowledge is found through self-reflection, projection, and imagination, Davis recalls Emerson's assertion, "I know that the world I converse with in the city and in the farms, is not the world I *think*."[15] Her images of inadequate vision and indeterminate information in "Life in the Iron-Mills" also anticipate the demise of confidence in self-knowledge in later nineteenth-century and early twentieth-century fiction. Unlike later figures, however, this narrator is not the ultimate subject of her own text.

Rebecca Harding Davis seems to have been well aware of the tension between romanticism and realism—that is to say, between essentialism and particularity in this story. In January 1861, as the story was going to press, her editor, James Fields, wrote to her, seeking a more "taking" title than "Life in the Iron-Mills." In response, Rebecca proposed calling it "Beyond?" She added, "I should like something suggestive of the subdued meaning of the story." As an alternative to that metaphysical title, she suggested naming it "The Korl Woman," which would have focused on the story's feminized symbolic center. In a wry defense of that title, she said, "*I* would be sure to read an article with that caption in the hope of discovering some new race,— of Hottentots perhaps."[16] In fact, Davis writes as if she has indeed discovered a new race, new at least to the readers of the *Atlantic Monthly*.

Thus, while the narrator can "scarcely see" the drunken Irishmen just outside her window, she makes it clear that we are dependent on her informed sensibility for new information and suggests that she can reveal the premises of industrial capitalism: "Not many even of the inhabitants of a manufacturing town know the vast machinery of system by which the bodies of workmen are governed, that goes on unceasingly from year to year" (7). Through Deborah's nighttime visit to the ironworks, Davis will expose the details of factory life. This was unique in American fiction. Davis's images of industrial activity and heat take us well beyond Herman Melville's symbolic portrait of factory work in "The Paradise of Bachelors and the Tartarus of Maids," published six years earlier, in which an extended sexual metaphor of the machinery in a paper mill subsumes his descriptions of female labor.[17] "Life in the Iron-Mills" more closely resembles the writings of George Lippard, author of *The Monks of Monk Hall* (1844) as well as in his newspaper, the *Quaker City* (1849) and twenty reform novels. Lippard was a journalist and novelist who mixed gothic horror and romantic eroticism with fierce social protest against the new industrial city. Although I cannot establish that Davis, situated in Wheeling, knew of the work of George Lippard, *The Monks of Monk Hall* was the best-selling American novel until the publication of *Uncle Tom's Cabin* in 1852.[18] By describing the "vast machinery of a system," Davis goes beyond the socialist Lippard.

Also unique to early fiction is Davis's description of the impact of industrialism on women's lives. As Deborah leaves the textile mill, she is described as "half-clothed" (5), a titillating detail for the contemporary reader that derives from the fact that early mill workers and miners often removed bulky garments because they posed a serious danger near machinery and hot furnaces. The visible nudity of women and men who worked in factories and mines contributed to demands for the abolition of child labor. Davis's reference to Deb's state of undress and spinal deformity, however, enables the narrator to express her feminine sympathy through the eroticized and denigrating representation of the mill girl, displacing sexuality and victimization onto a working-class woman.

After work, Deb returns to her basement dwelling, "low, damp,—the earthen floor covered with a green, slimy moss,—a fetid air smothering the breath" (6). There she finds Janey and Hugh's aged father, wrapped in torn horse blankets, asleep on heaps of straw. Her home, as stifling as the mill and the streets that spawned it, hardly offers refuge from the factory. Through this figure of Deb, a "mill girl" who works a twelve-hour shift and then tries to feed a family and remain responsible for the emotional connections within it, "Life in the Iron-Mills" introduced into American fiction the double oppression—the paid and the unpaid roles—of working-class women. In an era that idealized the home, as she prepares her meager meal for Hugh, it is clear that Deb has neither the time or the money for family life. Recurrent images of hunger and inadequate food in the story further question the nurturing endings typical of sentimental fiction and build toward a unifying image of female and working-class "soul starvation."

Davis is describing not just the iron works itself, but also the "vast machinery of system" that produces it.

> The hands of each mill are divided into watches that relieve each other as regularly as the sentinels of an army. By night and day the work goes on, the unsleeping engines groan and shriek, the fiery pools of metal boil and surge. (7)

Through images of time—hands, watches, night, day—the inexorable nature of factory work unfolds. The reified "hands" (a reductive word for a manual worker popularized during the rise of manufacturing in the eighteenth century) are dwarfed by the groaning and shrieking engines; while the workers in Davis's tale are portrayed as mute and insentient animals, exclamations of fatigue and resistance come from the "unsleeping engines." Thus, in this early study of industrial labor, Davis exposes the "system" of the twelve-hour night shift—the disruptive result of the new heat-intensive Bessemer process for making steel, invented in 1851, that made it too expensive to let huge vats of molten pig iron cool down each night.[19] On Sunday, however, "in half-courtesy to public censure, the fires are partially veiled" (7), but as

soon as the clock strikes midnight, "the great furnaces break forth with renewed fury, the clamor begins with fresh, breathless vigor, the engines sob
and shriek like 'gods in pain'" (8). Only the machinery itself shows feelings
and howls with sublime rage at the injustices of industrialism. The workers
are mute with exhaustion and ignorance.

Davis insists on giving us information, using her characters, partially
blinded by their histories, to rend the veil, to reveal the sham of Sunday
ethics. Within the language of myth and melodrama is one of the earliest detailed pictures of mills or factories in American fiction, seen through the
eyes of a tired young working-class woman who has brought her own dinner
to her beloved cousin:

> The mills for rolling iron are simply immense tent-like roofs, covering acres
> of ground, open on every side. Beneath these roofs Deborah looked in on a
> city of fires, that burned hot and fiercely in the night. Fire in every horrible
> form: pits of flame waving in the wind; liquid metal-flames writhing in tor-
> tuous streams through the sand; wide caldrons filled with boiling fire, over
> which bent ghastly wretches stirring the strange brewing; and through all,
> crowds of half-clad men, looking like revengeful ghosts in the red light, hur-
> ried, throwing masses of glittering fire.

Davis thus affiliates the iron workers with Vulcan, the god of fire and metal-
work who forges masses of flame and who is credited with the origins of art.

Critics such as Sharon Harris suggest that "Life in the Iron-Mills" hovers on the edge of naturalism.[20] Published six years before Émile Zola's early
and influential experiment in naturalism, *Thérèse Raquin* (1867), the story
launches Davis's lifelong exploration of the effects of heredity, race, economic factors, gender, and environment on character. To be sure, her early
characters appear dwarfed by their milieu. They must frequently navigate re-
lentless material pressures in a web of malevolent forces—economic, sexual,
or geographic. Without the power to enact their choices and incapable of
understanding the forces that control them, they seem to operate in a world
of malignant inevitability.

Nevertheless, unlike Stephen Crane's or Frank Norris's characters, Davis's
characters enact a realist's commitment to free will and rational choice; their
actions have meaning and shape the plots. Despite Deb's deformity, Hugh's

ignorance, or even his animalistic attributes, Davis's mill workers are never in danger of slipping into the grotesque. If in Davis we find impotent characters, we also find characters who can conceptualize their situation and who survive. More in the spirit of the urban fiction of Jack London or the later works of Theodore Dreiser, Davis pictures the economics of power. Destiny has little to do with chance and much to do with money. While the true naturalistic character is mainly driven by instincts of fear, hunger, and sex, Hugh and Deb retain a powerful self-consciousness, an ability to choose, and an incipient capacity to resist. Thus, unlike the alleged scientism or moral neutrality of naturalism, the female frame and the vocabulary of identification of "Life in the Iron-Mills" engages discourse derived from what I term sentiment, or what David Hume calls the logic of pain, the moral concern that is engendered when pain appears as if it were one's own.[21]

I also differ with those critics who consider "Life in the Iron-Mills" a protonaturalist text because of its images of rebellion. Deb and Hugh struggle to penetrate the fog of ideology through which they have hitherto accepted their poverty; as they defy the culture of industrial capitalism, they come to understand their natural rights—a consciousness lacking in literary naturalism. Furthermore, unlike naturalistic authors who aspire to scientific objectivity in narrative, Davis seeks to evoke ethical reactions in the reader through the intrusive presence of the sympathetic narrator. The theatrical images from melodrama and extended references to Dante's *Inferno* in the portrait of the mills also establish a moral referent that is absent or repressed in most works by naturalists such as Frank Norris or Stephen Crane.

The sympathy of sentimentalism rather than the inevitability of naturalism shapes both the structure and the desired reaction in "Life in the Iron-Mills." As Glen Hendler observes, sentimental narratives do not just describe sympathetic identification, they "perform" it, to encourage the reader to form "analogous attachments" to the characters.[22] Images of parallel forms of deprivation in the family, at the mills, and in the reader's own life structure the narrative of "Life in the Iron-Mills." Shared social repression forms the basis of the analogy between the narrator, the working-class characters, and the reader; sympathy flows across class and gender lines in a transcendent motif of female subjectivity. Endowed with superior sensitivity and emotional responsiveness, the female narrator gains access to the feelings and situations of the deprived mill workers. Davis, however, ascribes these emotional skills not to the narrator's womanly maternal function but rather to her recognition of female powerlessness. Thus one way to read "Life in the Iron-Mills" is to view the three central characters—the narrator, Hugh, and Deb—as a divided female subject. The frustrated narrator, torn between sentimental views of femininity and romantic views of genius, embraces elements of both Hugh and Deb. An "internally heterogeneous"[23] female, she suggests both the masculine self that sees itself as desiring, omniscient, and "set apart," and the feminine self, which sees itself as empathetic, plural, and representative.[24] The narrator, Deb, and Hugh embody the repression of the aesthetic, egocentric, and erotic female self. The story of "Life in the Iron-Mills" is a dialogue among these three identities.

Davis inherited a tradition of gender masquerading as class. In sentimental fiction gender and race represent class because, according to Amy Schrager Lang, "the conjunction of attributes that define class position are rendered so intrinsic or else so transcendent that they pass either below or above history . . . by means of a kaleidoscopic substitution of terms."[25] Although Davis represents Hugh and Deb as projections of the female narrator's artistic and sexual frustrations, her elision of gender and class does not disguise the concrete realities of the mill workers' lives. There is no female orphan in "Life in the Iron-Mills" who will either inherit "up" or marry "up" to conclude the story by dismantling class; even in the conclusion, the promise of female harmony is deformed by details of the dehumanization of industrial life.

Female sympathy is also modified by the upper-class position of the narrator. Although she identifies with the mill workers, she repeatedly invites the reader to "come down and look," to "judge" (11). Davis also absorbs the nativist stereotypes of Welsh immigrants that further undermine the culture of sympathy:

> You may pick the Welsh emigrants, Cornish miners, out of the throng passing the windows, any day. They are a trifle more filthy; their muscles are not so brawny; they stoop more. When they are drunk, they neither yell, nor shout, nor stagger, but skulk along like beaten hounds. (5)

In fact, in the mid-nineteenth century, the Welsh were not totally impoverished immigrants. With Britain's industrial revolution predating America's by about thirty years, England, Ireland, and Wales provided an important supply of skilled labor to the new American industries. During the antebellum years, Welsh miners and industrial workers crossed the Atlantic in both directions, paying their own fares, consciously responding to the laws of supply and demand. The Welsh sought work in the United States in the period between the abolition of indentured labor and American industries' postbellum recruitment of immigrant workers through bribes, agents, and utopian descriptions of American life. Usually able to pay their own way, the Welsh were mainly tempted to the United States by letters from other Welsh immigrants.[26]

Yet Davis persists in dehumanizing and dehistoricizing the Welsh as a group. The mill workers speak in Welsh dialect: "Begorra! on the spools. Alleys behint, though we helped her we dud. An wid ye!" (6) Meanwhile, the narrator uses elevated literary diction, occasionally tossing off sarcastic observations in French "the river, dull and tawny-colored (*la belle rivière!*)" (3). Interestingly, while Hugh speaks in dialect when he addresses the visitors, he generally speaks standard literary English to Deb, thereby encouraging our affiliation with her. Hence, "Life in the Iron-Mills" codifies at the same time it attempts to resist the values of its time.[27]

"Life in the Iron-Mills" exemplifies Davis's ambivalent relationship to sentiment. While she questions the tenets of sentimentalism—the joys of selflessness, motherhood, and the society of the family, the redemptive power of love, the home as refuge from the tensions of the workplace, and capitalism's protective covenant for women—she amplifies the rebellious strains in domestic narratives that on the surface portray women's willingness, in Henry Nash Smith's view, to "kiss the chastening rod."[28] Elaine Showalter locates such seditious themes in sentiment as female solidarity, sympathy for the unmarried woman, and feminized male heroes. Although we never see the cotton mill in operation and first meet the "mill girls" after they leave work, Davis describes an interracial collectivity that has developed among the female mill workers. They have covered for one of the women who is "alleys behint" in her work, they are sympathetic to Deb's fatigue and need for solitude, and they are going to celebrate their half day off together.

The figure of Deb, an unmarried woman suffering from unrequited love, reveals Davis's complex use of sentimental tropes. She assigns moral worth based on how various characters view Deb's body. The narrator, also a spinster, observes Deb with detachment: "When she walked, one could see that she was deformed, almost a hunchback" (6). A woman mill worker protectively calls hers a "quite [quiet] body" (6)—thereby speaking to Deb's repression rather than her disability. By contrast, when Deb creeps into the mill one of the men announces, "Hyur comes t' hunchback" (8). Typically, the unmarried woman is crippled. Seen through the eyes of the male ironworkers, "Miserable enough she looked, lying there on the ashes like a limp, dirty rag" (9). Both the narrator and mill worker associate Deb with the recurrent image of ashes, the extinguished fire and the waste of the mill. The female narrator, however, sees Deb, lying on the ashes taken from Wolfe's furnace, as a parody of a regal female in classical repose, and observes that the tired mill girl was "not an unfitting figure to crown the scene of hopeless discomfort and veiled crime" (9). The narrator then urges the reader to look "deeper into the heart of things,—at [Deb's] thwarted woman's form, her colorless life, her waking stupor that smothered pain and hunger."

Read thus, Deb's body becomes a metaphor for working-class oppression: she is "even more fit to be a type of her class." The narrator urges on: "Deeper yet if one could look, was there nothing worth reading in this wet, faded thing, half-covered with ashes? no story of a soul filled with groping passionate love, heroic unselfishness, fierce jealousy?" (9). The reader's class bias slips into a wider cultural critique; what is not seen is what is not read: "No one had ever taken the trouble to read" the "signs" of her "pale, bleared eyes and washed-out-looking face" (9). "No one" implicates both Hugh and, through the metaphor of reading, ourselves. In the figure of Deb, Davis ruptures the sentimental conventions of the female body, severs desire from appearance and historicizes the working woman's body.

Davis also uses images of Deb's body to cross class lines. As an unmarried woman herself, Davis was perhaps acutely aware of the loneliness of the spinster. The men at the mill see Deb as a "limp dirty rag," a "drowned cat" who painfully hides behind the machinery, knowing that Hugh is eating the food she brought only to please her because "it was his very nature to be kind, even to the very rats that warmed in the cellar: kind in just the same way" (9). The narrator comments, however, "One sees that dead, vacant look steal sometimes over the rarest, finest of women's faces,—in the very midst, it may be, of their warmest summer's day; and then one can guess at the secret of intolerable solitude that lies hid beneath the delicate laces and brilliant smile" (9).

But the lonely narrator, tapping at her window, backs off from her class analysis and suggests that it is Hugh's rejection that "had given to [Deb's] face its apathy and vacancy more than her low, torpid life" (9). Thus, Deborah is a doppelganger of the narrator, a romantic voyeur and romantic casualty. Deb's deformity, however, relegates her to the female realm of nature, of the body, and of the "other," and thus it locks her in her class. Except when we actually see through Deb's eyes, she functions as the object rather than the subject of consciousness. She is dependent on the consciousness of a middle-class female narrator who assigns her own bourgeois conventions to Deb and renders her both monster and angel. Because her subjectivity is defined through Hugh's desire, Deb is constricted as a romantic subject; her quest is never for autonomous selfhood, but rather for psychological intimacy. True female desire, impassioned "hunger," is reserved for the statue and the figure of the feminized artist. Yet because neither Deb nor the narrator is fixed within family or romance, the narrator also bestows dignity on Deb's single and isolated status. Thus, the reader takes up the subject position of the narrator and also identifies with Deb; the lives of both women expose the hollowness of the domestic promise.

Another instance of sentimental rebellion and another example of the fluidity of subjectivity in "Life in the Iron-Mills" is in the characterization of Hugh as the feminized hero. In the nineteenth century, the working-class male was frequently portrayed as effeminate.[29] Hugh is not only deficient by male standards, but also an unattractive parody of the Victorian view of the weak female body.

> He had already lost the strength and instinct vigor of a man, his muscles were thin, his nerves weak, his face (a meek, woman's face) haggard, yellow with consumption. In the mill he was known as one of the girl-men: "Molly Wolfe" was his *sobriquet.* He was never seen in the cockpit, did not own a terrier, drank but seldom; when he did, desperately. He fought sometimes, but was always thrashed, pommelled to a jelly. (10)

Unlike the feminization of male characters found in works by German romantics such as Goethe, who admires men's "feminine" capacity for pathos,

Davis represents Hugh's economic and political powerlessness as a sign of masculine and sexual inadequacy: the other mill workers only find Hugh "game enough, when his blood was up" (10). Hugh's delicacy, however, is also a sign of his class; typically, it signifies his status as victim, thereby defusing the threat of the working poor. What further feminizes Hugh and makes him unpopular with the men at the mill is that "he had the taint of school-learning on him,—not to a dangerous extent, only a quarter or so in the free-school in fact, but enough to ruin him as a good hand in a fight" (10). Through his initial political confusion, frustrated creativity, thwarted romance, worldly naivete, and aesthetic sensibility, Hugh anticipates several of Davis's female and slave characters.

In developing a discourse of the commonplace, Davis ultimately repudiated the epistemological and narrative procedures of romanticism, a repudiation shaped by her sense of gender. As early as "Life in the Iron-Mills," she used romanticism against itself to scrutinize the view that the masculine self can liberate itself from its own limitations. While critics such as Julie Elison and Susan Kirkpatrick argue that there is no inherent disjunction between feminism and romanticism, Davis associated the heroic, the sublime, the transcendent, and the mythic with a masculine and idealistic view of historical autonomy.[30]

In Davis's view, responsibility for the social and environmental decay caused in the mill town was due in part to the egocentric tendencies of romanticism, which blind the middle-class voyeur—the reader of the *Atlantic Monthly* or visitor to the mills—to the personal and ecological destruction caused by industrialization. In "Life in the Iron-Mills" she resolves the struggle that haunted Emerson and Thoreau, the conflict between duties to the self and duties to the world, between solipsism and commitment. If indeed, as the narrator asserts, "there is no hope that it will ever end" (11), it is because "you, Egoist, or Pantheist, or Arminian, busy in making straight paths for your feet on the hills, do not see it clearly" (4). The function of the artist—sculptor or writer—is to make us see historical change clearly. Clear vision provides a way of knowing that penetrates social veils, sees through fogs, and lifts curtains. Clear vision is thus a prerequisite for realism, for a language that acknowledges social barriers and deconstructs fantasies of pastoral transcendence and utopian digression. Yet paradoxically, it is the fantasy of transcendence that represents desire for harmony and commonality and links romanticism to feminism.

For Davis, female empathy forces the reader to see outside one's own world so that change may emerge. The egocentric, solipsistic male self of romanticism must give way to the limited but socially historicized female self of realism. The narrator scorns the isolated self who refuses to acknowledge what is both inside and outside her window, yet she is herself a parody of it. "Life in the Iron-Mills" is structured through images of vision. We are invited, indeed challenged, to watch the putative reader observe the narrator who examines Deb, who constantly watches Hugh, who in turn is observed by the group of visitors to the mill; and everyone examines the statue. But each of these visions results in faulty interpretation and erroneous conclusions of political impotence. This epistemological structure in itself harkens to the problems of a transcendent notion of fluid subjectivity. In constructing these visual relationships—between the narrator and the Wolfes, between Hugh and Deb, between the chorus of middle-class characters and the sculptor—Davis suggests that while we may sympathize, we will never know another subject as long as she remains hidden, repressed, or "veiled." Vision is thus inseparable from power. The genteel narrator, meanwhile, is the primary parody of the romantic self, whose masterful perspective deteriorates into an image of female isolation. In "Life in the Iron-Mills," identification and commonality are seen to occur only within the working class: "Their lives were like those of their class" whose "duplicates [are] swarming the streets to-day" (5).

Davis's critiques of the epistemology and politics of romanticism converge in the figure of the korl woman. Located at the center of "Life in the Iron-Mills," the sculpture represents a devastating attack on the cult of the true woman, on factory life, and on transcendentalism.

There was not one line of beauty or grace in it: a nude woman's form, muscular, grown coarse with labor, the powerful limbs instinct with some one poignant longing. One idea: there it was in the tense, rigid muscles, the clutching hands, the wild, eager face, like that of a starving wolf's. (15)

This statue is the first of Davis's many female figures whose body is not confined by bustle and bodice, whose existence is not defined by her maternal role, whose morality is not derived through avoidance of the outside world. This is a working woman's body, whose physique immediately contrasts with the frail figure of Hugh; created by the mills, her body is strong, tired, and dissatisfied. But none of the male characters, including her male sculptor, can say for sure what the korl woman wants. They can only interpret the statue by her absences: she wants "summat [something] to make her live" (16). Unique in American literature before works by such turn-of-the-century socialists as Theodore Dreiser, Jack London, and Ignatius Donnelly, the statue signifies the growth of a rebellious working-class consciousness. Perhaps this was the reason James Fields refused to let Davis entitle this story "The Korl Woman."

This massive female figure, without speech, action, or self-knowledge, awaits interpretation. Reluctant to reveal her meaning, the statue becomes a gendered mediation between the middle-class male spectators and her male creator. As such, she defies any closed or didactic reading of female representation and hence calls into question the romantic way of figurative seeing, the translation of life into generalized but unstable truths.[31] Instead, the body of the korl woman insists on specific political and economic responses which the visitors—who, in effect, become readers of the statue—refuse to provide. The doctor, ignoring Hugh, asks his companions, "What does the fellow intend by the figure?" When he asks the sculptor himself, Hugh answers, "She be hungry." The doctor tells him he is mistaken: "You have given no sign of starvation to the body." (15) The doctor refuses to see the female body as the romantic sign of Promethean desire. But Hugh in reply insists to the doctor that the statue is starving for "Summat to make her live, I think,—like you" (16). The phrase "like you" lifts this female body above class and gender particularities. She is universalized by her hunger, her lack, and her inherently undefinable meaning. Hugh's phrase "like you" harkens to his own feminization and thereby repudiates the ideology of female difference.

Initially, then, as each viewer seeks to assign meaning to the korl woman, the statue protests the romantic aesthetic—the need of the viewer to rewrite art according to his own image of desire as part of the constant desire of the subject to reconstruct itself.[32] Mitchell, invoking the trope of vision, snaps at the doctor, "Are you blind? Look at that woman's face! It asks questions of God, and says, 'I have a right to know.' Good God, how hungry it is!" (16).

Through her body, the korl woman suggests a Promethean hunger and a struggle against the culture that refuses it. For Mitchell, the korl woman is the romantic rebel who has burst through the refuse of the iron mill, out of which she is created, to conflate the body, the aesthetic, the female, and the economic. She exemplifies what Susan Kirkpatrick calls the "coincidence" of the erotic and the political in romantic Prometheanism, the "porousness that allows the seepage of the collective and the historical" into the unsatisfied romantic subject.[33] Thus, the meaning of the korl woman's hunger, debated only by male characters, suggests Hugh's transcendent hunger rather than Deb's longing for love and food.

Desire is still an attribute of the male artist. Like Mary Shelley, Davis has a male character create a figure to project the creative prerogative as his subject. Through the figure of the korl woman, Davis explores the ambiguities that arise when a man attempts to appropriate a woman in order to project his subjectivity. Ultimately, the visitors' debate about the meaning of the statue is a debate about the impossibility of men's defining female meaning. Thus, suggests Davis, the korl woman's hunger may never be appeased, both because of women's unequal status and because the romantic quest for fullness cannot be fully gratified through art. The aesthetic figure cannot resolve or subsume historical tension through the isolated pleasure of the lyrical self.

As an image of a naked and hungry female body, the korl woman also repudiates what Nancy Cott terms the "passionlessness" of mid-nineteenth-century representations of women, the assumption that only men are charged with sexual passion and that women experience their bodies primarily through maternal need and satiation. While the men view the korl woman (as they would any demanding and rebellious woman of their time) as bewildering, confusing, and overreaching, neither the female author, female narrator, nor the highly feminized artist manqué finds her mystifying or threatening. Unlike the subservient and genteel ideals expressed in the sickly bodies of many sentimental heroines, the korl woman's body is shaped by her activity and unsatisfied desire. Her muscles and tense posture insist that she is a producer, valued for her resistant energy. In contrast to the goals for women outlined in *Godey's Lady's Book* and represented in the constricted female clothing of the time, the statue does not mask the economics of women's bodies. As Dr. May observes, the statue is "a working-woman,—the very type of her class" (15).

Nonetheless, there are also hints of birth imagery implied in the posture of a naked crouching woman whose clutching hands suggest gestures of pain and drowning.

Ultimately, the visitors' reaction to the sculpture suggests the futility of realism and representation as instruments of change, or even communication. Standing in for the reader, the visitors to the mill have accepted the narrator's invitation to "come down and look." Although they are stunned by the urgency of what they see, they are unable to use their vision to find solutions. Just before the narrator introduces the visitors—the putative readers and voyeurs of life in the iron mills—she concludes, "There is no hope that it will ever end" (11). All she wants of the reader is to "see [Wolfe] just as he is, that you may judge him justly when you hear the story of this night." Her sentimental, as opposed to litigious, goal is compassion: "Be just,—not like man's law . . . but like God's judging angel, whose clear, sad eye saw . . . [how] his soul fainted in him" (11).

Morality resides in sympathy rather than justice. Ellen Moers suggests that the moral goal of women's social fiction is to reveal the humanity of a class or race by making its voice heard; the task of such fiction is to protect against the social risks of ignoring that voice.[34] Thus, Davis's most serious condemnation is the failure of the prosperous visitors (and, by extension, the comfortable reader) to show true sympathy for the new industrial working class. Sympathy, Glen Hendler observes, is the sentimental novel's utopia.[35]

The visitors' tour of the mill calls into question the romantic belief in the power of an individual mind to absorb the new social reality, what Emerson called the "contours" of the world. While Emerson believed that accurate information and correct seeing could renovate the individual and, in turn, society, and while abolitionists similarly hoped that the revelation of slavery's abuses would lead to its defeat, in "Life in the Iron-Mills" information and vision lead nowhere. Davis's description of the visit to the mill reveals her skepticism about the power of language and her doubts about the new literary form she is proclaiming. As the night wears on, the tired workers, anticipating the freedom of an impending day off, have grown noisy. Suddenly "they grew less boisterous . . . a silence came nearer" (11), and Deb notices that the "cause of the quiet" (12) is the group of visitors, who thereby personify the repression of their class. This repressive silence not only delimits their relationship with the ironworkers, but functions between themselves as well; when the mill owner's son, Kirby, observes to his overseer that the workers are "a desperate set," Davis comments, "The overseer did not hear him. He was talking of net profits just then" (12). Rather than expressing empathy, bourgeois speech is a species of domination. When one of the visitors asks whether the mill owner controls the workers' ballots, Kirby replies that his father delivered seven hundred votes in the last election, "No force-work, you understand,—only a speech or two . . ." (13).

In a story centered on images of language and repression, Davis makes it patently clear that utterance in and of itself is not freedom. Shaped by class, language itself is suspect. Each visitor's response to the question raised by the "dumb" statue—"What shall we do to be saved?" (17)—reflects the reification of language. For example, when the doctor asks Kirby if he thinks he could govern the world better, Kirby announces, "I do not think. I wash my hands of all social problems,—slavery, caste, white or black. My duty to my operatives . . . [is] the pay-hour on Saturday night. Outside of that . . . I am not responsible" (16). Mitchell, the spokesman for romanticism, replies, "Money has spoken!" He then asks the doctor, "What has the heart to say?" The doctor, believing that "much good was to be done here by a friendly word or two" (17), complacently tells Hugh that he is free to make himself into anything he chooses, although he refuses to help him. The doctor then "glows" in self-satisfaction at his prayers on behalf of "these degraded souls" (19), a "glow" that returns us to the threatening image of the furnaces as well as to the "blood-glow" of Mitchell's shiny ring. When the doctor in return asks of Mitchell, "what has [the] head to say?" he replies, "it would be of no use. I am not one of them" (19). Speech is not functional without transcendent "harmony."

Mitchell's observation that he is "not one of them" points to the political confusion within transcendentalism and shapes his complicated relationship with Hugh. From the first, there is an affiliation and attraction between Mitchell and Hugh. Their actions and images mimic and repel each other. Although Hugh cannot understand Mitchell's speech—"Greek would not have been more unintelligible"—he persists in identifying with him: "marking acutely every smallest sign of refinement, then back to himself, seeing as in a mirror his filthy body, his more stained soul" (14). Similarly, as Mitchell watches Hugh tend the fire, he comments, "'This is hot, with a vengeance. A match please?'—lighting his cigar" (12). While Hugh rakes away the ashes of the furnace, Mitchell knocks the ashes from his cigar. Sharon Harris suggests that the affiliation of Hugh and Mitchell implies that Hugh accepts the "capitalists' vision of Beauty"; hence, Hugh's fascination with Mitchell's ring symbolizes his unconscious attraction to the "blood drawn from workers like himself." As Hugh imitates Mitchell by sweeping away the ashes, he affiliates with the visitors' rejection of the korl woman.[36] In my view, while Hugh, the stoker and artist, is associated with fire, Mitchell, the nihilist, is associated with ash and ice. Mitchell has a detached light in his "cool grey eye"; "damp wind chills" his bones, and his temper is as "yielding and brilliant as summer water, until his Self was touched, when it was ice" (13)—attributes affiliated with the cold language of science as opposed to the impassioned vocabulary of sentiment.

Associated with nihilism and death, Mitchell takes Kant, Novalis, Humboldt "for what they were worth in his own scales"; he is "a man who sucked the essence out of a science or philosophy in an indifferent, gentlemanly way" (13). Mitchell would similarly deprive Hugh of his sentient self, arguing against an emotional and rational capacity in the working class:

> "If I had the making of men, these men who do the lowest part of the world's work should be machines,—nothing more,—hands. It would be kindness . . . What are taste, reason, to creatures who must live such lives as that?" (16)

Thus, while Hugh is attracted to the "blood-glow" of Mitchell's ring, a seductive but misleading light, Mitchell is attracted to the mill only when the fires are banked down.

> "Do you know," said Mitchell, "I like this view of the works better than when the glare was fiercest? These heavy shadows and the amphitheatre of smothered fires are ghostly, unreal. One could fancy these red smouldering lights to be the half-shut eyes of wild beasts, and the spectral figures their victims in the den." (14)

Despite Mitchell's romanticized and literary view of Hugh's labor, ultimately it is Mitchell who politicizes the images of light and fire surrounding Hugh. He concludes,

"Reform is born of need, not pity. No vital movement of the people's has worked down, for good or evil; fermented, instead, carried up the heaving, cloggy mass. . . . Some day, out of their bitter need will be thrown up their own light-bringer,—their Jean Paul, their Cromwell, their Messiah." (19)

For both Mitchell and Hugh, however, language itself is inadequate as a source of political growth. Mitchell remarks, "I tell you, there's something wrong that no talk of '*Liberté*' or '*Egalité*' will do away" (16). That is to say, talk cannot create change. Hugh, likewise, has "no words" for his radical thoughts.

In the end, Hugh faces the core choice of romanticism: duty to the world versus surrender to the temptations of solipsistic self. Hugh's tragic mistake is to identify with the nihilism and egoism of Mitchell and reject the Promethean passion expressed in his statue, in the social compassion of Deb, and ultimately in the realist discourse that encodes a dialectic between the individual and society rather than represents the individual as severed from culture. Thus Davis observes that Hugh found what he had been seeking "in this Mitchell, even when he idly scoffed at his pain: a Man all-knowing, all-seeing, crowned by Nature, reigning,—the keen glance of his eye falling like a sceptre on other men" (20). The Byronic man and his phallic and empowering "sceptre" seduce Hugh away from his vision of himself as a spokesman for his class: "Able to speak, to know what was best, to raise these men and women working at his side up with him: sometimes he forgot this defined hope in the frantic anguish to escape,—only to escape" (20). In contrast to Hugh's fantasy of romantic flight is Deb, "crying thankless tears, according to the fashion of women," who pleads with him to come home. But the domestic choice, as Hugh knows, is shaped by class, and he replies, "Home,—and back to the mill!" (20).

It is just at the moment when the visitors address the riddle asked by the korl woman, "What shall we do to be saved?" that Deborah commits the most defiant act in the story. She steals Mitchell's money and gives it to Hugh, insisting, "It is hur [your] right to keep it" (22). Only at this moment does Hugh acknowledge Deb's power and beauty. As the deformed mill girl describes the theft, Hugh sees that "she was young, in deadly earnest; her faded eyes, and wet, ragged figure caught from their frantic eagerness a power akin to beauty" (21), recalling the passion of the statue. If "timid, helpless" Janey, childlike, passive, and almost always asleep, offers Hugh the idealized feminine future, what George Eliot calls a man's "margin of dreams," Deborah embodies the material present. Yet at the same time, she suggests the feminized mythological Welsh past, offering the money as if it were a gift from one of the "witch dwarfs" (22).

Hugh's traumatic choice between returning or keeping the money emerges in a night of Faustian voices, a coda of images recalling the political and aesthetic tensions of the story. Sitting at the "mouth" of an alley, "mad with hunger; stretching out his hand to the world," he replicates the korl woman who also "wanted so much." Like Deb, he thinks "God made this money—the fresh air too—for his children's use" (23). And like both female figures, he too is invisible to the bourgeois world. Thus denied, Hugh slips into a dangerous affiliation with romanticism. Not only is he in possession of Mitchell's money; he is acting, like Mitchell, from his "brain" in order to be "cool" about returning the check. In this story centered in images of vision and veiling, Mitchell's money "blinded him to delirium,—the madness that underlies all revolution, all progress, and all fall" (23). Hugh's imagistic affiliation with Mitchell's cold nihilism and revolutionary heroizing is a movement into the consciousness of romanticism. Yet he never wakes Janey with a princely kiss; the sleeping and childlike female is never aroused into social adulthood.

During this night while "fierce devils whisper in his ear" (22), Hugh, in essence, struggles with the politics of aesthetic forms; he sees two competing visions and speaks in two competing discourses. As he wanders down the alleys where the mill hands lodge, he notes "with new eagerness the filth and drunkenness, the pig-pens, the ash-heaps covered with potato-skins, the bloated pimpled women at the doors,—with a new disgust" (24). But as he starts to look with his "artist's eye," he surrenders to the temptations and language of the sublime, seeing instead the "sun-touched smoke-clouds [as they] opened like a cleft ocean,—shifting, rolling seas of crimson mist, waves of billowy silver veined with blood-scarlet, inner depths unfathomable of glancing light" (24). This romanticized space, which would qualify for what Annette Kolodny calls the metaphorical landscape of someone else's imagination,[37] is a highly eroticized image of nature as female sanctuary. In this feminized interior red site, entered through "the gates of that other world," notions of private property dissolve: "What, in that world of Beauty, Content, and Right, were the petty laws, the mine and thine, of mill-owners and mill-hands?" (24). Hugh's fantasy of economic transcendence is, to Davis, a dangerous illusion based on a popular definition of female beauty.[38]

The romantic vocabulary, however, cannot endure. When he wanders into a church, a "sombre Gothic pile," where silent kneeling worshipers and mysterious music lift his soul with "a wonderful pain" (24), Hugh cannot even understand the sermon devoted to "incarnate Life, Love and the universal Man," even though it is delivered by a high-minded Christian reformer whose "outlook at man had been free, world-wide, over all time." The minister of the Social Gospel, "with a steady eye that had never glared with hunger, and a hand that neither poverty nor strychnine-whiskey had taught to shake," fails to reach Hugh. Without realism, commonality, and identity, Hugh cannot even grasp the minister's words, "toned to suit another class of culture." As Hugh leaves the church, he retrieves the realist's vision and sees that in fact the "night had come on foggy, damp; the golden mists had vanished, and the sky lay dull and ash-colored" (25).

The next morning Hugh is arrested. His only defense is to reiterate Deb's socialist understanding, "the money was his by rights" (26). Suffering from tuberculosis, he is sentenced to nineteen years at hard labor, a bitter paradox for a mill worker. A series of metallic images mark the ultimate failure of Hugh's quest as he makes two feeble efforts to escape; using a thin piece of tin, he is unable to carve through the bars of the prison window. Unable to sculpt his own freedom, he is, as an ironic consequence, chained in "irons."

Locked in his cell, through the iron bars of his window Hugh sees two last figures—a mulatto slave and an old lamplighter who uses his flame to bring light. Both fail to acknowledge him and, in effect, mock his life and point to the futility of vision. Hugh first notices the slave's "free, firm step," her "turban tied on one side, dark, shining eyes, and on the head the basket poised, filled with fruit and flowers, under which the scarlet turban and bright eyes looked out half-shadowed. The picture caught his eye. It was good to see a face like that. He would try to-morrow, and cut one like it" (30). While the slave's scarlet turban recalls the red pits of molten metal as well as Mitchell's ruby ring, her face and carriage transcend her subjugated status.

This is the first of many figures of a slave in Davis's opus, and it is complicated. On the one hand, the female slave is perhaps the most optimistic image in the story—tall, laughing, with a firm step, surrounded by her baskets of fruit and flowers. She certainly appears less oppressed and degraded than the factory workers. As Hugh romanticizes her and seeks to turn her too into a statue, she seems to confirm the southern view that chattel slavery is better than industrial slavery. In the figurative pattern of the story, she is outside the window, and Hugh, like the narrator, projects his own images of beauty and freedom onto her. Nonetheless, when the slave woman "caught sight of the haggard face peering out through the bars, [she] suddenly grew grave, and hurried by" (30). She, in essence, rejects his mistaken interpretation of her and their affiliation. She also recalls the only other reference to slavery in the story, the narrator's early metaphoric description of the Ohio: "When I was a child, I used to fancy a look of weary, dumb appeal upon the face of the negro-like river slavishly bearing its burden day after day" (3). Amy Schrager Lang comments that Davis tempers this image of enslavement with the observation that the river will flow out of town into "odorous sunlight . . . air, fields and mountains," exemplifying how "blackness is widely understood in the mid nineteenth century as a state of becoming."[39] Hugh, by contrast, is fixed in an interminable present, despite the obvious irony that he is white, male, and not a slave.[40]

In contrast to the river, Hugh finds freedom only in his cell, where he slices his own body with the piece of tin and bleeds to death in the cold and silent moonlight, his arms outstretched in a Christlike pose, separated from Deb, who lies helpless in the next cell. The tin, the cell, the money, and the ironworks themselves expose how human relations have become linked through metal—iron, coin, prison bars—rather than through love, blood, or human empathy. Hugh's suicide, however, is neither the "soteriological" death of Stowe's Uncle Tom, in which the highest human calling is to give one's life for another, nor the death of Little Eva, which offers a vicarious access to salvation.[41] Hugh's death is not redemptive. With the dissonance that Davis has drawn between Hugh's aesthetic needs and the realities of industrial poverty, she turns to literary convention for her resolution. Without an available tradition to represent success, survival, or even endurance, the (female) artist fails to survive.

Thus Hugh, a male romantic figure, dies alone, trying to aestheticize suffering. Not only are his Promethean aspirations frustrated by the realities of caste; his insistent solitude has isolated him from the collectivity of love or class. In that sense, his lonely death is self-constructed. Hugh's romantic and artistic autonomy has led him to what Susan Kirkpatrick terms the "dialectic of Promethean desire" in which the self-defining and the self-destructive urges conflict.[42] What Hugh lacks is true identification and empathic relation with any other person, represented by Deb who can only listen from the next cell as he slashes his veins. Hugh's sculpture, suggesting the possibility of transcendence through the freedom of the imagination, has not provided him true freedom, and the prison becomes a symbol of his psychic isolation. His romantic impulse toward detachment has sundered passion from compassion. And hence his alienated self, his artistic self, is incapable of transforming the world.

To the degree that Hugh is a feminized artist, we must also read his isolation, like that of the narrator, as a form of involuntary confinement. Even though he suffers from tuberculosis, an incurable illness associated at the time with hunger and poverty, it is confinement that inevitably destroys Hugh. Unlike Deb's suffering, Hugh's quest for knowledge renders his death heroic. Clearly Davis's own creative ambitions are marked on his rebellious and artistic sensibility. Through the figure of Hugh, Davis penetrates the aesthetic silence that separates women from the artistic and verbal authority of men.

In Hugh, the ideology of gender—the sentimental respect for dependency and community—confronts the masculine individualism of romanticism. Hugh's attraction to Mitchell, the romantic Nietzchean ego willing itself into power, is defeated by the realist self, one ultimately contingent on society. Hugh is thus unlike many of Davis's later female artists who strive to nourish their self-identity and at the same time struggle, as did Davis, to maintain their commitment to duty, dependency, and community.[43]

In contrast to Hugh, Deb's pattern of development represents a movement toward female attachment, continuity, and fusion. After serving a three-year sentence, Deb goes into the hills to live with the Quakers, "pure and meek . . . more silent than they, more humble, more loving" (33). She is "waiting: with her eyes turned to hills higher and purer than these on which she lives" (33). In this figure of female endurance, the hope for eternal life and the ascetic peace of self-denial subsume the political thrust of "Life in the Iron-Mills." Although the silent woman in gray suggests the failure of worldly desire, rural life is regenerative. But it is important to qualify the common interpretation of this ending as a fantasized escape from industrial history; during the 1860s the Quakers were well known to readers of the *Atlantic* as social activists and leaders in the movements for abolition and prison reform.

"Life in the Iron-Mills" suggests that in industrial society, while thirst cannot be quenched and desire cannot be satisfied, neither can they be stifled. There are three endings in "Life in the Iron-Mills" that mark the choice between solipsism and commitment—Hugh's suicide, Deb's joining the Quaker community, and the statue's insistent demand for fulfillment. In the end, the korl woman parodies the sentimental figure of the repressed narrator and decries the frustrations of Davis's own life.

The narrator closes the story in her own dark room. She has tried to hide the korl woman behind a curtain, like Mary Shelley's "hideous progeny." Sometimes, however, when the curtain is accidentally drawn back, she sees Hugh's thwarted and hungry spirit in the statue's look, the same look "in the eyes of dumb brutes,—horses dying under the lash. I know" (34). The final image of desire resides in the sculpture, upon whom the narrator again bestows her own suffering. Although she tries to treat the sculpture the way Hugh treated Deb, in the end the korl woman insists on a final glimpse of her "soul starvation," the terror of the self buried alive in the social history of class and gender. "Its pale vague lips seem to tremble with a terrible question. 'Is this the End?' they say,—'nothing beyond?—no more?'" (34)—a question recalling the story's epigraph. At last, the statue can utter her question. In "Life in the Iron-Mills" Davis represents and seeks to repress this image of the social shape of desire, an image that refuses to remain hidden.

In the end, because the narrator remains trapped in her house, her womanhood, and her middle-class aestheticism, she fails to answer the "terrible dumb question." She is Davis's first portrait of a romantic self whose masterful perspective has deteriorated into an image of female isolation. Confined in her room at the close of her story, she reveals for the first time that she too is a sculptor, but of a different sort than Hugh. As the dawn rises, she lists her tasks for the coming day: "a half-moulded child's head; Aphrodite;

a bough of forest-leaves; music; work; homely fragments, in which lie the secrets of all eternal truth and beauty. Prophetic all!" (34). But prophetic of what? Reclaiming art and nature as "homely fragments" of women's daytime endeavors, she erases their romantic and insurgent capacity. Taken together, the figures of Aphrodite and the half-molded child's head hint at love and motherhood; sublimated through art, they suggest female incompletion and sterility. And they undercut the terrible question of the korl woman, whose "dumb woful face seems to belong to and end with the night" (34). In the domestic rhetoric of daytime, the female sculptor will birth the child; for the time being, sentimental convention will stabilize and contain Davis's social and aesthetic rebellion. Yet the politicization of sympathy and the feminization of public life would be subjects for narrative exploration for the rest of Davis's long career.

3 ❦ The Common Story
of *Margret Howth*

IN A ROLE he would play throughout his tenure at the *Atlantic Monthly,* James Fields, Rebecca Harding Davis's literary mentor, attempted to contain her narrative radicalism. In May 1861, one month after the successful publication of "Life in the Iron-Mills," Fields rejected Davis's next piece, "The Deaf and the Dumb,"[1] as too gloomy for the *Atlantic.* Davis wrote back, apparently abject and insecure about the literary direction she was taking:

> I am sorry. I thank you for the kindness with which you veil the disappointment. Whatever holier meaning life or music has for me, has reached me through the "pathetic minor." I fear that I only have the power to echo the pathos without the meaning. When I began the story, I meant to make it end in full sunshine—to show how even "Lois" was not dumb, how even the meanest things in life, were "voices in the world, and none of them *without* its signification." [Lois's] life and death were to be the only dark thread. But . . . in my eagerness . . . I "assembled the gloom" you complain of."

At this early point in her career, Davis seems conciliatory: "[Do] you think I could . . . make it acceptable by returning to my original idea. Let her character and death (I cannot give up all, you see) remain, and the rest of the picture be steeped in warm healthy light. A 'perfect day in June.'"[2] Eight weeks later, she sent Fields a revised manuscript; he accepted it immediately and published it anonymously.

Like the insistent statue of the korl woman, the "rough ungainly thing" that remains hidden behind the curtains at the end of "Life in the Iron-Mills," *Margret Howth* embodies competing tendencies. Jean Fagan Yellin argues that in writing *Margret Howth* Rebecca Harding Davis suffered from a deep self-division, a consequence of her attempts to conform to the expectations of the Brahmin world of the *Atlantic* on the one hand and her ambivalence about her artistic self-assertion on the other. Reading through Davis's letters to Fields, Yellin astutely re-creates Davis's editing process and concludes that throughout the summer and early fall of 1862 Davis reluctantly acceded to many of Fields's editorial suggestions, apparently adding ninety sunny pages to placate him.[3] In my view, however, *Margret Howth*, like the korl woman, both expressed and repressed Davis's own Promethean desires as she struggled to create a literary form that could embody her growing social anger.

I believe that *Margret Howth* burst open the optimistic foundations of American romanticism. Even though Davis wrote Fields that she was "afraid to touch forbidden subjects so only the husk of the thing was left,"[4] powerful images of the degrading effects of slavery, the reactionary arrogance of secessionists, the social myopia of organized religion, the hardships of industrial life, the suppression of women's work, and in particular the transcendental attraction to solipsism waft through the novel—written, as Davis insists, "from the border of the battlefield, and I find in it no theme for shallow argument or flimsy rhymes."[5]

The story of life in a new factory town in Indiana is hardly a portrait of a perfect day in June. Although she promised Fields a summertime story "steeped in warm healthy light," her tale opens with these words: "Men have forgotten to hope, forgotten to pray"; they survive only through "the bitterness of endurance"; in the morning they say, "'Would God it were even!' and in the evening, 'Would God it were morning!'"(3). Throughout the text, the narrator realigns the reader's romantic expectations as she explodes the epic and public themes of the first year of the Civil War: "Let me tell you a story of To-day,—very homely and narrow in its scope and aim. Not of the To-Day whose significance in the history of humanity only those shall read who will live when you and I are dead." Having preemptively killed off her reader (whom I allege to be Fields), she adds, "Neither I nor you have the prophet's vision to see the age as its meaning stands written before God." Further, she goes on, the Civil War did not assure a happy ending for the war-torn nation: "Those who shall live when we are dead may tell their children, perhaps, how, out of anguish and darkness such as the world seldom has borne, the enduring morning evolved of the true world and the true man. It is not clear to us" (4).

Rejecting nationalistic rhetoric, Davis turns to affectional discourse, the language of "mercy and love," to tell her "story of today." The narrator announces that she has renounced the language of "patriotism and chivalry" in order to record "less partial truths . . . that do not speak to us in bayonets and victories." Insistently reiterating, "Do not call me a traitor," she returns to the female vocabulary of sentimentalism to forge a social and realistic rhetoric, and along the way she repudiates the solipsistic and overreaching will of romanticism.

Sentimentalism was a tradition that linked private feeling to public action, moral faculties to social activity, and emotion and ethics to law and economics. As modern readers consider Davis's choice of discourse, it is important to bear in mind that sentimental ethics held a highly political charge. In the mid-nineteenth century, sentimentalism was viewed as unmediated expression of human nature, *socially defined*. As Fred Kaplan observes, "Most Victorians believed that the human community was one of shared moral feelings, and that sentimentality was a desirable way of feeling and of expressing ourselves morally."[6] *Margret Howth* portrays how the new industrialism was challenging visions of a shared national morality by encouraging assertive individualism. In Davis's view, individualism is a political identity that sits rather comfortably with the egoism of literary romanticism. In her first full-length novel, the discourse of feelings confronts both the vocabulary of romantic egoism and the emerging imagery of utilitarianism, invention, and political economy.

Davis believes that male energies—equally necessary to patriotism, narcissism, capitalistic self-advancement, and romantic self-discovery, threaten female drives—gestures toward self-growth through friendship and family bonds. She holds that the greatest danger to the commonweal is ego, which she pictures in the willingness of male characters to buy and sell people through slavery, wages, marriage, and utopian visions of political omnipotence; her best hope for social change lies in "harmony," which she sees as "faith in God, faith in her fellow-man, faith in herself" (77). Harmony to Davis is the sine qua non of a better society. In assigning harmony to female characters, Davis suggests that women's right and capacity to express social outrage derives from their social authority *as women*. Only visions of community, whether utopian, socialist, pastoral, or familial, can resist the pressures of industrial capitalism toward atomization, expressed in terms of character as selfishness, loneliness, and greed. Paradoxically in *Margret Howth*, each communal dream is found seriously wanting, contaminated by the system that has spawned it. In *Margret Howth*, the debate over the true course of social change thus emerges as a political expression of the tension Davis finds between the egotistical love of men and the self-denying love of women.

Viewing sentimentalism as a species of mid-nineteenth-century discourse may account for the considerable dissonance between the modern and the contemporary receptions of *Margret Howth*. Nineteenth-century reviewers received the book enthusiastically, specifically praising its social concerns. A reviewer for *Peterson's Magazine*, a popular journal with a mostly female audience, observed,

> On some of the deepest problems that agitate humanity [Davis] has evidently thought much and deeply; and she has come back, from the solemn quest . . . full of heaven-like faith. . . . Such characters as Holmes and Knowles, in their robust strength and originality, exist nowhere in the novels of female writers, except in those of Charlotte Bronte; and we would say that Holmes and Knowles are more powerful creations than even the best of Charlotte Bronte's if we were not afraid of being too eulogistic.

The reviewer goes on to predict that the anonymous author of *Margret Howth* "will eventually be confessed to be the greatest of American novelists."[7] Likewise, the *Continental Monthly*, a new journal with strong abolitionist sentiments and a commitment to early realism, praised *Margret Howth* as a realistic exploration of "a new field, right into the rough of real life, bringing out fresher and more varied forms than had been done before."

Echoing the narrator of "Life in the Iron-Mills," the *Continental's* reviewer observed that "few, especially in the Atlantic cities, know what becomes of culture among men and women who 'work and weave in endless motion' in the counting-house, or factory, or through daily drudgery and the reverses from wealth to poverty."[8] This review admired Davis's pictures of "incidents" of industrial life and her portrait of the "inner being" of residents of industrial towns, that is, the relationship between the new economic system and subjectivity:

> One may believe, in reading it, that the author, wearied of the old cry that the literature of our country is only a continuation of that of Europe, had resolved to prove, by vigorous effort, that it *is* possible to set forth, not merely the incidents of our industrial life in many grades, in its purely idiomatic force, to make the world realize that in it vibrate and struggle outward those aspirations, germs of culture and reforms that we seldom reflect on as forming a part of the inner-being of our very practical fellow-citizens.[9]

The reviewer saw that in Davis's portrait nationalist struggles for reform reside, in part, in consciousness and desire.

By contrast, Sharon Harris finds *Margret Howth* "ultimately a failure in artistic terms precisely because of the incongruous insertions of 'full sunshine' into an otherwise stridently realistic work."[10] Jean Fagan Yellin accounts for this incongruity by suggesting that Davis "trimmed" *Margret Howth* to conform to the requirements of the literary establishment surrounding the *Atlantic Monthly*. In privatizing public problems, ignoring economic hunger, and eradicating spiritual hunger, Yellin argues, Davis made the revisions that would placate Fields and thereby she "feminized" and weakened her tale.[11]

In my view, the tension between realism and sentiment in the novel marks Davis's definition of social responsibility as active participation in a sympathetic community. With the Civil War raging around her, with industrialism polluting both the air and the social fabric of Wheeling, overawed by the abolitionist and secessionist passions that she saw rending her town, in *Margret Howth* Davis launched her lifelong theme of political desire and elevated the Promethean theme of "Life in the Iron-Mills" to social debate. Influenced by the ideology of sentiment, she suggested that if political hunger is not regulated by family, love, and the female definition of true community, it could degenerate into a destructive and hungry egoism that uses others as it promotes its unfulfilled desire in the name of social progress. *Margret Howth* confronts the politics of romantic egoism through a literary convention in which the give-and-take of domestic relationships regulates desire.[12]

It is this tension that may have raised Davis's concern about a comparison between herself and Charlotte Brontë. In August, as she was undertaking minor revisions to *Margret Howth*, she wrote to Fields, "You did not think I imitated Charlotte Bronte, did you? I would rather you had sent it back than thought that, but tell me candidly if you did. I may have done it unconsciously."[13] Davis's unease in fact points to the transnational influences of women authors that forged an "imagined community"[14] and suggests that she, along with other nineteenth-century American women authors, did not write in intellectual isolation. As in *Jane Eyre*, in *Margret Howth* sentimental motifs confront patriarchal assumptions within the reform tendencies of romanticism. Rather than a story of female capitulation (in the tradition of Ann Douglas, who bemoans the "feminization" of American literature), *Margret Howth*, like *Jane Eyre*, should be read as a gendered paradigm of the social tensions embodied in the movement from romanticism to realism, from the "egotistical sublime" to a genre based on the growth of individuals who interact with an expanding industrial society.

Romanticism, Nina Baym reminds us, promises an *idea* of America where individuals can achieve complete self-definition because they can exist in some meaningful sense prior to and apart from history. Romanticism inscribes a confrontation between the American individual, the pure American self divorced from specific social circumstances, and the promise offered by the idea of America:

> This promise is the deeply romantic one that in this new land identity is untrammeled by history and social accident. Behind this promise is the assurance that individuals come before society, that they exist in some meaningful sense outside the societies in which they happen to find themselves. The romantic myth also holds that as something artificial and secondary to human nature, society exerts an unmitigatedly destructive pressure on individuality.[15]

Further, as Mary Poovey suggests, the romantic absence of social regulation and the egotistical drive to assert and extend the self, deny—to use Kant's phrase—the otherness of others.[16] In *Margret Howth*, as in *Jane Eyre*, women's identity is enmeshed within the network of family and community; the Emersonian idealization of autonomy represents a masculine threat to communal sensibility. The power of sentiment can contain egoism, but usually at the price of repressing men's and women's deep hunger for "summat to make them live."

By appending a sentimental resolution to a realist novel, by appending a June ending to her wintry tale, Davis appealed to two democratic literary traditions: the vernacular characterization of farmers and factory workers, and the sentimental discourse of female emotionality, piety, and moral commitment. The sentimental novel, as Jane Tompkins reminds us, saw itself as an "agent of cultural formation," a blueprint for women's survival under a specific set of political, economic, social, and religious conditions.[17] Sentimental authors adopted a familiar idiom, assured that a contemporary audience would know how to respond. In these terms, readers of *Margret Howth* would have recognized that the ending, dissonant though it may be to us, left Margret in a familiar context of common female opportunities and oppressions. Thus, I think that the apparent tension between the sections, voices, and discourses of *Margret Howth* partakes of what Susan Harris, in Bakhtinian terms, calls the "heteroglossia" of women's fiction of the time, the frequent use of multiple discursive modes within one text to represent a female author's ongoing debate about how to live in the world.[18]

In this way, *Margret Howth* also recalls "The American Scholar," in which Emerson, a great influence on Davis, finds no tension between such discourses when he said that the office of the scholar or "poet" is "to cheer, to raise, to guide men by showing them facts amidst appearances. . . . He is the world's eye. He is the world's heart."[19] *Margret Howth* works through both the eye and the heart, conflating Davis's industrial topic and her realist technique through the metaphor of literary language itself:

> My story is very crude and homely, as I said,—only a rough sketch of one or two of those people whom you see every day, and call "dregs," sometimes,— *a dull, plain bit of prose*, such as you might pick for yourself out of any of these warehouses or back-streets.

Perhaps addressing Fields himself, she notes sardonically,

> I expect you to call it stale and plebeian, for I know the glimpses of life it pleases you best to find; idylls delicately tinted; passion-veined hearts, cut bare for curious eyes; prophetic utterances, concrete and clear.

Responding to Fields's insistent pressure to revise her gloom, Davis persists:

> You want something, in fact, to lift you out of this crowded, tobacco-stained commonplace, to kindle and chafe and glow in you. I want you to dig into this commonplace, this vulgar American life, and see what is in it. Sometimes I think it has a new and awful significance that we do not see. (6)

She then goes on to summon this reader, whose "manlier nature" has been awakened by the trumpet of the Civil War, to the other great "warfare" going on, a war that also "has its slain. Men and women, lean-jawed, crippled in the slow, silent battle, are in your alleys, sit beside you at your table; its martyrs sleep under every green hill-side." From this class war, she insists, "money will buy you no discharge" (7).[20]

Davis also disagreed with Fields about the title of her novel. Originally she wanted to call it either *The Deaf and the Dumb* or *A Story of Today*, either one a more appropriate title than *Margret Howth*, which Fields bestowed on the manuscript.[21] Her preferred title, *A Story of Today*, and her frequent references to "today" also echo Emerson, who said, "I do not ask for the great, the remote, the romantic; what is doing in Italy or Arabia; . . . I embrace the common, I explore and sit at the feet of the familiar, the low. Give me insight into to-day."[22]

Margret Howth is a highly contemporary story about a raw mill town in Indiana. Hunger and poverty have forced Margret, a spinster daughter of a retired and blind schoolmaster, to take a man's job as a bookkeeper in a large woolen mill. The mill is owned by Dr. Knowles, an abolitionist and romantic reformer who is selling the property to Stephen Holmes, one of the new men who will mold the age, like "all men around him . . . thrusting and jostling and struggling, up, up" (121). The penniless but ambitious Holmes, living for "self-salvation, self-elevation," ends his romance with Margret so he can use the dowry of a young heiress to buy the property. But before he can pay for the mill, it burns down, torched by an angry ex-convict, Joe Yare, an African American who works in the mill as a night stoker. Eventually Knowles, Holmes, and Margret redesign their personal and social visions through the humble and self-sacrificing love of Joe's daughter, Lois, a deformed mulatto peddler, who dies from the toxic fumes breathed while rescuing Holmes from the fire. Her death instructs them in the power of sympathy and the values of humility, duty, and family; thus it redeems them all.

Margret Howth is also the story of the breakup of rural social structures in an emerging industrial capitalist economy. The novel begins with an image of one of the most profound changes of industrialization, the painful and repressive adjustment of a young woman who leaves home and enters the workplace for the first time. It explores how new relationships of production surrounding the woolen mill—wages, contracts, and competition—are replacing the rural networks of family, barter, gossip, and charity. Thus Davis contrasts the atomized and defensive personalities spawned by the economy of the mill—Knowles, Holmes, and Joe Yare—to the caring and responsible relationships of dependency sustaining those who work and live in the surrounding countryside, outside the economic aura of the mill—the Howths, local farmers, and, in particular, the peddler Lois. In contrast to the sham utopianism embraced by Knowles, Lois unites the community by trading its garden produce, a role that links her to its preindustrial economy. By comparing the new manufacturing town with the rural life of the farms (the Howth farm is still just a long walk from the mill), Davis exposes the tensions in the early stages of capitalist development. Mercantile and farm ethics of hard work, thrift, attachment, honesty, and community are yielding to individualism, secularity, self-interest, competition, alcoholism, and petty crime.

The novel begins on Margret's first day of work, her twentieth birthday, when she enters the mill as a bookkeeper in order to "support a helpless father and mother; it was a common story" (19). Clearly, her status has worsened. Margret's climb onto her stool on October 20, 1860, in a small "closet," a dark seventh-floor office, is mainstream American literature's first record of a young rural woman leaving home to work in a factory. The floors shake with the incessant thud of the looms, and the office is heavy with the smell of dye and copperas, a sulfate of copper, iron, and zinc used in woolen dyes. Seated uncomfortably on her stool which is, metaphorically, "too high for a small woman," the American heroine is no longer looking out a window, but finds herself fully occupied by the world of work within. As in "Life in the Iron-Mills," images of artistic repression define industrial work. Unwilling to "dramatiz[e] her soul in writing" (8), she has taken up ledger work, the uncreative and monotonous copying from one book to another. With her steel pen "lining out her life, narrow and black," she soon wipes the ink from her pen in a "mechanical fashion" (10)—reified by her task. Through the imagery of writing itself Davis replaces sentimental fiction's metaphoric and literal closet of the house with the realist's enclosed office: female confinement endures.[23]

In contrast to her own anonymous "cramped quiet lines," Margret soon discovers a series of charcoal sketches drawn on the office walls by her predecessor, P. Teagarden, who has boldly emblazoned his name on the ceiling with the smoke of a candle—an interesting literary gesture from a woman novelist who is pleading with her publisher to keep her work anonymous.[24] Teagarden has also left behind a doleful chicken pecking the floor of a wire cage, which, along with the drawings, prompts Margret to recall how, as an aspiring and imaginative young girl, she planned to "dig down into the middle of the world, and find the kingdom of the griffins, or . . . go after Mercy and Christiana in their pilgrimage" (11). As Margret walks past soot-stained warehouses toward her home in the hills after her first day of work, the narrator observes, "One might have fancied her a slave putting on a mask, fearing to meet her master" (17)—an image of alienation and self-disguise that fuses wage slavery, chattel slavery, and the repressions of domestic life. These images of mechanical confinement and artistic inhibition anticipate such images as the caged parrot of Kate Chopin's *The Awakening*, who incessantly chants, "Allez-vous en!" ("Go away!" "Get out!") and the wallpaper in Charlotte Perkins Gilman's "The Yellow Wallpaper," whose design becomes a frightening projection of female repression.

Despite Fields's title for her novel, Davis always saw Dr. Knowles as the center of the story.[25] Influenced by his readings of early European socialists, Knowles, like Hollingsworth in Hawthorne's *Blithedale Romance*, plans to use the profits from the sale of the mill to launch a utopian community made up of the most degraded and impoverished residents of the town—alcoholics, prostitutes, and abandoned women—and he hopes to recruit Margret (suggesting Margaret Fuller, perhaps) as his aide. The relationship between Margret and Knowles, rather like that between Hollingsworth and Zenobia, distills the tensions between the telos of sentimentalism and the telos of romanticism. Knowles presumes that Margret "had been planned and kept by God for higher uses than daughter or wife or mother. It was his part to put her work into her hands." Like her mother, who thinks that "Margret never had any opinions to express" (29), Knowles presumes that her desire is a species of his own, which he fantasizes as incestuous and repressed intimacy: "Between the two there lay that repellent resemblance which made them like close relations,—closer when they were silent" (19).

While Margret views her office job as a consequence of her father's financial incompetence and of Holmes's rejection—"perhaps life had nothing better for her, so she did not care"—Knowles, who consistently misreads Margret, sees her work as a romantic test. Intending to "make use" (23) of her in his utopian community, "he must know what stuff was in the weapon before he used it. He had been reading the slow, cold thing for years,—had not got into its secret yet. But there was power there, and it was the power he wanted" (19). He is convinced that Margret is an emanation of his best self and that if he can control her it will assign them both significance. To Knowles, Margret is a "Damascus blade which he was going to carry into battle" (23). But only in his phallic projection is she dangerous; in fact, Margret's repression and plainness undercut Knowles's egoistic fantasies: "There were no reflected lights about her; no gloss on her skin, no glitter in her eyes" (22).

In my view, a central problem with Davis's novel comes from a contradiction within transcendentalism itself: how to reconcile egoism with the dissolution of self that allows for political engagement. Like Bronson Alcott, Knowles tries to resolve this profound impasse by linking his ambitious quest to the universal good, a fusion of the personal and the public at the core of utopianism. In assigning political righteousness to his dominating fantasies of Margret, Knowles legitimizes her powerlessness at the same time that he blesses it with historical possibility. Margret's social vision, by contrast, derives from sentimentalism. Fred Kaplan explores how sentimentalism inherited the Enlightenment faith in the redemptive power of emotions over self-calculation. He cites David Hume, for example, who argues that "the ultimate ends of human actions can never . . . be accounted for by *reason*, but recommend themselves entirely to the sentiments and affections of mankind, without any dependence on the intellectual faculties."[26] Kaplan thus distinguishes sentiment, an "access of feeling," from the romantic "excess of feeling," which, almost by definition, must deny the world. Furthermore, he suggests, while sentiment offers an optimistic vision overall, it nonetheless takes its force from a keen awareness of human nature that, paradoxically, jeopardizes its claims to an ideal world.[27] Margret's dilemma is thus to find a way to defend the sentimental woman against the self-sufficient romantic imagination on the one hand, and the post-Calvinist forces of philosophical realism on the other. If sentimentalism sought to atrophy woman in her emotions and traditional social duties, realism sought to limit woman as the dubious product of her social conditions and biology. To Davis, neither race, gender, class, nor region should be prescriptive.

For Davis, the split between preindustrial and industrial values has a gendered valence. She believes that transcendentalism prompts patriarchal self-interest, which fits comfortably with the industrial breakup of rural and familial communities. In Knowles and Holmes, both mill owners, she portrays men who assert their self-reliance while they remain emotionally and financially dependent. The romantic man needs the sentimental woman, typified by Lois, as an enduring sign of the living gospel, and as an apostle of anti-egotistical and anticapitalistic values that can heal the culture as a whole. In *Margret Howth*, it is as the vessel for men's salvation that women's essential nature takes on a transformative role in the ongoing social debate about American industrialism.[28] In this Davis again echoes Emerson, who holds that self-reliance is not a paradigm of freedom from duty, but rather a model of an internalized standard of duty.

Thus, rather than a protonaturalist text, *Margret Howth* belongs to a discursive category that Thomas Laqueur terms the "humanitarian narrative," a hybrid of sentimentalism and early realism in which details of suffering, particularly bodily suffering, prompt compassion—understood in its time as a moral imperative to undertake social change.[29] Sentiment thereby shapes Davis's vision of social goals. For example, Margret, despairing of her plight, agrees to accompany Knowles on a visit to a crowded railroad shack, a "haunt of the lowest vice," where he hopes to recruit members for his celibate community. In this passage Davis recalls the nighttime visit to the mill in "Life in the Iron-Mills," but this time the witness is female, as are the homeless Irish women and fugitive slaves who live in the shack; as an empathic female, the narrator repudiates Knowles's romantic appropriation of suffering.

True to the lineaments of sentimentalism, the suffering of the industrial poor is pictured as an imprisoning and confining female site where gender transcends class. Knowles views poverty as erotically female: "'Come here!'

he said, fiercely, clutching [Margret's] hand. 'Women as fair and pure as you have come into dens like this,—and never gone away. Does it make your delicate breath faint?" (150). Knowles and Margret stand over women who are prostrate and drunk, incompetent as mothers and incapable of taking action on their own behalf: "Women, idle trampers, whisky-bloated, filthy, lay half-asleep, or smoking on the floor, set up a chorus of whining and begging when they entered. Half-naked children crawled about in rags."

The destitute women are further distinguished by their Catholic faith, which, to Davis, marks them as recent immigrants: "On the damp mildewed walls, there was hung a picture of . . . Pio Nono, crook in hand, with the usual inscription, "Feed my sheep" (151). This ironic reference to Pius IX (the pope who whose betrayal of the Italian revolution of 1848 was bitterly described by Margaret Fuller)[30] points to Davis's lifelong hostility to Catholicism as well as to Protestant churches that were unwilling to engage in the Social Gospel. Davis conflates the Irish women with runaway slaves, who are mutually eroticized: "In the corner slept a heap of half-clothed blacks. Going on the underground railroad to Canada. Stolid, sensual wretches" (151). The narrator's racial discourse is indistinguishable from that of Knowles, who, while viewing the slave women as his future utopians, is trapped in the rhetoric of human commerce, and who observes, "so much flesh and blood out of the market, unweighed!" (151). When Margret, by contrast, picks up a slave child and kisses her face, Knowles responds, "Would you touch her? . . . Put it down" (151). Locked in their own discursive systems, Margret and Knowles appropriate the poor in different ways.

Eventually Margret agrees to join the community, a reluctant choice that mainly stems from her plight as a lonely single woman who is tired of taking care of her pettish mother and her bigoted father. Margret is repulsed by Mr. Howth's dreams of secession, his admiration for Napoleon, and his tiresome investigations of the Middle Ages when commoners still believed in the "perfected manhood in the conqueror" (31). Unlike Knowles, her father believes that now "the world's a failure. All the great dreams are dead" (34). Even in a novel that prioritizes affectional bonds, Davis, like Susan Warner in *The Wide Wide World*, satirizes a father who is self-interested, unreliable—indeed, "blind." Margret's decision to enter Knowles's "House of Refuge," a parody of the idealized home, reflects the disempowerment of domesticity and frustrations at her parents' house, "in which her life was slowly to be worn out: working for those who did not comprehend her; thanked her little, —that was all" (61).

Davis, herself a single woman taking care of her parents, is unromantic about the trials of housewifery on a meager income, the "white leprosy of poverty" (38). She pictures how Mrs. Howth forages in the harvested fields for late peas or corn, until Margret "could see the swollen circle round the eyes, and hear her [mother's] breath like that of a child which has sobbed itself tired" (37)—a role reversal that exposes the protective covenant of motherhood. Not only is the family vulnerable to economic pressures outside its moral sway; Davis's satiric representations of Margret's family as conflicted and inept—indeed, her very act of ironizing the family—destroys it as sentiment's utopian telos. Thus, Margret's choice to follow Knowles is based not only on her poverty, but also on her own isolation as a woman whose lover has rejected her, whose dog has run away, and whose mother prefers the company of her father. Compared to the House of Refuge, her parents' home offers neither Margret nor her mother female authority, emotional transcendence, or the moral significance of domestic work. Margret also turns to a life of social duty because Jesus (often shaped in sentiment as a consoling figure who protects women from isolation)[31] also "had been alone" (159).

Unlike Margret, but also unlike the romantic figure Mitchell in "Life in the Iron-Mills," Knowles has a political role: "Fanatics must make history for conservative men to learn from" (180). Knowles is a follower of the French utopian socialists Fourier (1772–1827) and Saint-Simon (1760–1825) and of the German romantic and founder of "absolute idealism," Johann Gottlieb Fichte (1762–1814), whose works Davis probably read with her brother, Wilson, a student of European romanticism. From Fourier's design for phalansteries, Knowles planned a community that would work "like leaven through the festering mass under the country he loved so well" (154–55). From Fichte, who was influenced by the "ethical activism" of Jean-Jacques Rousseau and Emmanuel Kant, Knowles inherited the view of a morally empowered ego. Unlike the solipsistic strain found in many transcendentalists, Fichte believed in a socially ethical self that could withstand pressures from the competitive and aggressive world of nature. History, once a prerogative of God, now belonged to the individual, who had a duty to create a rational, moral, egalitarian, and self-sufficient community free from the "anarchy of trade." Organized into guilds, the tightly organized community would provide each member with tools, the value of one's labor, and the right to a full creative life.[32] While Davis never develops Knowles's utopian design, in his plans to "make use" of Margret, however, he also exhibits the authoritarianism of Hawthorne's Hollingsworth and of Saint-Simon, who argued that leadership belongs to the educated elite—scientists, physiologists, historians, and economists—who can best design and supervise a technocratic but providential state on behalf of the poorest and most numerous classes.

Unlike Margret, Knowles identifies with social as well as personal suffering. On the one hand, the details of the humanitarian narrative touch his Fichtean sense of moral empiricism: "All things were real to this man, this uncouth mass of flesh that his companion sneered at; most real of all, the unhelped pain of life, the great seething mire of dumb wretchedness in streets and alleys, the cry for aid from the starved souls of the world" (49–50). On the other hand, still reiterating the word *real,* Davis locates Knowles's political drive in his own racial oppression. In her first reference to the plight of Native Americans, the narrator explains that Knowles's mother was a Creek Indian and notes: "You and I have other work to do than to listen,—pleasanter. But he, coming out of the mire, his veins thick with the blood of a despised race, had carried up their pain and hunger with him: it was the most real thing on earth to him,—more real than his own share in the unseen heaven or hell" (50).

In contrast to the social egoism that compels Knowles is Stephen Holmes's "self-existent soul" (160). Holmes, who has purchased the mill with his fiancée's dowry, is driven by economic self-interest. He has "turned his back on love and kindly happiness and warmth, on all that was weak and useless in the world" (139), that is, everything he identifies with Margret. A representative of the emerging ideology of bourgeois individualism, Holmes views his new fiancée, the mill, its workers, and Margret as his property, which he will try to transform into an aspect of his self. Since purchasing the mill, he has become so mechanized that to Margret his familiar footsteps now sound like an "iron tread, . . . so firm and measured that it sounded like the monotonous beatings of a clock" (87). Now, "in the mill he was of the mill" (117). Eventually he even decides to sleep in the mill, where his hard bed and chairs are made of iron—"here was discipline" (120). Only money, he finds, is erotic: "it made his fingers thrill with pleasure to touch a full pocket-book as well as his mistress's hand" (104).

Fusing his utilitarian belief that "all things were made for man" (105) with a romantic vision of the self, Holmes seeks "a savage freedom, . . . the freedom of the primitive man, the untamed animal man, self-reliant and self-assertant, having conquered Nature" (107). As Margret realizes that she must leave Holmes to his "clear self-reliant life,—with his Self, dearer to him than she had ever been" (62), Davis marks the dangers of romanticism through a character who has chosen solitary wholeness over communal fragmentation. Nonetheless, even in a sentimental narrative that values nurturance and concern, both Margret and Dr. Knowles are attracted to Holmes whose credo is *Ego sum* (112). Margret finds Holmes "a master among men: fit to be a master" (62), and Knowles likewise observes "If there were such a reality as mastership, that man was born to rule" (80).

Holmes rather than Knowles thus inherits the mantle from Mitchell in "Life in the Iron-Mills." Pictured, like Mitchell, through images of coolness and ice, Holmes is an exponent of the "great idea of American sociology,—that the object of life is *to grow*" (121). Unlike the korl woman, however, who is "hungry to know," Holmes has a "savage hunger" (137) that drives him to transcend his childhood in the slums and become a "merchant prince." In contrast to the statue, he believes that "endurance is enough" for the slaves and destitute factory workers who work at his mill (113). Images of slavery surround Holmes; he believes that he has been "bought and sold" by his fiancée, who "held him a slave to her fluttering hand." While she is "proud of her slave," he resents the fact that "there were no dark iron bars across her life" (139). It is tempting to think that having promised Fields a perfect day in June, Davis was mocking her publisher when Miss Herne masquerades as June in a tableau vivant. Anticipating the tableaux vivants in Edith Wharton's *House of Mirth*, Miss Herne dresses as a seductive, dangerous, and serpentine figure who, in Holmes's view, glows with a "smothered heat beneath the snaring eyes" and whose "unclean sweetness of jasmine-flowers mixed with the . . . smells of the mill . . . Patchouli or copperas,—what was the difference? The mill and his future wife came to him together" (126–27). Miss Herne's decadent sexuality, a form of promiscuity earlier associated with aristocratic excesses that threatened middle-class virtues,[33] has in *Margret Howth* evolved into a female metaphor for the seductive power of industrial capitalism itself. Margret's chastity, by contrast, emerges as a trope for bourgeois morality, which, in the end, prevails.

In *Margret Howth*, true community arises through the understanding of shared suffering rather than through the design of any single individual. In the figure of Lois Yare, Davis's first African-American character, the politics of pathos bridge the discourses of sentimentalism and realism, mobilizing democratic sentiment through the values of domesticity.[34] Lois embodies the tension between personal pain, inscribed in the language of sentimentality, and industrial oppression, inscribed in the language of vernacular realism. To signify the loss of preindustrial innocence, Davis invokes the racist stereotype of a childlike, physically handicapped, mentally retarded mulatto woman: "Her soul, being lower, it might be, than ours, lay closer to Nature" (65). Nonetheless, when speaking for herself Lois insists that it is the mill (where she had worked from the time she was seven until she turned sixteen), not her nature, that has ruined her mind and her health. Like Stephen Holmes, she was "of" the mill: "I kind o' grew into that place in them years; seemed to me like as I was part o' the' engines, somehow."

Countering the narrator's racist observation that Lois's "tainted blood" had "dragged her down" is Lois's own clear insistence on the erotic force and toxic ecology of the mill:

> Th' air used to be thick in my mouth, black wi' smoke 'n' wool 'n' smells. In them years I got dazed in my head. . . . 'T got so that th' noise o' th' looms went on in my head night 'n' day,—allus thud, thud . . . th' black wheels 'n' rollers was alive, starin' down at me, 'n' th' shadders o' th' looms was like snakes creepin',—creepin' anear all th' time. (69)

Lois's sense of defilement by the mill marks her passage to adulthood and affiliates her narrative with that of other girls in sentimental fiction (such as Ellen Montgomery in Susan Warner's *Wide Wide World*, 1850), who are initiated into a culture that has abused their bodies and repressed their emotions. Lois recalls that before she went to work on the looms she used to play house in the lumberyard at the mill; now she realizes that her "crushed brain and unawakened powers" were caused by the "mass of iron and work and impure smells" of those years (171).

But for Davis, writing from a slave state in 1861, the traditional midcentury fictional ending of marriage and home is historically and imaginatively unavailable for a black woman character—a tension that Davis seems to have understood. Initially Margret identifies with Lois, the disfigured and bitter survivor of years of slavery and brutal child labor, through their common female suffering, acknowledging that her own "higher life" was also "starved, thwarted" (71). As Julie Elison observes, in the nineteenth century pain (which is always gendered) serves as the link between the body and power.[35] However, Margret soon recognizes a crucial distinction: unlike Lois she "was free,—and liberty . . . was the cure for all the soul's diseases" (72). Thus Davis refuses to let slavery and blackness serve as a generic metaphor for many other sorts of pain.

Although permanently deformed, Lois recovers spiritually through her relationship to nature. In the figure of Lois we can trace the profound influence of Emerson on Davis. Lois is indeed a nature scholar who, in Emerson's sense, "can read God directly."[36] In a series of passages that adhere rather closely to the prescriptions of "The American Scholar" and "Nature," Lois reveals what Emerson calls an "original relation to the universe."[37] Emerson argues that a primal contact with nature allows one to experience God firsthand, unmediated by corrupt churches or biblical interpretation; able to be "read" by anyone, nature can replace the Bible as the greatest spiritual text. Further, a nature scholar is unalienated because he is infantile:

> Few adults can see nature. Most persons do not see the sun. At least they have a very superficial seeing. The sun illuminates only the eye of the man, but shines into the eye and heart of the child. The lover of nature is he whose inward and outward sense are still truly adjusted to each other; who has retained the spirit of infancy even into the era of his manhood . . . In the presence of nature a wild delight runs through them, in spite of real sorrows.[38]

In *Margret Howth* Lois is a child-artist who reads nature as a great spiritual text; she becomes the world's eye. For Davis, Lois's primal ability arises from the fact that she is black and female. Even though Lois is clearly a young adult, the narrator and various characters refer to her as a cheerful child. Unlike Knowles and Holmes, Lois has eyes quick to know the other light that "went into the fogs of the fetid dens from which the coarser light was barred" (91). Like the scholar-artist, she has the simplicity of character to become an "interpreter" of nature who understands that nature is (in Emerson's phrase) a "remoter and inferior incarnation of God, a projection of God in the unconscious."[39] Thus Lois, says the narrator, can see glimpses of the "heavenly clearness" of God's light: "Was it weakness and ignorance that made everything she saw or touched nearer, more human to her than to you or me?" (93). Surrounded by Emersonian images of sunlight, Lois "liked clear, vital colours . . . the crimsons and blues. They answered her somehow. They could speak. There were things in the world that like herself were marred,—did not understand—were hungry to know: the gray sky, the mud streets, the tawny lichens" (92).

Emerson's scholar inevitably becomes a realist artist whose unmediated sensibility is shaped not by tradition or imagination but by the eye: "To the human eye that the primary forms, as the sky, the mountain, the tree, give us . . . a pleasure arising from outline, color, motion, and grouping."[40] Lois is such an artist, fulfilling Emerson's requirement that art should become an epitome of the real world, a "result or the expression of nature, in minia-ture."[41] Lois instinctively composes her cart along such lines: "Patched as it was, [it] had a snug, cosy look; the masses of vegetables, green and crimson and scarlet, were heaped with a certain reference to the glow of color . . . What artist sense had she,—what could she know—this ignorant huckster— of the eternal laws of beauty or grandeur?" (64–65). Davis frequently judges her characters by this transcendent artistic capacity. Like Hugh Wolfe, Lois, an "ignorant huckster," has built her sculpture from the materials of her work. By contrast, despite his humanitarian inclinations Knowles is "blind to the prophecy written on the earth," and, similarly, in his isolated myopia Holmes sees that "the windless gray, the stars, the stone under his feet, stood alone in the universe, each working out its own soul into deed. If there were any all embracing harmony, one soul through all, he did not see it" (161).

While Davis masculinizes society, she feminizes nature which, as such, is vulnerable to male exploitation and definition. Viewed in relation to urban life and industrial control, nature in *Margret Howth* becomes a projection of woman's unconscious and an image of her recurrent need for mothering. Like Emerson, who sees nature as a "beautiful mother,"[42] Lois finds in na-ture a new mother who "longs to take her uncouth child home again" (263). Onto this maternal sensibility Davis layers a feminized sense of erotic unity.

While Holmes's impetus is toward separation, discontinuity, and self-denial, Lois moves toward a transcendent sense of nature that erases boundaries— "Why, sometimes, out in the hills, in the torrid quiet of summer noons, she had knelt by the shaded pools, and buried her hands in the great slumberous beds of water-lilies, her blood curdling in a feverish languor, a passioned trance, from which she roused herself, weak and tired" (93)—a romantic and erotic erasure of the self and others, subject and object. The surrender to the romantic universal also removes the entranced child-woman from the in-evitability of history, represented by the mill. Marianne Hirsch suggests that in female romanticism sleep not only signifies withdrawal into the symbolic landscape of the innermost self; it also suggests the one-dimensional nature of a woman's development. Excluded from social interaction, she is thrown back into herself, where she can explore her spiritual or emotional sides, but only at the expense of other aspects of her selfhood.[43]

For Emerson, Lois's transcendent capacity would have had a social func-tion: "The office of the scholar is to cheer, to raise, to guide men by showing them facts amidst appearances."[44] In contrast to Knowles, who is ineffectually trying to forge a utopian society in his own image, Lois, the peddler, through her "Great Spirit of love and trust" (77) and her romanticized trinity of "a faith in God, faith in her fellow-man, faith in herself," offers the enduring possibility of a true preindustrial community. One morning, for example, as Margret walks alongside Lois into town, they stop and visit at each farm-house, collecting produce and butter and enjoying several breakfasts. Repudiating the imagery of mechanical time that surrounds Holmes, Lois's leisurely work connects Margret, the isolated bookkeeper, with her neigh-bors. For the first time "the two women were talking all the way. In all his life Dr. Knowles had never heard from this silent girl words as open and eager as she gave to the huckster about paltry, common things" (72). As she shares "disjointed" womanly talk with Lois, Margret feels "keenly alive" (73) for the first time. Even in the town, where Margret used to see the houses as closed and silent, she discovers through Lois a sisterhood of servants, house-maids, and news vendors.

In the end, rage generated by racism and poverty brings down the indus-trial house—a danger that Davis believed the North must heed. Lois rescues Holmes from a fire that her angry father, Joe, has started at the mill, and dies after inhaling the fumes of burning copperas. But her death does not represent the Christian martyrdom of Stowe's Uncle Tom or Little Eva. Lois's pre-oedipal attachments, her allegiance to childhood, her dissolution of boundaries, and her sense of the dangers of industrialism render her death an inevitable effect of the adult world of industrial and chattel slavery. Her death actualizes sentimental rage, reiterating the novel's choice between romance and self, community and ego. As Lois lies dying, the community, black and white, comes together and invests her death with the power of social redemption. In *Margret Howth* Davis revises the theme of much female fiction from the mid-nineteenth century—the endless attempt to achieve self-sacrifice[45]—by viewing women's submission as a tragic consequence of masculine assertion and romantic egoism. Eventually Margret quits the House of Refuge and forgives Stephen Holmes, who has repented of his ambitious romance and returned to Margret, announcing, "I need warmth and freshness and light: my wife shall bring them to me. She shall be no strong-willed reformer, standing alone: a sovereign lady with kind words . . . only to that man whom she trusts" (242). The narrator notes, however, that Margret "paid no heed" to this final comment.

Davis was quite disappointed with Margret, and wrote to James Fields that she did not want the novel named after its heroine because "she is the completest failure in the story, besides not being the nucleus of it." Whether Margret dissatisfied her author as a woman or as a literary achievement is tauntingly unclear.[46] If Margret's betrothal and reentry into her family sanction what Davis took to be available forms of female adulthood for middle-class women, Lois's death from the brutality of child labor and the toxic waste of the mill suggests the sorrowful fate of mill girls and former slaves. Since Fields had vetoed Davis's plan to "kill Dr. Knowles at Manassas,"[47] in the end, she leaves Knowles and Holmes mutually penniless from the fire. Knowles abandons his utopian plan and quietly builds the House of Refuge as a homeless shelter. The impoverished Howth family, however, is ironically rescued by their slave, Joel, who discovers oil on their farm—a portentous omen of industrial inevitability in a book that marks its risks.

Margret Howth critiques transcendentalism's investment of the egotistical imagination with social power. In this early novel Davis challenges literary and philosophical systems that, in their formal structures and social textures, divorce the reader from life in the commonplace. Midway through the novel, as Davis prepares to satisfy Fields and "come to the love part of [her] story," she speaks to her place in literary history: "I am suddenly conscious of dingy colors on the palette with which I have been painting." She compares her ambivalent characters, who must navigate difficult choices in their public and personal lives, to figures in "once upon a time" fiction, when readers "had no fancy for going through the world with half-and-half characters." Nature, she reminds herself, no longer turns out "complete specimens of each class." Refusing to write of a heroine who "glides into life full-charged with rank, virtues, a name three syllabled, and a white dress that never needs washing," she announces that her heroines will never be "ready to sail through dangers dire into a triumphant haven of matrimony." Thus, Davis introduces the reconciliation of Margret and Holmes with a manifesto on realism: "I live in the commonplace. Once or twice I have rashly tried my hand at dark conspiracies, and women rare and radiant in Italian bowers; but I have a friend who is sure to say, 'Try and tell us about the butcher next door, my dear'" (102). This became her lifelong literary charge.

In *Margret Howth* Davis extends her discourse of realism and talks about "the butcher next door," seeking to challenge the restrictive tenets of sentimentalism—its illusion that domestic culture can transcend political culture, that the self can be divorced from social circumstances, and that domestic life can guarantee women status, autonomy, economic security, and moral redemption. Romanticism, she found, severed the individual from history just as the imperatives of slavery and industrialism were threatening the American illusion of community. Indeed, autonomy became a snare that threatened women's identity as social subjects. Exploring subjectivity in the history of slavery and early industrialization, Davis finds that her characters face aesthetic frustration and emotional repression. In fastening the emerging strategies of literary realism onto felt experience, Davis reclaims from sentimentalism its subjectivity and intensity of feeling. In *Margret Howth*, her first novel, the social practices of domesticity, female labor, free black labor, and nascent industrialization authorize emotional appeals, shaping American realism as an indigenous and heartfelt political narrative.

4 ❧ The Savage Necessity of
Abolition and Civil War

IN JULY 1867 William Dean Howells concluded, "Our war has not only left us a burden of a tremendous national debt, but has laid upon our literature a charge under which it has hitherto staggered very lamely."[1] Until quite recently, critics from Edmund Wilson to Daniel Aaron to Hazel Carby have tended to agree: in terms of literature, the Civil War was barren. In their view, a profound literary silence stemmed from the narrative conventions of antebellum literature, from the hidden history of abolition fiction, and, most particularly, from the nation's historical ambivalence about race.

Nonetheless, in 1862 the *Atlantic Monthly* published three stories by Rebecca Harding Davis that picture the brutality of the war, the national fratricide that it implied, and the system of slavery that spawned it. In these stories Davis marks the contradictions between the brutal reality of slavery and the narrative configurations of domesticity within which slavery was pictured at the time.[2] "John Lamar" is a story of a slave who murders his master; "David Gaunt" is a pioneering antiwar story in which the Civil War becomes an example of the romantic conflict between individualism and community; "Blind Tom" is a character sketch of a deformed musical genius, a slave child suffering from savant syndrome, who is displayed by his master as a stunning oddity in concert halls all over the South.[3] These stories challenge Jane Tompkins's assessment that women confronted slavery only in the "'closet' of the heart."[4] Although occasionally Davis is still trapped in the era's reductive stereotypes of African Americans as alien and bestial, she rigorously describes the brutality of slavery. In these stories, written early in the Civil War, literary representation itself becomes the site of Davis's conflicted racial understanding and regional loyalties.

Davis believed that she was able to write in ways that many other Unionists could not because she had a closer knowledge of slavery and the Civil War than most northerners did.[5] When she began to write on slavery, she still lived in her hometown of Wheeling, where nearby farms and small plantations supported an active slave trade. Located across the river from the free state of Ohio, Wheeling was also the site of much underground railroad activity.[6] Davis's own memories of slavery are contradictory. In 1903 she recalled, "I came from a slave State, and the evils that I saw in slavery made me an Abolitionist before these excitable young men probably were born."[7] Elsewhere, however, she noted,

> Abolitionism was a burning question in that part of Virginia. Nothing lay between any slave there and freedom but the Ohio River, which could be crossed in a skiff in half an hour. The green hills of Ohio on the other side, too, were peopled by Quakers, all agents for the Underground Railway to Canada. Hence the only slaves we had were those who were too comfortable and satisfied with us to run away. We knew "the institution" at its best, and usually listened to the furious attacks on it with indifferent contempt.[8]

By 1861 Wheeling had become the center for the division of Virginia after the area's painful debate over the issues of slavery and union. Just a few blocks from Rebecca's house, a citizens' convention voted to nullify Virginia's Ordinance of Secession, and in October a small voter turnout endorsed a new state that came into being early in 1862. West Virginia swiftly passed a constitution that granted gradual emancipation to slaves, who represented about 4 percent of the state population.[9] Soon thereafter, General Rosecrans headquartered the Mountain Garrison across the street from the Harding house. Near the end of her life, Davis recalled the tensions of this ambivalent site:

My family lived on the border of Virginia. We were, so to speak, on the fence, and could see the great question from both sides. It was a most unpleasant position. When you crossed into Pennsylvania you had to defend your slave-holding friends against the Abolitionists who dubbed them all Legrees and Neros; and when you came home you quarrelled with your kindly neighbors for calling the Abolitionists "emissaries of hell." The man who sees both sides of the shield may be right, but he is most uncomfortable.[10]

Meanwhile, in the divided town, young girls were arrested from playing "Dixie" on their pianos:

> Some of our friends who were secessionists were in an old theatre just in sight which had been turned into a jail. Others were in a prison camp on a pretty island in the river. The change in the drowsy town was like that made in those little vine-decked villages on the flanks of Vesuvius after the red hot flood of lava had passed over them. Nothing but gloom and suspicion and death were real to us now. The range of mountains just out of sight was alive with rebel guerrillas, quite as little minded to peace and mercy as our guards.[11]

Rebecca's need to see "both sides of the shield" endured even after her marriage in 1863 to L. Clarke Davis, a man with strong antislavery views, and her move to Philadelphia where she met other abolitionists, Quakers, and leaders of the underground railroad[12]—the men and women who, in her words, "kindled the fire under the caldron."[13] For two decades she had been listening to speakers such as John C. Fremont, Horace Greeley, F. Julius Le Moyne, the vice-presidential candidate in 1840 on the Abolition ticket, Sara Clarke, the "Liberty Poetess" (who later wrote under the name of Grace Greenwood), and Frances Harper, whom Davis remembered as "an able, ambitious woman, who lectured with a strange, bitter eloquence."[14] In Philadelphia Davis came to know John Greenleaf Whittier, Mary Grew, and Elizabeth Burleigh, and she became close friends with Lucretia Mott. Yet despite the influence of radical friends and his own abolitionist leanings, Rebecca's husband did not want to be drafted, and it appears that the Davises bought his way out of the Union Army for three hundred dollars—not an uncommon act.[15]

The view that the war over slavery was "unwritten" was initially popularized by Daniel Aaron, who holds that the literature of the American Renaissance was able to portray only "unsoldierly" activities. Giving shape to "soldierly" activities required a genre that could emphasize action over speech, avoid ambiguity and ambivalence, and address war "kinds of experience."[16] Moreover, argues Aaron, the Civil War appeared to lack the sort of noble purpose that gives holy wars the "epic character" that yields great fiction. In Aaron's view, "The 'emotional resistance' blurring literary insight, I suspect, has been race."[17] Aaron's recipe of violence, clarity, and closure would have been particularly unsuitable, however, to those female authors at midcentury who wrote from within the traditions of sentimentalism, inscribing in their works omens of domestic insurrections. Initially, Hazel Carby tended to agree with Aaron's later judgment: "Slavery is rarely the focus of the imaginative physical and geographical terrain" of American fiction.[18]

Slavery itself contributed to the literary repression of the Civil War. It certainly appears to have confounded Nathaniel Hawthorne, for example, who announced in 1852 that it was "one of those evils that divine Providence does not leave to be remedied by human contrivances" but which, one day, "by some means impossible to be anticipated," will "vanish like a dream."[19] In 1860 Hawthorne had returned from England to write a new romance, only to find himself "mentally and physically languid" in the fervid surroundings of his abolitionist neighbors.[20] By 1862, after a tour of the battlefields at Harper's Ferry, Newport News, and Manassas, Hawthorne wrote his last major piece, "Chiefly About War Matters," in which he concluded,

> We . . . have gone to war, and we seem to have little, or at least, a very misty idea of what we are fighting for . . . [so] that the Great Arbiter to whom [we all] so piously and solemnly appeal, must be sorely puzzled how to decide.[21]

That same year, in a letter to Horatio Bridge, he sardonically observed,

> I ought to thank you for a shaded map of Negrodom, which you sent me a little while ago. What a terrible amount of trouble and expense, in washing the sheet white!—and, after all, I am afraid we shall only variegate it with blood and dirt.[22]

Hawthorne never wrote his next romance.

Ambivalence about slavery was not solely a matter for literature. Despite pressure from abolitionists, during the first two years of the war President Lincoln tried to deny that slavery was the war's "noble purpose." He insisted (in the words of Horace Bushnell, a northern conservative) that the war was solely about "the religious crowning of our nationality."[23] Southerners such as Davis, however, saw the connection between war and slavery more clearly. As James McPherson points out, by 1861 the South understood that "slavery and independence were each a means as well as an end in symbiotic relationship with the other, each essential for the survival of both."[24]

Despite Walt Whitman's assertion to the contrary, slavery was a written atrocity and the Civil War did "get on the books."[25] In recent years, the intense interest in Harriet Jacobs's *Incidents in the Life of A Slave Girl* (1861) and Harriet Wilson's *Our Nig* (1859), as well as in Frederick Douglass's *Life and Times of Frederick Douglass* (1845), has revised the national narrative of slavery to include the perspective of nineteenth-century African-American authors. It has also renewed attention to the representation of slavery and the Civil War in the works of such authors as Herman Melville, Harriet Beecher Stowe, Louisa May Alcott, and Lydia Maria Child. Yet many midcentury tales of slavery and the Civil War, although written by white authors committed to abolition, reveal the profound dissonance between the realities of slavery and its construction in the white imagination. Some northern authors not only repressed the black character as "an uncomfortable reminder of abandoned obligations, or a pestiferous shadow, emblematic of guilt and retribution,"[26] but also wrote from within a domestic ideology that hinged on transcendent empathy and commonality. A sense of commonality, however, challenged the midcentury axiom of racial difference, typified in an observation by Edgar Allan Poe, a defender of slavery: "We must take into consideration the peculiar character (I may say the peculiar nature) of the Negro. . . . [Some believe that Negroes] are, like ourselves, the sons of Adam and must, therefore, have like passions and wants and feelings and tempers in all respects. This we deny and appeal to the knowledge of all who know."[27]

Thus, to picture slavery Davis needed to find a discourse that could accurately represent the lives of African Americans, who, for the most part, figure only peripherally in fiction written around the time of the Civil War. How to reconcile the particularities of slavery and the Civil War with literary stereotypes? Aaron suggests that at the time there were three ways to represent the black: with contempt, with dread, or with sympathy[28]—always a fertile ground for condescension. Despite the informative rhetorics of abolition tales and slave narratives, most popular literature—domestic fiction as well as plantation fiction—still pictured the African American as the contented slave, the comic minstrel, the fulsome mammy, or the wretched freedman. As Werner Sollars reminds us, stereotypes reflect a form of universalist or essentialist thinking that is always a "thin camouflage of power relations."[29] Essentialism, however, was a perspective not only of sentimental fiction but also of abolitionism, which frequently argued through the politics of sympathy and the needs of the family. To the degree that the domestic novel attempted to represent the suffering of slaves, a sweeping racial determinism took over. In turning to the discourses of sympathy, sisterhood, and community, abolitionists also frequently absorbed sentimental assumptions about female biology and motherhood that projected women as instinctively caring, moral, protective, and committed to putting the needs of family and society above their own.

Tales of slave resistance by white women were often couched in these terms. Carolyn Karcher suggests that in antislavery fiction written by men, rebellion tends to be the central theme, whereas in antislavery fiction by women, the focus is on the sexual exploitation of female slaves.[30] In my view, however, these perspectives merge in both men's and women's narratives that connect white supremacy and patriarchy. For example, in Frederick Douglass's "The Heroic Slave" (1853), Madison Washington, leader of a well-known slave revolt, is driven by his love for his wife, who is in danger of rape.[31] In Lydia Maria Child's "Slavery's Pleasant Homes" (1843), a slave murders his master, his "quadroon brother," in revenge for the rape of his slave wife, while the plantation mistress passively endures her husband's nightly rape of her mulatto slave sister. Child's ironic title points to the myth of the protective plantation.[32] In Louisa May Alcott's "The Brothers" (1863), a slave soldier, recovering in a Union hospital, contemplates the murder of his white brother, a captain in the Confederate Army who lies in a nearby bed, because his brother has raped his enslaved mulatto sister-in-law.[33] "Ray" (1864) by Harriet Prescott describes how a fugitive slave fighting for the Union Army kills his Confederate white brother in battle and returns to marry his white cousin.[34]

Aside from Herman Melville's "Benito Cereno" (1855), most stories of slave resistance written before the war were published in antislavery journals such as Garrison's weekly *Liberator* or Maria Weston Chapman's abolitionist annual *Liberty Bell*.[35] During the 1860s, however, under the editorship of James Fields, the *Atlantic* published Davis's, Alcott's, and Prescott's stories of slave revenge alongside Thomas Wentworth Higginson's historic series on the slave insurrections of Gabriel Prosser, Denmark Vesey, and Nat Turner. Also published in the *Atlantic* was Fitz-Hugh Ludlow's "If Massa Put Guns Into Our Han's," an essay that urged northern readers to recognize slaves' outrage at rape, whipping, starvation, and separation of families. Even in the era of intense self-censorship about slave militancy, southern newspapers also occasionally published stories about slaves who killed a master, a mistress, or an overseer by poison, arson, or whipping.[36]

Despite Davis's claim that abolition was never a "burning issue" in Wheeling, she too was keenly aware of local underground railroad activities and reported that a neighbor was recruited by John Brown and died in the abortive slave uprising in nearby Harper's Ferry. She recalled how a farmer, known to be a believer "in spiritualism, divorce and woman's rights," was visited by Brown in 1859; she remembered Brown as "a tall gaunt old man . . . who came into town sometimes, stalking up and down the streets with his eyes fixed and lips moving like a man under the influence of morphia."

> After he had disappeared it was told that he was a poor farmer from the West who was insane on the question of slavery, and that he had brought a quantity of huge pikes and axes . . . with which the slaves in town were to kill their masters whenever there should be an uprising. . . . The children used to tease the old black aunties and uncles to show them how they meant to stab them with pikes or behead them with axes when the day came. We thought it a very good joke. But five months later, when the old farmer died at Harper's Ferry on that bright October day, the whole world looking on with bated breath, the pikes were brought out of hiding by his friends, who declared that they never had meant to give them to the negroes to use, and had thought the old man mad.[37]

At the same time, the southern states made it increasingly difficult, if not impossible, for masters to free their slaves. John Garraty notes that during 1859 in all the South only about 3,000 slaves in a slave population of nearly

4 million were given their freedom. Many of these were elderly and hence had little economic value. In Virginia, where manumission was legal, only 277 out of half a million slaves were set free in 1859.[38]

Davis, well aware of the urgency of her topic, wrote to Fields, "Won't you publish 'John Lamar' as soon as you can? I have a fancy for writing of *today* you see."[39]

In the (albeit slim) tradition of studies of slave resistance, Davis extended her experiment in representing life in the commonplace to include the issue of slavery. But her depiction of slaves in "John Lamar," "David Gaunt," and "Blind Tom" was complicated by the heritage of sentimental assumptions about character. As Georg Lukács observes, realism relies on free will; realist characters have the capacity to make choices that both affect their destiny and have an impact on their environment. Yet Davis understood that slavery and war depend on totalizing ways of being and knowing. At the same time, she relied on racial stereotypes that persistently undermine her belief in free will, human rationality, conscience, and the capacity for self-improvement, and returned to sentimental forms that predetermine moral behavior and shape narrative endings toward racist systems of belief—challenged though they might be by an ironic narrator, resistant imagery, and rebellious peripheral characters. In these three stories, Davis suggests that ethical behavior arises from social as opposed to theological systems. At the time she was deeply averse to Calvinism and evangelicalism of all sorts and hostile to the hypocrisies she found in most organized religions. Influenced by European romanticism, she saw the individual as the moral center of an ethical universe. Like many abolitionists, she believed that domestic work rather than innate moral superiority gave women an understanding of the best needs of the community. Hence, Davis's antislavery fiction emerges as a blend of realism, Quakerism, transcendentalism, the Social Gospel, and domestic ideology.

Davis's sense of the limitations of domesticity, however, positioned her to write about slavery as repression and exile. In "Life in the Iron-Mills," the grasping female figure carved from the refuse of the ironmaking process expresses the human right for "summat to make her live," a motif of "soul starvation" that reappears in Davis's studies of slavery.[40] In *Margret Howth*, female suffering offers a way to understand industrial oppression and environmental pollution. In her Civil War fiction, Davis extends to slaves her conviction that no one thrives in confinement; the plantation, like the home, cannot promise refuge. With the spheres of private life and economic life separated in ideology but so patently fused in slavery, the plantation erases the sentimental distinction between the home and the workplace. In these stories, acts of female survival inscribed in domestic fiction—endurance, lying, manipulation, creativity, and succumbing to madness—emerge as gestures of slave resistance. Slaves in Davis's tales dissemble, run away, enlist in the Union Army, commit violent acts against white slaveholders, and still survive.

Davis was raised in slaveholding Virginia, and her portraits of slaves are tinged with ambivalence. When in 1862 she began to focus on race and the brutality of slavery in her fiction, she rejects the sentimental view of slavery as a form of martyrdom. Instead, as she investigates analogies between racial and gender differences and between slavery and domesticity, she undermines their mutually enforcing romanticization. As William Chafe observes, the parallels between race and sex function "not in the substance of material existence that women and blacks have experienced but in the *forms* by which others have kept them in 'their place.'"[41] In Davis's stories of slavery, these parallel forms of control include physical abuse, psychological intimidation, economic deprivation, unrealizable goals, and painful limits on aspirations.

In "John Lamar" Davis describes a master and his slave who are both psychologically and physically imprisoned by slavery. The plantation has become the locus of abandoned children, physical abuse, intellectual loss, confinement, separation, and sexual exploitation, undercutting the fantasy of a sheltering home. Even so, the stereotype of the "brute Negro" competes with images of the brutality of slavery. The action takes place in a makeshift guardhouse, once a cider shed on a small farm in the "Rebel counties" of West Virginia—a liminal space that is neither North or South, indoors or outdoors, slave or free.[42] Here John Lamar, a Confederate officer from Georgia, is held prisoner, an image that both parodies the trope of female confinement in domestic fiction and points to the fact that whites were morally, psychologically, and economically "imprisoned" by the system of slavery.

Lamar is accompanied by his slave, Ben, who is not considered a prisoner, and he plans to have Ben help him escape so they can both return to the South. Hence Ben must choose whether to secure his master's freedom at the expense of his own—an irony underscored by Lamar's comment, "We will be free to-night, old boy!" (47). At first, the Union soldiers guarding Lamar see his loyal slave as a "white nigger," and on his side Ben views them as "miss'able Linkinite[s]" (36). Ben's first contact with abolitionists, however, immediately complicates his abject identity; the Union soldiers encourage his dreams of freedom, teach him Methodist hymns, and then give him a knife. For their part, the soldiers see Ben both as "a man, wifeless, homeless, nationless, hawked, flung from trader to trader for a handful of dirty shin-plasters" but also as "a human brute" (48–49). The slave's first awareness of the injustice of slavery and the notion of freedom thus derive from his con-tact with northerners rather than from a rebellious subjectivity shaped by en-slavement—a perspective that suits the southern view that abolitionism rather than slavery itself stimulates black rage. Severed from the deliverance promised in the abolitionist hymns, Ben's fury becomes a rational act insti-gated by abolitionists who have bestowed their belief in freedom on a man whom, they believe, lacks rationality.

We first see Ben, "crouching outside, his knees cuddled in his arms to keep warm: a field-hand, you could be sure from the face, a grisly patch of flabby black, with a dull eluding word of something, you could not tell what, in the points of eyes,—treachery or gloom" (35). The "dull eluding word," however, is not stupidity; to Davis the unuttered word suggests the repressive silence and hidden meaning of slavery. While the nature of Ben's labor and poverty is defined and definite, his character is unknowable to the presum-ably white narrator and reader. Ben has also learned "the reticent eye, the mastered voice"; his face cannot be read. Survival for the black slave, as for the white woman, demands the ability to understand power, to dissemble, to mask emotions and impressions that are nonetheless intense and skillful: "It is a trait of serfdom, the keen eye to measure the inherent rights of a man to be master. A negro or a Catholic Irishman does not need 'Sartor Resartus' to help him to see through any clothes" (41). Yet although his inscrutable eyes render Ben a difficult text and distance him from the narrator, his body, scarred "where the lash had buried itself" (49), patently exposes his brutal servitude. For Davis, Ben's rage derives not from an inherent feature of his biology but from his slave origins, his illiteracy, his lost family, and his long-ing for his father, a runaway slave who, "whipped into heroism, had betaken himself into the swamp, and never returned" (42). Davis's conflicting images reflect not only Ben's divided cultural inheritance but also her own divided regional loyalties that test her claim that she always opposed slavery.

The abolitionist impulse in "John Lamar" also derives from the commonality between Ben and the other characters, and between Ben and the reader. When Ben first observes that the Union sentry's "trousers were in rags like his own, and his chilblained toes stuck through the shoe-tops," he calls the soldier "cheap white trash" (35). Ignoring their shared poverty, Ben ironically echoes a proslavery epithet. James McPherson points out that even if the dichotomy of "rich man's war/poor man's fight" lacked objective reality, it remained a powerful symbol to be manipulated by southern Democrats who made conscription a partisan and class issue.[43] The narrator, however, insists on commonality in both emotional and economic terms. Of Ben's father, she sardonically remarks,

> He was this uncouth wretch's father,—do you understand? The flabby-faced boy, flogged in the cotton-field for whining after his dad, or hiding away part of his flitch and molasses for months in hopes the old man would come back, was rather a comical object, you would have thought. Very different his, from the feeling with which you left your mother's grave,—though as yet we have not invented names for the emotions of those people. We'll grant that it hurt Ben a little, however. (42)

Universalized through his sense of parental loss, Ben's profoundly American longing for an absent father is shaped by the particularities of the slave family. Ben has also lost his "ole woman," Nan, the woman whom slavery did not allow him to marry. Nan fled North after receiving her free papers and, like Ben's father, never returned. In the representation of fathers, "John Lamar" is closer to texts by black women wherein white men usurp patriarchal control from the black man, and hence symbolically deprive him of other forms of political, social, and economic power, than it is to domestic novels in which the protective father mediates patriarchal control over women. As Hazel Carby observes, images of an absent black father paradoxically repudiate patriarchal power per se.[44]

In Ben's character Davis also pictures the internalization of servitude. Contemplating the murder of his master, Ben daintily (like a woman?) bends down to polish Lamar's boot, "holding Lamar's foot daintily, trying to see himself in the shoe, smoothing down the trousers with a boorish, affectionate touch,—with the same fierce whisper in his ear, Would the shoes ever be cleaned again?" (46). A black narcissus, Ben sees his image, shaped by dependency, in his master's boot. The domestic caretaking codes of projection, protection, and selfless identification serve, as in the literature of sentiment, to enhance the morality of martyrdom.

The fate of a young white girl further points to the dangers of Ben's marginality and explodes the notion that the "peculiar institution" of slavery was paternalistic and compatible with domesticity. Lamar has a sickly orphaned sister, Floy, left on the Georgia plantation in charge of three hundred slaves, "a heavy weight for those thin little hands to hold sway over,—to lead to hell or heaven" (38). Davis's image suggests the inevitable disorder and the impossibility of social governance under plantation slavery. Lamar wants to escape from the Federal prison shack in order to protect Floy, or, as he puts it, "to keep his brawny body between these terrible realities and Floy" (39). By 1863, fearing slave insurrections and the disintegration of the southern work force, the Confederacy allowed any soldier who owned more than twenty slaves to return to his plantation.[45] But Davis adds a twist to these southern fears that points to the hypocrisy of the sexual contract. Lamar carries a small portrait of Floy in which magnolia buds surround her face, "unstained, as yet, as pearl. It angered Lamar, remembering how the creamy whiteness of the full-blown flower exhaled passion of which the crimsonest rose knew nothing,—a content, ecstasy, in animal life" (38). While the explicit sexual threat is from the unsupervised blacks—"Up North they could have worked for her, and gained only her money"—the magnolia also establishes Floy's sexual appeal to her brother, who thinks of her alternately as "my baby" and "my darling" (38). Slavery threatens the protective covenant of patriarchy and exposes the myth of plantation chivalry. Male sexual fantasy, posed as chivalric romanticism, exposes the false security of the plantation code. In "John Lamar," the midcentury ideology of sexuality—of virginity, chastity, and infantilized women—becomes a factor in the representation of ethnicity.

Carby suggests that the "narrative of slavery" has three possible conclusions: the slave's narrative ends with escape, the historian's narrative ends with emancipation, and the rebel's narrative ends with death.[46] Rebecca Harding Davis, however, deconstructs these narrative closures as historical closures; in her stories, slavery undermines the possibility of any comfortable ending or resolution and moves us "beyond the ending" in particular and historical ways.[47] The ending of "John Lamar" is, in fact, "open." On the night that Lamar hopes to escape, he falls asleep, dreaming of Floy in her white nightgown. Nearby, Ben is encouraged by the avenging hymn of the Union soldiers:

> That in the blood of enemies
> Thy foot imbrued may be.

Ben creeps back into the hut. Muttering, "It's for freedom, Mars' Lord!" he stabs Lamar and flees. Paradoxically, Jesus' name ("Lord") fuses with the slaveowner's epithet, "Mars'" (Master, and, possibly, the name of the god of war), as history undermines stereotype. "Free now! The best of them despised him; the years past of cruelty and oppression turned back, fused in a slow, deadly current of revenge and hate, against the race that had trodden him down" (50). In turn, typology undercuts history and a religious metaphor subsumes the political discourse: just as Ben knifes his master, "A belated bird swooped through the cold moonlight . . . with a low fearing cry, as though it has passed through Hades" (50). A parody of the dove that escapes from the dying Jesus, the bird portends further war. The allusion to Hades, however, paradoxically recalls the Union sentry, an abolitionist boatman, a figure of liberation and escape by the underground railroad. Thus, this image has strong southern overtones, echoing the proslavery position that abolitionists (the "best of them") not only were racist, but also incited slaves to murder their masters.

As soon as Ben slays Lamar, an erotic stereotype replaces the portrait of the angry slave; a sexual fantasy of little Floy replaces Ben's fantasy of freedom:

> He ploughed his way doggedly through the snow,—panting, as he went,—a hotter glow in his gloomy eyes. It was his turn for pleasure now: . . . He did not need to choose a wife from his own color now. He stopped, thinking of little Floy. . . . He had watched her climb up into [her brother's] arms and kiss his cheek. She never would do that again! He laughed aloud, shrilly. By God! she should keep the kiss for other lips! Why should he not say it? (51)

When interpreting this passage, one should bear in mind that within the sexual ideology of the mid-nineteenth century, civil marriage and the family were supposed to regulate the sexual passions of both black and white men. By codifying sexual repression, the family was to bring restraint and stability to civilization as a whole. Still, as Elizabeth Fox-Genovese observes, "Sex broke through the barriers of civility within which slave holding conventions tried to contain it. The primary culprits were men, whose self-control was widely acknowledged to be much more fragile than that of women."[48] Herbert Gutman adds that such sexual beliefs reinforced racial beliefs about African Americans, who, as slaves, were denied relationships sanctioned by law and hence appeared to lack the restraints of moral and religious culture.[49] Indeed, abolitionists such as Charles Whipple argued that slavery failed to contain white men's "licentiousness."[50] Nonetheless, as Ralph Ellison observes, the myth of unrestrained black sexuality, advanced by both abolitionists and proslavery figures, was "idealized . . . into a symbol of sensation, of unhampered social and sexual relationships."[51] In Gutman's view, this myth "made a ghastly mockery of the family life and behavior, much less the moral and social beliefs, of the slaves and the ex-slaves."[52] Thus, in "John Lamar" slavery mutually victimizes the slave and the white female.[53]

Interracial sexuality has long been a source of ambivalence in the white imagination.[54] Sterling Brown once commented that "the closer a Negro got to the ballot box, the more he looked like a rapist."[55] In "John Lamar," as elsewhere, black sexuality resides in a fantasized rape, an eroticization of the violence of slavery that reverses the real sexual danger—white men's freedom to rape their slaves. The consequences of "amalgamation," as miscegenation was termed in the mid-nineteenth century, informs the fiction of slavery, even when it is not its subject per se. In an age that revered chastity, the presence of biracial children—living proof of rape and concubinage—called into question the protective pretenses of plantation chivalry.

Abolitionists often invoked the image of the mulatto as evidence of the betrayal of the ideology of domesticity; nonetheless, miscegenation also provided a window into the erotic. And a reference to black eroticism was a sanctioned reference to eroticism per se. The fusion of the ethnic with the erotic in stories such as "John Lamar" projects both figures as distanced, other, and mutually unacceptable. The ethnic and the erotic are tainted by their literary attraction to each other. Sander Gilman thus suggests that when white women authors assign sexual images to black characters, these authors become the objects of their own sexual fantasies.[56] At the least, Ben's sexual fantasy undermines Davis's implication that racism is more powerful than patriarchy.

Davis thus taints Ben with what would become the most racist stereotype of Reconstruction fiction: a black man who seeks to ravish a white girl. Ben's first consciousness of himself as a free man is to think of himself as a gendered, sexual, and patriarchal being, but the ultimate promise of freedom is the sexual possession of a white woman of higher caste. In this synthesis of sex, gender, and race, the actual history of interracial rape disappears. As does literary realism.

There is no documentation of the prevalence of the rape of white women by slaves or former slaves; there is some evidence that women who owned slaves had voluntary sexual relations with black men.[57] Nonetheless, Ben conforms to the cultural stereotype of "Buck," the oversexualized and virile male slave. In accounting for this gender convention that both caricatures the economic value of male slaves' strength and reflects an attribute that white men sought in themselves, Fox-Genovese notes,

> Buck . . . represented a reversal of the notion of the cavalier. It encoded white male fears of black sexuality in particular and of virility in general . . . [and] emphasized white views of the single, sexually active black male as divorced from other social roles. As a shadow image of the cavalier, it reflected whites' bad faith about the master-slave relation. Since slave law denied the legality of black marriage and ownership of property, it is hardly surprising that the white image of the black man should have divorced sexuality from reproduction and social responsibility. . . . The Buck evoked a sexually active, perpetual adolescent. Implicitly, it also evoked the threat of black sexuality to white women—a fascinating reversal since the main interracial sexual threat was that of white predators against black women.[58]

Betrayed by a stereotype, Ben no longer appears as the abused slave; his fantasy of Floy has eclipsed Davis's justification for his murder of Lamar.[59] Not only has the murder violated compassion, the ethical core of sentimental politics; Ben's erotic dream has also transformed slavery into an institution that makes southern women its victims, not its perpetrators. His fantasy reinvokes domesticity in order to point to female vulnerability. Race slips into gender to picture a white female as a vulnerable child left alone in a house without male protection; a final bond appears between the woman narrator and white female child, not between the woman author and slave. In "John Lamar," the male world of slavery, war, and abolition cannot guarantee female safety. The figure of Floy may also serve as a projection of the author's own fears of wartime death and separation. Furthermore, anxiety concerning power always seems to stimulate a desire to establish a clear demarcation between the self and the other—hence, it undermines commonality. Stephen Heath observes, "Where a discourse appeals directly to an image, to an immediacy of seeing, . . . [for] its argument or demonstration, one can be sure that all difference is being eluded, that the unity of some *accepted* vision is being reproduced."[60] In "John Lamar," the "accepted vision"—that is to say, a stereotype—has replaced a realistic or accurate perception of the other.

Nonetheless, "John Lamar" calls into question Mary Ryan's observation that the "domestic argument" always "constricted the oppression of slavery into the narrow vision of sentimental womanhood and contained neither a clear conception of freedom for the black man or woman nor a rational purpose for civil war. The principle of human freedom stood on a shaky foundation of domestic priorities."[61] Even though Davis acknowledges that Ben's murder of Lamar and his sexual fantasy about Floy arise in the context of historic cruelty, we are meant to identify with Ben as a man suffering from the lack of a mother, wife, daughter, or sister of his own—hence without the reforming power of love. Slavery is a domestic issue. Davis's messy synthesis of domesticity and slavery redefines the capacity of the private sphere to reshape the public sphere; domesticity offers no sanctuary from masculine activity. Slavery thus is not simply an alternative or replacement economy; rather, as Gillian Brown observes of *Uncle Tom's Cabin*, it confirms the absence of white women's authority and makes domesticity dependent on the whims of whatever economic practice it adjoins.[62] For Davis, the situation of the woman and the slave may be read as mutually empowering; together they call for the repudiation of many forms of masculine mastery. Nonetheless, her sexual metaphor does not simply displace the racial. Instead, the erotic allusion confirms the subject's right to control his or her body. And control of the body means the annihilation of slavery. Davis's fusion of gender and race suggests that all relationships forged without consent are unacceptable. Hence Ben's violence gives moral purpose to a reluctant war.

With the murder of Lamar, Davis preempts the homecomings and family reunions that mark the conclusions of domestic fiction, leaving the reader without an ending of ascribed meaning. As Lamar lies dying, he hears Ben's "wild, revengeful laugh" in the distance, and the narrator observes, "In that dying flash of comprehension, it may be, the wrongs of the white man and the black stood clearer to his eyes than ours: the two lives trampled down" (52), a suggestion that slavery has brutalized whites and blacks similarly—a troubling but common equivocation. Writing from a battlefield town, Davis believed her task was to transform the nation, not the home or the heart. John is dead, Ben escapes, and Floy, a child, remains incapably and tenuously in charge of the plantation. Dave Hall, the abolitionist boatman, has the millennial last word: "The war, which had become a daily business, stood suddenly before him in all its terrible meaning. God, he thought, had met in judgment with His people" (53). The final merger is not the male-female synthesis of domesticity, but a black-white apocalypse brought on by the sins of the white father.

With the debate over union and the preparations for war raging around her, and with preparations for her marriage to Clark stymied by family illness, Davis wrote to James Fields: "You may expect a *very* abolition story in David Gaunt. How can I help it? Here is [sic] Gen. Fremont confiscated one of my friends houses for headquarters just across the street. And Zag [?] is charging continuously past the windows. . . . My secession proclivities (if I had any) are oozing out at my elbows."[63] Still, Davis was encouraged because Fields had readily accepted "John Lamar" exactly as she wrote it: "I am glad that my poor Georgian [John Lamar] could find so warm a welcome in Massachusetts. Perhaps I need not have written it 'with one hand tied behind my back' as Artemus Ward says, after all."[64] Pained by the tension between her Virginia roots and her growing abolitionist sensibilities, Davis understood that the Civil War portended national fratricide and would soon render political actions in personal terms and personal actions in political terms. With its insurrectionist and, at the same time, interfamilial overtones, the war would become a metaphor for resistance to many forms of social proscriptions—racial, theological, and patriarchal.

Despite Davis's growing antipathy to slavery, she nonetheless rejected facile and romanticized images of the Civil War itself. She was haunted by the personal and domestic suffering she saw on both sides:

The histories which we have of the great tragedy give no idea of the general wretchedness, the squalid misery, which entered into every individual life in the region given up to the war. Where the armies camped the destruction was absolute. Even on the border, your farm was a waste, all your horses or cows were seized by one army or the other, or your shop or manufactory was closed, your trade ruined. You had no money; you drank coffee made of roasted parsnips for breakfast, and ate only potatoes for dinner. Your nearest kinsfolk and friends passed you on the street silent and scowling; if you said what you thought you were liable to be dragged to the county jail and left there for months. The subject of the war was never broached in your home where opinions differed; but, one morning, the boys were missing. No one said a word, but one grey head was bent, and the happy light died out of the old eyes and never came to them again. Below all the squalor and discomfort was the agony of suspense or the certainty of death. But the parsnip coffee and the empty purse certainly did give a sting to the great over-whelming misery, like gnats tormenting a wounded man.[65]

In her next story, "David Gaunt," Davis represents the debate about se-cession as a debate about domesticity; her discourse shifts between national and familial struggles as each becomes a meditation on the situation of women. But unlike most sentimental fiction, in which domestic values tri-umph over public pursuits, in this story both the public and private domains grow from confrontations over union, religion, and the role of women. "David Gaunt" is a story of a Rebel truck farmer, Joe Scofield, his lonely and devout daughter, Dode, and her two suitors: David Gaunt, an ignorant and rigid itinerant preacher, and Douglas Palmer, a pragmatic, passionate Union officer who is a religious doubter. Peripheral to the narrative but central to the meaning of the story is Bone, Joe's slave, who grows from unquestioning loy-alty to his master to an understanding that freedom will give him the right to be his "own man."

Davis's pacifist thesis emerges from the competing voices in her own imagination about public identity. The tragic ironies of war force all the characters to become open to new ways of thinking—that is, to openness itself. Living in rural West Virginia, a location of indeterminate politics, Dode Scofield and David Gaunt learn from the war to question their as-sumptions about Christianity, father-daughter attachment, female activity, political allegiance, and romantic love. The war redefines sentimental fiction's conventions of romance, reunion, and reform, only to leave open the issue of sacrifice: does any goal—romantic, political, moral, or religious—merit the loss of a father, brother, or friend?

The central characters in "David Gaunt" converge along two battle lines: the war and Dode's hand in marriage. The story opens with a reference to *Pilgrim's Progress*: "What kind of a sword, do you think, was that which old Christian had in that famous fight of his with Appolyon, long ago? . . . Where is . . . the sword which Christian used, like a man, in his deed of derring-do?" (54). Davis questions whether the contemporary sword, the Civil War, has the moral legacy of Christian's, and she explores how this legacy is viewed by men and women. Rescripting the relationship between violence, religion, and masculinity set out by Bunyan, she situates male activity against images of Dode's home. Dode has decorated her small brick house with wreaths of dried flowers that mock death "in indignant life, purple and scarlet and flame, with no thought of dying; . . . the rough wire-baskets filled with mould, . . . grew living, and welled up, and ran over into showers of moss" (66). Unlike Gaunt and her father, "There was not a dead atom in her body: something within, awake, immortal, waited, eager to speak every moment" (66). Images of fertility associate womanhood with speech—lying in wait, atrophied but kinetic. At the same time, the house, Dode's "snuggery" (102), resists isolation, certainty, and death.

Contrasting images of male and female activity are complicated, however, by contrasting images of male and female confinement. Joe's narrow world has nourished the rigid certitude of his southern loyalties: "You could see that it need not take Prospero's Ariel forty minutes to put a girdle about this man's world: ten would do it, tie up the farm, and the dead and live Scofields, and the Democratic party, with an ideal reverence for 'Firginya'" (55). The death of his son at the Battle of Manassas has further constricted Joe's vision. By contrast, Dode is surrounded by images that defy confinement: "Her soul was tired of sitting at her master's feet, like Mary. [Her] passion-fits were the only events of her life. For the rest, she washed and sewed and ironed. If her heart and brain needed more than this, she was cheerful in spite of their hunger" (57). Female hunger, pictured again as soul starvation, defines the isolation of domestic life for another of Davis's single women: "Almost all . . . women, before their life-work is given them, pass through such hunger,—seasons of dull, hot inaction, fierce struggles to tame and bind to some unfitting work the power within" (57).

The phrase "hot inaction" implies the sublimation and repressive quality of spinsterhood. As Rebecca Harding Davis prepared to leave her family at age thirty-one to marry, the story also carries oedipal overtones. Joe repeatedly denies his daughter's intelligence and independence. Refusing to see that she's a "tad abolitionist," he announces, "She don't take sharp sides in this war" because "she a'n't smart . . . got no public sperrit" (58), an error echoed by every man in the story. Within the narrative, Dode is not free to love and marry until Davis has killed off this father, whose "ruled heart leaped with a savage, healthy throb of jealousy" (63) when he suspects his daughter may be in love, the father who "kissed her mouth passionately" (60) when he tells her goodbye. Joe worships his daughter as an idol of sentiment: ignorant, intuitive, passive and as chaste as a "clean well" (58).

At first affiliated with the house, Dode and her "snuggery" promise the three men a utopian reward for their claims on behalf of the masculine nature of war. As "David Gaunt" develops, however, the traditionally privileged story of men in battle yields to a story of a woman who refuses to be the prize for valor or political rectitude; she will not allow the men to fight for her per se, even if she is the impulse that defines their rectitude and certainty. Ultimately, Dode suggests that the moral claims of the war cannot be categorized as female.

Having located her story during the Battle of Blue Gap, Davis pictures how, along gender lines as well as along regional lines, the Civil War tore asunder the image of United States as a national family. Sympathy, the sphere of women, confronts political certitude, the terrain of men. As Davis wrote to Annie Fields,

> These are sad lonesome days for us here. The war is surging up close about us. O Annie, if I could put into your and every true woman's heart the irrepressible loathing I have for it! If you could only see the other side enough to see the wrong the tyranny on both! God rules. Yes I know. But God in His inscrutable wisdom suffered great wrongs to work out His ends. And this is one of them. . . . I am glad you are so far away from it. I could tell you things I *know* would make your heart sick.[66]

The action centers on the tragic night when Joe Scofield, Douglas Palmer, and David Gaunt face each other in battle. Seeking revenge for the death of his Rebel son, Joe sneaks off to warn the nearby Confederate guerrillas of an impending Union attack. In the woods he inadvertently encounters his minister, David Gaunt, a "cloudy brained enthusiast" who had converted Joe by preaching "bigotry, gross likings and dislikings" (59). Gaunt has just enlisted in the Federal Army, motivated neither by allegiance or conviction but by religious cliches: "It was God's cause, holy: through its success the golden year of the world would begin on earth. . . . The pillar of cloud, he thought, moved as in the old time, before the army of freedom" (60).

A man who holds "nothing irresolute," Gaunt announces that Christ has called on him to "choke down his carnal nature,—to shut his eyes to all beauty and love,—to unmake himself, by self-denial, voluntary pain" (61) and fight the South. "Being a Calvinist, and a dyspeptic, (Dyspepsia is twin-tempter with Satan, you know,) [he had] sold his God-given birthright, like Esau, for a hungry bitter mess of man's doctrine" (62). Believing that Jesus seeks "peace by murder," Gaunt shoots the unwitting Scofield, who dies ironically wishing that Gaunt were there to pray for him.[67] In contrast to Gaunt, who suffers from "feminine unable" nerves, is Douglas Palmer, Dode's other suitor, a confident and manly Unionist whose "very horse . . . caught the spirit of its master, and put down it hoofs with calm assurance of power" (64). Yet he too is shot in battle; fallen from his horse, Palmer lies wounded and bleeding in a deep ravine.

As Dode is mourning the death of her father at the hands of the Union Army, she hears that Palmer is missing. Braving sniper fire from both sides, she rides out alone on an icy mountain trail until she comes upon a gulley "covered with muddy ice; there was a split in it, and underneath, the black water curdled and frothed" (95). Pursuing a trail through the snow, she continues to search for the fallen Palmer. "She pushed her way through the thicket: the moon did not shine there"; she finds a "dark crevice in the hill" where Gaunt is tending the wounded Palmer in a crude shed (96). With its allusions to female eroticism, this hidden crevice becomes a transforming female space, a refuge in which Gaunt decides to surrender his weapons, go west, and become a military nurse, and where Dode agrees to marry Palmer. As Philip Fisher observes, sentimental fiction offers no real redress, but rather provides training in how to feel.[68]

"David Gaunt" questions whether the Civil War has a moral purpose. For example, a villager who had held the contract to supply the army with meat becomes a recruiting officer, calculating that he earns "pay better than pork, especially in damp weather." He knows that his new Union recruits are at heart secessionists, but he also understands that "the twenty dollars a month on one side, an' the test-oath on t' other, brought loyalty up to the scratch" (77). He too has quit "the hog-killing for the man-killing business, with no other motive than the percentage" (76). In her memoirs, *Bits of Gossip*, Davis recalls:

> I had just come up from the border where I had seen the actual war; the filthy spewings of it; the political jobbery in Union and Confederate camps; the malignant personal hatreds wearing patriotic masks, and glutted by burning homes and outraged women; the chances in it, well improved on both sides, for brutish men to grow more brutish, and for honorable gentlemen to degenerate into thieves and sots. War may be an armed angel with a mission, but she has the personal habits of the slums. (445)

For the women of Romney, West Virginia, the war marks the intellectual and social deprivations of domestic isolation.

> They had taken the war into their whole strength, like their sisters, North and South: as women greedily do anything that promises to be an outlet for what power of brain, heart, or animal fervor they may have, over what is needed for wifehood or maternity. . . . These women . . . had no poetic enthusiasm about it, did not grasp the grand abstract theory on either side. . . . Their sleazy lives had wanted color and substance, and they found it in a cant of patriotism, in illuminating their windows after slaughter, in dressing their tables with helmets of sugar, (after the fashion of the White House)—delicate *souvenirs de la guerre!* (77)

For men and women alike, the war has less to do with slavery and regional loyalty, freedom and union, and more to do with poverty, tedium, isolation, ignorance, and repression. Even so, Davis focuses on the reactions of women who see "their door-posts slopped with blood—that made a difference. This woman in front had found her boy's half-charred body left tied to a tree by Rebel scouts" (77–78). Even as she accepts her Union suitor, Dode resolves that nothing can be holy that turns honest men into assassins, and she remains a pacifist.

In "David Gaunt," the battle at Blue's Gap is a senseless tragedy. The victorious Union soldiers

> had work to do on their road back: the Rebels had been sheltered in the farmers' houses near; the "nest must be cleaned out": every homestead but two from Romney to the Gap was laid in ashes. It was not a pleasant sight for the officers to see women and children flying half-naked and homeless through the snow, nor did they think it would strengthen the Union sentiment; but what could they do? As great atrocities as these were committed by the Rebels. The war . . . was a savage necessity. (87)

Within a week, however, the Union Army evacuates Romney, leaving the wounded, the town, and the surrounding hill in full possession of the Confederates because, as Palmer explains to Dode, such acts "must be, while men were men" (78).

Nonetheless, the ending of "David Gaunt" is abolitionist in spirit. At the beginning of the story, Bone fulfills the stereotype of a politically unaligned and loyal slave. After the battle, however, when Dode's house becomes a Union infirmary, the soldiers urge him to think of himself no longer as "'ole Mars' Joe's man." With profound joy, Bone discovers that "dar's somefin' in a fellah's 'longin' to hisself, af'er all!" (102). Influenced by Palmer, Dode realizes that she too is "half-Abolitionist" (102). In this powerful story, in which a father and son die, a community is torn apart, a minister—the one man who fails to conform to gender expectations—kills his only friend and flees to the territories, the war becomes a metaphor for rigidity and dogma. Before the battle of Blue Gap, David and Dode "thought that they were Christian, and Rebellion and infidelity Appolyon" (54). Afterward, each has learned that neither Christianity, rebellion, or loyalty provides a fixed identity.

Rather, political morality lies in the recognition of commonality. As the old comrades prepared to go to battle on opposite sides, secessionist Joe had reaffirmed his friendship with Unionist Douglas. Now Gaunt seeks a way to serve his God without the rigid prescriptions of revivalism; distraught at the sin of killing his friend, he plans to become an army nurse so as to reach a different understanding of "blood on his hands" (103). Finally, Dode marries Palmer even though he is an "infidel." "David Gaunt" attacks social hypocrisy on all sides, satirizes any religion that is dogmatic, and questions any view that supports the war for reasons of cant patriotism and unanalyzed sentimentality. To Davis, political meaning is fluid and is found in experience and friendship. With her career taking shape during a moment of great political upheaval that was painfully felt at the most local level, and with her marriage only a few months away, she believed that the home was still the space of intellectual closure and political safety. With this story we also see Davis growing in self-confidence as a writer. In a note to Fields, acknowledging receipt of the $200 which the *Atlantic Monthly* paid for "David Gaunt" Davis states, "I have 'one request' like Queen Esther. Don't leave anything out of it in publishing it. Deformity is better than a scar you know."[69]

In posing analogies between white women and slaves, however, Davis does not simply appropriate slavery, but rather posits a reciprocal discourse of repression and liberation. Marianna Torgovnick holds that the needs of the present determine how society defines the value and the nature of the ethnic person. Ethnicity, she says, is pliable. It does what we ask it to do: "Voiceless, it lets us speak for it. It is our ventriloquist's dummy—or so we like to think. . . . The ethnic can be—has been, will be . . . —whatever Europeans want it to be. It tells us what we want it to tell us."[70] Finally haunted by slavery but committed to transcendent commonality, Davis never viewed race as a clear trope of ultimate, irreducible difference.[71]

In "Blind Tom," also written in 1862, a slaveowner attempts to make a slave his "ventriloquist's dummy," channeling the culture of white society through the slave's musical talent. "Blind Tom," based on an actual person, is both a study of white projection and a critique of popular assumptions about the black performer as a "comic Negro."[72] Thomas Greene Bethune, the fourteenth child of a field hand, was born blind and seriously deformed.[73] When a Georgia slaveowner, Colonel Bethune, purchased Tom's mother from a trader in 1851, the crippled baby was tossed into the bargain "for nothing." Initially perceived as an "imbecile," Tom grew up in the main house, an affectionate if irritable "family pet" who was allowed to sleep in the halls and listen to the colonel's daughters play the piano. One night, when he was four (or, by some accounts, seven), he awakened the family by ecstatically playing complicated music on the piano. He was soon performing for the plantation, accurately reproducing any melody he heard; however his fingers fell on the keys, "cadences followed, broken, wandering, yet of startling beauty and pathos" (106). Anyone manifesting this triad of genius, disability, and mental confusion was once called an idiot savant, but the condition is now variously termed savant's syndrome, monosavantism, or autistic mnemonism.[74]

Tom's owner soon realized that his slave offered him "a more fruitful source of revenue than tobacco-fields" (107) and exhibited him in concert halls in Savannah, Charleston, Richmond, and other principal southern cities, although never in a free state or Europe. At each performance Tom demonstrated his creativity and his astonishing capacity to mimic and memorize, playing works of Beethoven, Verdi, Thalberg, Gottschalk, and Mendelssohn, repeating accurately long new compositions proffered by local musicians, and composing perfect accompaniments to any melody heard for the first time. According to a contemporary report, he could also improvise on given thematic ideas, such as a rainstorm or the battle of Manassas.[75] Tom also performed musical contortions, sometimes playing with his back to the piano.

When he was sixteen, Tom Bethune was examined by Dr. Edward Seguin, who diagnosed him as an "idiotic genius." In a 1866 report, Seguin concluded that in addition to biology and genetics (the common etiologies of the time), isolation and sensory deprivation had produced sizable "intellectual defects" in Tom. With a vocabulary of less than a hundred words, he had a musical repertoire of over 5,000 pieces. As a young child, noted Seguin, Tom was fascinated with sounds, and although he could scarcely walk and refused to speak, he would play beautiful tunes if someone seated him at a piano—a somewhat less sudden debut than that recorded by Davis. Although apparently incapable of learning in any area other than music, by age six Tom could improvise as well as repeat. By age seven, Bethune took him on a tour that is said to have earned $100,000 in the first year. At age eleven, Tom played at the White House before President James Buchanan. After the Civil War, Tom continued to appear on stage, but his career ended at age fifty-three with the death of the colonel. Tom Bethune died in 1880, apparently lonely and alone, a tragic victim of dependency and exploitation. I have been unable to discover what happened to the profits from his many performances, but his isolated death suggests that the money did not go to him.[76]

Davis was fascinated by the history of Tom Bethune. En route to Boston in 1862 in the "heat . . . of Southern sultriness and secession,"[77] she saw him perform in Baltimore, undertook research into his biography, and gathered information about his case. She even sought a phrenologist to "read" Tom's "bumps," that is, the configuration of his skull.[78] Tom raised critical issues for Davis that engaged her ongoing critique of domesticity. His story showed how love and protection can be redefined in terms of ownership, how the body can be at once a source of creative freedom and an object in an involuntary transaction, the physical hunger for artistic expression; and it presented the slave's body in particular as a contested site of nature versus nurture, a representation colored by Davis's racist assumptions about black nature.

In Davis's portrait, through seemingly mindless self-expression Tom frees his consciousness while his body remains enslaved. Like Deb Wolfe in "Life in the Iron-Mills" and Lois Yare in *Margret Howth*, Tom signifies both physical subjugation and exclusion from intellectual discourse. Anticipating many of Davis's later female characters, he defies his designated identity and creates a form for his own freedom that in the end guarantees his enslavement.

Tom's subjectivity becomes the means of his appropriation and display. Initially Tom's deformed body is perceived as a reliable sign both of his race and of his meager abilities:

> The boy, creeping about day after day in the hot light, was as repugnant an object as the lizards in the neighboring swamp, and promised to be as little use to his master. He was of the lowest negro type, from which only field-hands can be made,—coal-black, with protruding heels, the ape-jaw, blubber-lips constantly open, the sightless eyes closed, and the head thrown back on the shoulders, lying on the back, in fact, a habit that he still retains, and which adds to the imbecile character of the face; . . . we find no other outgrowth of intellect or soul from the boy. (105)

Distancing herself from Tom's body through highly racist rhetoric, Davis also confirms the sentimental notion that the body offers a stable grammar of social and psychological signs. She attempts to account for Tom in terms (not uncommon at the time) that anticipate social Darwinism: "Generations of heathendom and slavery have dredged the inherited brains and temperaments of such children tolerably clean of all traces of power or purity,—palsied the brain, brutalized the nature" (105). It is likely that by 1862 Davis was aware of Charles Darwin's *Origin of Species* (1859), published in the United

States in 1860 and widely reviewed. Hers is a conventional abuse of the notion of natural selection, shaped here to define the wrongs of slavery. Nonetheless, the figure of Tom uniquely fuses the mind and the body in the midcentury representation of slavery. As Lora Romero observes, "If people could be made into just bodies, slavery would seem less appalling than it is." Further, suggests Romero, a mind-body binarism allowed authors such as Harriet Beecher Stowe to "imagine the self in a relation of complete exteriority" to political power exercised in an act of rebellion.[79] Paradoxically, the very union of mind and body, intellect and physicality in Tom, deformed though both might be, resists those pressures in abolitionist literature that produced such phrases as Stowe's original subtitle for *Uncle Tom's Cabin*, "The Man That Was a Thing."

By attacking slavery through the figure of a child, abolitionists implicitly transferred the responsibility for eradicating slavery to women, pictured frequently as the mothers of America. The figure of child-slave thus disguised slavery's market relations and stressed the ways slavery severed and distorted family relations. By equating slavery with improper stewardship of children, abolitionists also appealed to the legal and physical vulnerability of free white women, who lacked a title to their own bodies.[80] Like a woman's, Tom's purity derives not only from his childhood condition but, paradoxically, from the absence of culture and education:

> His comprehension of the meaning of music, as a prophetic or historical voice that few souls utter and fewer understand, is clear and vivid: he renders it thus, with whatever mastery of the mere material part he may possess, fingering, dramatic effects, etc.: these are but means to him, not an end, as with most artists. One could fancy that Tom was never traitor to the intent or soul of the theme. What God or the Devil meant to say by this or that harmony, what the soul of one man cried aloud to another in it, this boy knows, and is to that a faithful witness. His deaf, uninstructed soul has never been tampered with by art-critics who know the body well enough of music, but nothing of the living creature within. The world is full of these vulgar souls that palter with eternal Nature and the eternal Arts, blind to the Word who dwells among us therein. Tom, or the daemon in Tom, was not one of them. (108)

Davis also undermines the assumption about black performers embodied in the caricatures and the structure of the minstrel show: slaves can shrug off their worries to play.[81] Not only does Tom, as a slave, have a double market value; his performances have a titillation, a fascination with bondage that Tom attempts to resist when he refuses to perform. In "Blind Tom," the narrative seduction based on exhibition and display is shifted to narrative seduction, which works by evoking female empathy and subjectivity.

Davis here invokes sentiment to deconstruct the cultural stereotype of the black man. Yet by emphasizing Tom's talent, deformity, isolation, and haunting pain, she takes him outside of what Werner Sollars terms "universal categories"[82] and thereby depletes them of meaning. Davis, who saw herself as unattractive, identified with a series of homely but artistic characters whose creative and sexual passions are stymied by their bodies—as female, plain, or deformed. Tom's enslaved and misshapen body both is and is not a sign of who he is; hence, Tom signifies a complex paradigm of how Davis reads the body. In describing such paradoxical mergers of reciprocity and appropriation, Karen Sanchez-Eppler observes that abolitionist images of a bound and silent figure of a slave often symbolized all women's oppression and thus granted the white woman access to political discourse that was denied to the slave, exemplifying how slave labor produced—both literally and metaphorically—even the most basic of freedom's privileges.[83]

Images of silence, both historical and personal, frame and contain the story of "Blind Tom." Because Tom has been purchased through a slave trader, Davis cannot initially identify his family, establish his full name, or discover when or where he was born:

> This idiot-boy, chosen by God to be anointed with the holy chrism, is only "Tom,"—"Blind Tom," they call him in all the Southern States . . . and yet—nothing but Tom? That is pitiful. Just a mushroom-growth,—unkinned, unexpected, not hoped for, for generations, owning no name to purify and honor and give away when he is dead. (104)

In fact, Davis wrongly identifies Tom's owner as Mr. Oliver (the man who owned Tom's mother when he was born), perpetuating his confused identity. In a tradition that centers on identity and family, slavery further complicates the figure of the sentimental orphan. Paradoxically, Davis insisted that this story be published anonymously. When, in response to Fields's later inquiry as to whether he could name her as a contributor to the *Atlantic*, she replied,

"In my most emphatic tones I write NO. My best friends and advisers hearing of Mr. Fields's wild proposition say, 'Not yet—if ever.'"[84]

Eventually, Davis, as narrator, becomes a member of Tom's audience, which she pictures as a degenerate reflection of the interracial character of the nation as a whole:

> Beaux and belles, siftings of old country families, whose grandfathers trapped and traded and married with the Indians,—the savage thickening of whose blood told itself in high cheek-bones, flashing jewelry, champagne-bibbing, a comprehension of the tom-tom music of schottisches and polkas. (109)

The image of the hybrid nature of popular music exposes Davis's own racism, as well as her sense of the racial and ethnic mix of slavery, immigration, and frontier expansion—pictured as democratic yet debased.

The ending of "Blind Tom" reinvokes what Philip Fisher terms the "sentimental procedure," the conflation of the categories of class and gender into figures of prisoners,

> children of their parents, animals of their owners, . . . slaves of their masters. Each was subject to abuse and tyranny. Each was, by moral and legal custom, deprived of that degree of self-hood that is dependent upon rights and freedom, autonomy and the primacy of self-interest.[85]

By means of this sentimental analogy, "the weak and the helpless within society gain . . . full representation through the central moral category of compassion." Fisher warns us, however, to distinguish the successful politics of sentimental representation from the representation itself. Sentimentalism, he proposes, extends "normal states of primary feeling to people from whom they have been previously withheld. . . . Each achieves, or rather earns, the right to human regard by means of the reality of their suffering."[86] In other words, sentimentalism attempts to reverse the process of representing slavery as difference.

In the end, when Davis finally sees Tom play, she discovers that his performance offers an incomplete reading of the slave child. It cannot erase his condition. While his owner talks on stage,

> Tom was left to himself,—when a weary despair seemed to settle down on the distorted face, and the stubby little black fingers, wandering over the keys,

spoke for Tom's own caged soul within . . . tender or wild, a defiant outcry, a tired sigh breaking down into silence. (III)

Through the metaphor of silence, Davis projects Tom's isolation across lines of gender and class. Her image of the universalized mute annihilates caste:

You cannot help Tom, either; all the war is between you. . . . But (do you hate the moral to a story?) in your own kitchen, in your own back-alley, there are spirits as beautiful, caged in forms as bestial, that you *could* set free, if you pleased. Don't call it bad taste in me to speak for them. You know they are more to be pitied than Tom,—for they are dumb. (III)

It remains unclear whether Davis is suggesting that the people who are "more to be pitied than Tom" are poor whites or free northern blacks. The ending certainly harkens to the conventional southern view that impoverished whites and free blacks in the North were worse off than slaves. However, for Davis, clearly what distinguishes and empowers Tom is the fact that he has not been silenced; Tom is not "dumb." Rather, Davis's fascination and identification with an exceptional state of being and her image of the articulation of pain, intensified to the point of hysteria, anticipates the protomodernist vision of control and repression in Gilman's "The Yellow Wallpaper."[87]

In "John Lamar" and "Blind Tom," Davis presumes to speak for the black person, to represent the slave, to put presumably unspoken assumptions and histories into words, to interpret through representation. The white woman has given the black man his voice. But because this is the voice of the slave, it lacks the reassurance of domesticity. Davis has severed the practice of virtue from the promise of material success. Subservience is repression, not reward. She explodes the confines of private space to raise public questions that insist on political responses. The private space, projected as private pain, is made public in order to show that it cannot transcend slavery. Jane Tompkins observes that domestic fiction is "preoccupied, even obsessed" with the nature of power.[88] In Davis's stories of slavery, power is economic, physical, political, and gendered. Unlike the martyrdom of Uncle Tom, power is not a spiritual predicament. The suffering of Ben, Bone, and Blind Tom insists on a secular telos. Through realism Davis avoids what Werner Sollars terms the typology of ethnicity, the assumption of reciprocal events that transform and elevate history into a shared biblical drama. Through realism, Davis confronts the sentimental imagination that pictures prison, including the prison of the home, as bliss. She deconstructs the Calvinist tendencies in domesticity that express suffering as heavenly wrath. In the figures of Ben, Dode, and Tom, Davis has externalized suffering, which she represents as historical, political, institutional, and public. Thus she compels her readers to conceive of the destruction of slavery as the true role of the Civil War.

5 ❧ The Soul Starvation of the Domestic Woman

IN DAVIS'S EARLIEST writings, female suffering was frequently a metaphor for the abuses of slavery and industrialism, caste and class. In stories written from 1863, just before her marriage, through the 1870s, Davis wrote about patriarchy itself. Despite the changed roles for women during and after the Civil War and their new opportunities in an emerging industrial society, Davis found that most women were still illiterate, uneducated, unemployed, lonely, impoverished, and frequently dependent on ineffectual or abusive men. In a group of stories published during and just after the Civil War, she invoked and portrayed fervent emotions as appropriate reactions to women's plight, splicing the political and the sentimental through her understanding of misogyny and female inequality. By depicting the daily details of working women's lives through the conventions of domestic fiction, Davis kindled sympathetic and compassionate emotions to condemn a culture of masculine individualism. In these stories, women recognize the false utopia of their lives—the isolation of housework and child rearing, the conflict with immature husbands, the loneliness of single women, their limited professional and educational options, and the silence of female poverty. Neither marriage nor the family provides a retreat from worldly consciousness.

Instead, home offers a realm of somewhat limited female power that can, through sympathy, stimulate affection and model communal responsibility.

In these stories focusing on the social realities of women during and soon after the Civil War, Davis also exposes the tension between sentimentalism, a genre predicated on the repression of the self, and realism, a genre predicated on the search for individual identity. Narrative friction—between realism and repression, authenticity and sentimentalism, history and literary tradition—shapes her female bildungsromans. Early in the development of American realism, an aesthetic that attempts to represent common social practices and languages, Davis borrows literary tropes from the popular domestic novel—plots about orphans, broken families, class barriers, physical disfigurement, and unjust imprisonment—and infuses them with intense feelings—abandonment, isolation, and inadequacy—to stimulate our sympathy for female workers, unpublished writers, sexually frustrated single women in celibate utopian communities, lonely women doctors, and a female circus performer. Intense feelings of confusion, isolation, and rage emerge as appropriate reactions to social and economic frustration. Thus the link between sentiment and realism in Davis's fiction hinges on her conceptualization of patriarchy.

At the same time that she invokes sentimentalism, Davis questions its tenets—the joy of selfless love, motherhood, and the society of the family, the redemptive power of love, the home as a refuge from the tensions of the workplace. In her representations of houses, factories, farms, and streets, capitalism's promise of a protective covenant for women is often broken. Images of deprivation, loss, silence, and confinement build toward unifying patterns of "soul starvation" and deconstruct the nurturing endings of sentimental fiction. Davis's early stories support Jane Tompkins's view that domestic fiction of the nineteenth century is "remarkable for its intellectual complexity, ambition and resourcefulness, and . . . offers a critique of American society far more devastating than any delivered by better-known critics such as Hawthorne and Melville."[1]

What is missing in Davis's early stories of female suffering is the compensation of aestheticized celebrations of the "bonds of womanhood," "female worlds of love and ritual," or "empires of the mother"[2] proffered, for example, in works by Susan Warner and Louisa May Alcott. Living at the edge of a battlefield in a western town and writing only for the *Wheeling Intelligencer* made Davis acutely aware of her geographical distance from New England. In her early years of writing, she was excluded from contact with the literary sorority of the East, and thus her instinct toward realism was allowed to thrive. The most influential woman in Davis's early development as a realist was her mother, Rachel Leet Harding. Rebecca declared that her fascination with history, her love of literary style and meticulous description, and her plots and characters from the "commonplace" came from her mother.

Also an eager storyteller, Rachel told Rebecca tales about the frustrations and isolation of lonely and impoverished southern women "who did not lead the picturesque idle life which their Northern sisters imagined and envied."[3] For example, Davis recalled her mother's recollections of her early years on a frontier plantation in Alabama:

> I . . . often heard my mother describe the mixed magnificence and squalor of the life on the plantations among which we lived; the great one-storied wooden houses built on piles; the pits of mud below them in which the pigs wallowed; the masses of crimson roses heaped high on the roofs; . . . the bare floors, not too often scrubbed; the massive buffets covered with magnificent plate, much of it cups and salvers won on the turf.[4]

Clearly, Rachel was an early regionalist and realist who sought to explode the myths of southern romanticism.

Davis's other confidante and literary guide was Annie Fields, wife of James Fields. Davis's correspondence with Annie began in 1861 when Annie wrote to the unknown author, praising "Life in the Iron-Mills" and inviting her to Boston. Although the outbreak of war delayed the visit, letters between the two women flowed with great frequency. When Davis made the trip in 1862, she met Emerson, Bronson Alcott, and Louisa May Alcott, and she formed a friendship with her childhood literary hero, the elusive Nathaniel Hawthorne, who invited the shy author to his home. Ultimately the friendship between Rebecca and Annie was unfortunately dependent on Davis's dealings with James Fields, a connection that waned in the late sixties with Davis's difficult departure from the *Atlantic*. Only Rebecca's side of the correspondence remains, but these hundred letters, along with her public reminiscences in *Bits of Gossip* (written in 1904 near the end of her life), provide our only intimate view of the author. As she wrote to Annie, "I would rather tell other women's stories than my own."[5] Rebecca's letters to Annie reveal a woman halting, pragmatic, repressed, proud of her southern mountain culture, and yearning for intimacy. At first, Rebecca naively sought Annie's interference with James on publishing matters; by the late 1860s she had grown increasingly assertive about her editorial wishes and her financial rights.

The only other significant woman to appear in Davis's personal writings was Lucretia Mott, the well-known abolitionist, who befriended Davis soon after her move to Philadelphia. Mott, who Davis noticed kept a copy of Mary Wollstonecraft's *Vindication of the Rights of Women* on her sewing table, became as "kin" as "a woman and a sister."[6]

With her marriage only months away, Davis wrote one of the more daring stories she would undertake for publication in the *Atlantic*, "The Promise of the Dawn," a winter's tale pointedly subtitled "A Christmas Story."[7] In this first of her many Christmas stories, Davis tells of a young prostitute whose mother has recently died "of starvation and whiskey" on the docks of New York, seduced and abandoned by a wealthy man who had brought her from Wheeling. Lot (for "harlot"; she is also called Charley) has brought her small brother Ben back to Wheeling, only to discover that her elderly Uncle Adam and his new young wife, Jinny, will not even acknowledge them. When Jinny, a revivalist obsessed with the conversion of slaveholders and the Sioux tribes, hears of the sordid death of Lot's mother, she comments, "God sent an angel to bring her up, an' have her soul washed clean." Adam bitterly replies, "That's not the way men told the story" (16).

"The Promise of the Dawn" is about the differences in how men and women tell the story of a prostitute—if the masculine story is of an eroticized and diseased woman, the feminine story is of an infantilized and sexualized female victim. "The Promise of the Dawn" is shaped both by how the Victorians imagined the harlot, and how, in the name of Christianity, society denied her real conditions, trapped as she was by poverty, drug addiction, and venereal disease. "The Promise of the Dawn" was written during an interregnum between two periods of social concern about prostitution.[8] The 1830s and 1840s, troubled by ethical questions, saw the rise of organizations that sought to end prostitution by rescuing "fallen women" and reforming their male clients. The Magdalen Society and the New York Female

Moral Reform Society, for example, offered prostitutes refuge in rural areas where they could learn new skills in forced isolation from men; the societies also listed the names of male clients in the police columns of urban newspapers. Following the Civil War—an era more concerned with slavery and its aftermath than prostitution—and the rise of the male medical profession, doctors returned to the issue. Male health became the leading motive for the abolition of prostitution, as "regulationists" sought to protect men through the licensing and medical inspection of prostitutes. The shift away from the rescue of "fallen women" prompted an intense reaction from female reformers such as Susan B. Anthony, who argued for the elimination rather than the institutionalization of prostitution.

The contemporary debate surrounding the causes of prostitution emerge in "The Promise of the Dawn," a story that predates the literary fascination with prostitution in the 1870s. Prostitution, Ruth Rosen observes, functions as a "lens through which we gain a detailed magnification" of a society's organization of class and gender.[9] It serves not only as a marker of women's biology and economic status, but also as an emblem for contemporary views of sexuality, both inside and outside of marriage. In the 1830s, as young women entered the public sphere as mill workers and domestic servants, they were suddenly living and working in close proximity to large concentrations of single men in the new mill towns, such as Wheeling, which had lost preindustrial traditions of community morality.[10] Highly vulnerable, poor, and isolated from their families, the "mill girls" were frequent victims of rape, seduction, alcohol abuse, unwanted pregnancy, opium addiction, and prostitution. Along with thousands of other young working women, prostitutes suffered from syphilis, gonorrhea, assault, and dangerous abortions. In 1859, Caroline Healey Dall, a reformer who addressed the economic plight of working women, proclaimed, "Seven thousand eight hundred and fifty ruined women walk the streets of New York—five hundred ordinary omnibus-loads. . . . What drives them to it? The want of bread."[11] Davis similarly insists on poverty as the source of Lot's "fall," satirizing characters who punitively talk about the "wages of sin." Unlike Stephen Crane's Maggie, Lot became a prostitute in order to feed her little brother; as she explains, "My God! I had to live!" (19). By exonerating her, however, Davis also reaffirms woman's asexual and innate moral nature.

Davis's portrait of Lot reflects the widely publicized results of a study undertaken in the late 1850s by William Sanger, the resident physician at Blackwell's Island Prison, who surveyed 2,000 prostitutes in New York. Sanger found that the largest number of prostitutes were young, age eighteen to twenty-three; over half were foreign-born, mainly from Germany or Ireland; 30 percent had children; and nearly half "confessed" to suffering from syphilis and/or gonorrhea. They were all desperately poor: 534 women said that as prostitutes they earned one dollar per week; at the most, 127 earned four dollars per week at their trade. In explaining why they became prostitutes, 525 said they were destitute, 258 were seduced and abandoned, 181 cited alcohol, and nearly 200 others listed "ill treatment" by parents and husbands. Twenty-seven said they had been "violated."[12] Typical of Sanger's findings, Lot was entrapped into prostitution by fraud; she is uneducated, addicted to drugs, suffering from venereal disease, desperately poor, and supporting a child. And, true to Sanger's demographics, she died only four years after first becoming a prostitute at age fifteen.[13]

There were many fewer prostitutes in the South, where Lot and her brother have fled in search of familial and rural sanctuary. (The purchase of sex was generally unnecessary for southern white men, given their license to rape their slaves, and indeed, there is little documentation of black prostitution during the mid-nineteenth century.) In Wheeling, however, the presence of the iron mills and the massing of soldiers—both Union and Confederate—encouraged prostitutes and camp followers, women who unofficially accompanied military units to perform both sexual and domestic duties for the soldiers. In the eyes of the good citizens of Wheeling, Lot, as a prostitute and as a diseased female, figures as an infectious carrier of northern urban values.

In "The Promise of the Dawn" Davis beguiles her reader into thinking this is a Christmas story. Not only does the title hint at rebirth and redemption, but also the narrator observes that with the foul mills closed for the winter, the city has "clothed" itself again in "spotless" snow. Images of winter purity, however, fail to cloak eros: unlike the "sea-breath in the New-England states" that "sucks the vitality out of Nature . . . to put it into the brains of the people" in the West, "the earth every day of the year pulses out through hill or prairie or creek a full, untamed animal life,—shakes off the snow too early in spring, in order to put forth untimed and useless blossoms, wasteful of her infinite strength" (10). Resisting the rarified New England theologies imaged in the "wan and washed-out" sky of the North is the West Virginia sky of "sensuous yellow langour" (10).

Tempting images of permissible eroticism and consumable treats shape the Christmas Eve story of sexual and religious hypocrisy. Lot first encounters her Uncle Adam as he "stopped before the confectioner's: just for a moment, to collect himself; for this was the crowning point, this. There they were, in the great, gleaming window below: the rich Malaga raisins, bedded in their cases, cold to the lips, but within, all glowing sweetness and passion." A female image of hidden delicious orality is exposed for the pleasure of Adam's gaze. Indeed, a group of boys shoves Adam away from his vision: "Let's have a look, boys!" (14). Adam then observes the "delicate, pure women" going into the concert hall for the holy carol ceremony: "It made his nerves thrill into pleasure to look at them" (14). But lurking at the edge of images of countenanced eroticism are darker references to this wartime Christmas, when "the most plentiful harvest which the States had yielded that year was one of murdered dead" (10). Adam's tempted gaze is parodied by that of the grimy and tattered Confederate prisoners being held in an old theater, who peer at the Christmas delights from behind barred windows.

It is at this moment of Adam's lawful eroticism—desire of observation or purchase—that his niece Lot, desperate to provide some holiday decorations for her brother, tries to steal a small bunch of Christmas flowers that Adam has just purchased for his wife. As Lot grabs at his flowers, Adam notices that her hand is covered with venereal sores and sees her young face, "deadly pale, on which some awful passion had cut the lines; lips dyed scarlet with rank blood" (14). The repeated imagery of disease that surrounds Lot desexualizes her as it insists on her material reality. To protect Jinny's flowers—that is to say, her innocence—Adam strikes Lot. The narrator comments, "A woman? Yes; if it had been a slimy eel standing upright, it would have been less foul a thing than this" (14)—a phallic displacement prompted by Adam's disgust at his own temptation. By assigning eros to Lot rather than to Adam, Davis affiliates female sexuality with disease. In a world of female passionlessness, contagion deconstructs the prostitute as a sanctioned figure for male desire and rescripts female frailty as contamination. In describing Lot through her foul sores and lips "dyed scarlet with rank blood," Davis renders her unavailable, even while she asserts her historical presence. Lot's body substantiates the view uttered by a contemporary male physician that a woman is "a moral, a sexual, a germiferous, gestative and parturient creature."[14]

Repudiated by her uncle, Lot tries to earn some money for Christmas, only to encounter a town of "stingy souls" who believe that "us uns is outsiders" (13). The manager of the theater, hence a man who works at the edge of the sexual demimonde, refuses to allow Lot to sing for a small pittance in the Christmas chorus, explaining, "There's no place for such as you . . . when a woman's once down, there's no raising her up" (19). Even the black porter at the theater draws his coat aside, loath to touch Lot, and chases her out of the theater with a stick. Increasingly desperate to provide for Ben's Christmas, Lot approaches Jinny's house, begging for work in her kitchen, but when she is turned away, Lot concludes, "There's not one of those Christian women up in the town yonder 'ud take Lot into their kitchens to give her a chance to save herself from hell" (19).

Lot has defied the ideals of chastity, exposing the double standard of sexual behavior for men and women and severing female sexuality from Jinny's fecund imagery of reproduction, the appropriate emblem of the female body. As the theater manager tells her, "Those that have made you what you are hold good stations among us" (19). The era was well aware of this hypocrisy. C. E. Rogers, in his popular study *The Secret Sins of Society* (1881), examined such contemporary "social evils" as cosmetics, the prevention of conception, mesmerism, eating salt, "foeticide," and prostitution, and concluded,

> We may reasonably expect seduction to be frequent, and prostitution from this cause unabated, so long as our social system recognizes in the weak, confiding victim an object for all its contempt and abhorrence . . . while society throws open its doors to the offender, but brands with shame and disgrace the outraged victim of his perjury and crime.[15]

In her portrait of the marriage of Jinny and Adam, Davis satirizes the class pretensions, social myopia, and religious hypocrisy of the cult of true womanhood.

In December, as "The Promise of the Dawn" was going to press, Davis wrote to Annie Fields, "You were right not to let Mr. Fields think the Christmas story overdrawn." Hinting at James Fields's Brahmin myopia, she commented, "You know, here in a town like this it is easy to come into direct contact with every class" and concludes, "'Lot' is from life."[16] Even so, Lot is desexualized, a victim of the belief that men lead unwitting and unwilling women into sexual promiscuity.[17] Despite the many letters and diaries of the time that testify to mid-nineteenth-century women's forthright desire for sexual intimacy with their husbands and lovers, the image of the victimized prostitute was part of the double standard that posited men as naturally lustful and uniquely in need of sexual gratification.[18] The social purity movement of the 1870s and 1880s and the demand for "age of consent" legislation would perpetuate the view, typified by Davis, that prostitutes (and by implication, other sexually active young women) were unwitting and uneager victims of unbridled male passion. Lot's martyrdom contests her bodily significations of female depravity and subverts the idea that women possess a potential for depravity even greater than that of men. There is no whore lurking inside this self-sacrificing and passionless madonna. In the end, Lot's social history is collapsed back into her biology—what G. M. Goshgarian terms the "female within the female."[19] She is a divided subject who projects Davis's understanding of the incoherence of the ideology of domesticity. Depicted as a child prostitute (who is actually nineteen), Lot suggests female suffering and sexuality, incest and refusal, eros and pathos, victimization and resistance.

The resolution of a story that had attempted to represent a prostitute in fact erases her. Banished by Adam and Jinny on Christmas Eve, Lot covers herself with her cloak and returns to the street. There she encounters an urchin, a friend of her little brother, and urges him "never to tell that child that his 'Charley' was Lot. . . . When you play with Ben, I wish you'd call me Charley to him, and never—that other name" (22). In obliterating her body and purging the name that defines her as a prostitute, Lot colludes in her social invisibility. She returns to the tenement room in an old cotton factory, creeps into the cold bed with her little brother, and swallows an overdose of opium and dies, so that Benny will be rescued by Adam and Jinny on Christmas morning—"it was the promise of the Dawn." In a conclusion unlike anything else in Davis's fiction, the "vile worm Lot" goes to heaven where she meets Jesus:

> The child that might have been, came to His feet humbly, with bitter sobs. . . . "I'd like to try again, and be a different girl." That was all. She clung to

His hand as she went through the deep waters. . . . Jesus took the child Charley in His arms, and blessed her. (24)

Davis has not merely allowed the narrator to assume a sympathetic stance in a drama of seduction in which there is no possibility for reform—a woman without her "virtue" must die. By escaping from her body, Lot is also literally eliminated from the narrative. Davis has erased the sexualized body of an adult woman, as well as the social economics that constructed her, and in their place literalized a spiritual vision of a maternal and forgiving Christ tending an errant child.[20]

The sordid aspects of women's lives that Davis explores in her stories of the mid-1860s were not yet common topics of fiction. Perhaps because they appeared for the most part in the *Atlantic*, Davis was granted a certain measure of respectability. In 1881 the American Library Association Cooperation Committee sent a questionnaire to seventy major libraries asking if they had ever held or withdrawn the works of sixteen authors, including Mrs. E. D. E. N. Southworth, Ann Sophia Stephens, and Augusta Jane Evans Wilson, for reason of "sensational or immoral qualities."[21] Although Davis was not on the list, she shared with her peers the choice of such "immoral" topics as the rejection of masculine authority in domestic life and religious faith, the dangers of weak or ignorant men, and the precarious economic position of both single and married women. Davis however was more explicit about women's public vulnerability, more pointed in her expose of evangelical hypocrisy, and more condemning of the economic ethos of urban culture, than the writers the Library Association sought to discredit. Indeed, stories such as "The Promise of the Dawn," "The Second Life," and "Paul Blecker" would put her closer to the group termed by Dee Garrison the "sensational school" —William Harrison Ainsworth (1805–1882), Mary Elizabeth Braddon (1837–1915), and Ellen Price Wood (1814–1887)—authors who, with considerable zest and in lurid detail, focused on the urban underclass and the criminal character.

Writing on the eve of her marriage to L. Clarke Davis, if Davis introduces the figure of Lot to explore her own conflicts about the sexual woman and the pure woman, she likewise uses Jinny to picture the abject gratitude of a lonely spinster finally beloved. It is hard not to think of Rebecca, thirty-one years old, burdened by an ill father and aging mother, leaving home to marry a man she scarcely knows, in her description of Jinny, "How faded and worn and tired-out she was, how hard the years had been,—to show him how his great love for her was thickening the thin blood with life, making a child out of the thwarted woman [whose heart had become] a contracted tenement . . . adapted for single lodgers" (15).

Yet marriage is never a sanctuary for Davis's women. From late 1862 and through the early spring of 1863, as Rebecca was anticipating her wedding while tending to her family and navigating her first few months of marriage while tending to her new in-laws, she wrote two stories about women trapped in abusive and loveless marriages. "The Second Life" (January–June 1863) was Davis's first serialized novel for *Peterson's Magazine*, a journal with a largely female audience.[22] Written in an era fascinated by female murderers,[23] "The Second Life" is the story of Esther Lashley, who has been accused of murdering her cruel husband. This detective novel, narrated by a lawyer, raises the issue of self-defense as a justification for killing an abusive husband and calls into question the ethos of female masochism and endurance.

Esther is a shy, grateful, and childlike woman who honors her guardian's deathbed wish to marry his alcoholic son, Clayton. Once married, Esther is frequently the object of her husband's violent rage; she becomes "dumb," silent, gloomy, and given to "wild bursts of frantic pain, as if driven to insanity" (293). One night Clayton rapes her, then refuses her pleas for divorce and disappears. Days later, when his belongings are found in a creek, Esther is arrested for murder. Although Esther is acquitted on a technicality, the lawyer-narrator seeks to clear her name. Eventually Clayton reappears. Crazed and helpless, he must be hidden and confined for his own protection—a gendered twist of narrative revenge. Although Davis allows Clayton to die of natural causes soon after his reappearance, she clearly believes in Esther's right to self-defense. Similarly, in "The Promise of the Dawn," Lot vows to herself that even though Adam is her uncle, "I'll kill him, if he strikes me agin" (20).

In "Paul Blecker" the issue of a woman's entrapment in a loveless and degrading marriage emerges in rhetorics that identify the merits of divorce with the abolition of slavery.[24] Set in abolitionist mountain towns in western Pennsylvania and the Civil War battlefields of Harper's Ferry and Fredricksburg, this story of marital abuse is patently rooted in the history of antislavery crusades. This is the story of the romance between Paul Blecker, a surgeon for the Union Army, and Grey Gurney, a married woman from a "poorgenteel" (593) family in the hills of western Pennsylvania, who believes that her husband, a tyrannical man who has abused and abandoned her, has died in Cuba. Although Paul insists that Grey's mother "sold" her daughter into a foul marriage, Grey reminds him that her mother had ten children and was "not selfish, more than other women. There were very many mouths to feed" (593). Grey explains that she too saw no other options: "I am very dull about books, . . . I could not teach; and they would not let me sew for money, because of the disgrace." When Paul mumbles that he understands, Grey persists, "'No man can understand,'—her voice growing shrill with pain. 'It's not easy to eat the bread needed for other mouths day after day, with your hands tied, idle and helpless'" (593). Besides, as Davis herself understood, Grey says she was tired of being a spinster; even her difficult marriage "was like leaving some choking pit, where air was given to me from other lungs, to go out and find it for my own . . . living on suffrance, always the one too many in the house" (593). Believing that her husband is dead, Grey has returned home, taking up her late mother's burden of caring for not only for many sisters and brothers but also her self-indulgent father, an unemployed geologist, a "tadpole of a man, rooting after tracks of lizards . . . while the country is going to mash, and his own children next door to starvation" (64).

Paul's plan to marry Grey is blocked when they discover that Gray's husband, John, is a Confederate prisoner lying wounded in the hospital at Harper's Ferry. John "did not care especially to torment the woman . . . unless, indeed, he needed her pain" (690). Desiring his own freedom, John offers to let Grey seek a divorce and sue him for wilful desertion. Davis's description of this marriage suggests analogies between slavery and patriarchy. The narrator reiterates that Grey was "sold" to John; she suggests that there are "slaveries in society, and false marriages are the worst" (55). Grey is "sorry that the slaves are slaves . . . as sorry, being unpatriotic, for the homeless women in Virginia" (596). When Grey is finally willing to consider divorce, she stands in the guardhouse where John Brown defended himself during his aborted slave rebellion at Harper's Ferry:

> The marks of bullets were in the walls. She tried to think of all that had followed that defence, of the four millions of slaves for whom he died, . . . it

seemed to her she was more to be pitied than they. Chained to a man she hated. Why, more than four millions of women had married as she had done: society drove them into it. (52–53)

At the time of "Paul Blecker," divorce was an issue contested in ideology but not in law. As early as 1827 the Virginia legislature authorized the court of chancery to annul marriages based on impotency, idiocy, or bigamy, and to grant divorces for adultery and cruelty. By 1853, ten years before the publication of "Paul Blecker," Virginia law was liberalized to include as just causes for divorce imprisonment, prostitution, evidence that a wife was pregnant by another man at the time of the wedding—or, most relevant to Grey, desertion for at least three years. In explaining the apparent paradox of the ease with which divorce became available during the peak of the cult of domesticity in the 1850s, Roderick Phillips argues that divorce law reform was actually a conservative movement to preserve a system of values and behavior that was believed to be at risk. Divorce was designed to reinforce the conventional family, under threat from adultery, desertion, wife beating, and drunkenness.[25] Phillips also notes that divorce reform was supposed to shore up the notion of separate spheres if a man or woman failed to perform the tasks expected of them—such as John Gurney.

Nonetheless, at midcentury, as the debate between Grey and Paul reveals, divorce was still a highly contentious topic. There was no consensus on divorce, for example, at the Seneca Falls Conference in 1848. Susan B. Anthony feared that demands for divorce reform could frighten other reformers; Lucy Stone grouped divorce with abortion and infanticide as topics too sensitive to be discussed.[26] Many other women's rights reformers shared Grey's view that the family was inviolate. Despite the legal access to divorce at midcentury, it is thus not surprising that the overall numbers remained low. In 1860 there were 7,380 divorces, separations, or annulments in the United States. The number fell by about 500 in 1863, the year of "Paul Blecker," probably because the Civil War separated husbands and wives and because the enormous death toll inevitably terminated hundreds of thousands of marriages. Not surprisingly, the number of divorces nearly doubled with demobilization in 1865 and 1866.[27]

There are two endings to "Paul Blecker." The first resists the possibility of divorce and the related metaphoric texture of female enslavement: despite

Paul's valiant attempt to save his life, John Gurney dies a fortuitous death on the battlefield of Fredricksburg, freeing Grey to marry Paul and buy a small farm in the Allegheny Mountains—in Grey's eyes a pastoral reward from God for her self-sacrificing decision to "submit" (58). But the story moves beyond this ending and closes in a coda, with the tale of Grey's younger sister Lizzy, whose destiny undercuts and comments on Grey's marriage to Paul (which has not solved the problem of the ten hungry and motherless sisters and brothers). In contrast to Grey, the narrator observes of Lizzy,

> You do not like this Lizzy Gurney? . . . I chose her purposely. I chose a bilious, morbid woman to talk to you of, because American women are bilious and morbid. Men all cling desperately to the old book-type of women, delicate, sunny, helpless . . . mere crumpling of the rose-leaves. But how many of them do you meet on the street? (677)

Unlike Grey, Lizzie suffers from "unrest . . . there was a consciousness that with a man's body she would have been more of a man than her brother" (677); her soul starvation gives vent in "perpetual self-analyzing" and in "embracing the chimera of the Woman's Rights prophets" (678). But more than gaining the right to vote, what Lizzie really wants to do is sing. Faced with the death of her lover in the war and the fierce economic needs of her family, she takes a job in New York in a second-rate opera company—despite the threat from her brother-in-law, Paul, who "hates" women who display "vitality and pain and affection" (66) and who warns Lizzie that her dead lover will reject her in heaven. Lizzie, however, perseveres with her musical career, and the story concludes with her performance on Broadway. Although on opening night she starts to pity herself that "she, a woman, should stand before the public for them to examine and chatter over her soul and her history, and her very dress and shoes" (68), the moment passes when she recalls not only the hungry mouths she is feeding with her earnings, but also the "quiet and useless" home life she has escaped.

"Paul Blecker" thus situates women's personal choices in a complex web of economic and political pressures. The story challenges the view that romance, marriage, and family are a self-enclosed realm in which men are competent and money does not matter. At the time she wrote "Paul Blecker," the precarious financial situation of many women was becoming very clear to

Davis. In an undated letter to James Fields, she describes her fatigue and, for virtually the first time, asks for an advance. With polite desperation, she reveals her new sense of the economics of publishing:

> Here are "The Gurneys"—I hope they will please you better than they do me. The pages read "fagged" to me and I *am* tired and need rest. . . . I want to ask a favor of you. Can you *if the story pleases you* advance me now $225 on it? At 8 dollars a page it will be worth more than that, but I would like to have that now. . . . I am sorry to ask you this . . . but it would be very *convenient* for me to have that much just now, and I can ask *you* to oblige me so far. Nobody else.[28]

Within months of her marriage to Clarke and her move to Philadelphia, Rebecca suffered from a nervous collapse. At age thirty-one, she had suddenly found herself living with in-laws, tending to Clarke and his sister, who were both ill, and she was pregnant. When long walks and patent medicines failed to restore her energy and spirits, she turned to the prominent physician S. Weir Mitchell who recommended the same cure of rest and sensory deprivation that he later prescribed for Charlotte Perkins Gilman. The restorative effects on Davis, however, differed radically from the mind-destroying terrors described by the narrator of Gilman's "The Yellow Wallpaper" (1891).

As she began to recover, for the first time her letters to Annie become open and self-disclosing, confiding that she was "still weak enough to feel [her] heart beat and the tears come at a little petting." She remarks that she was deeply moved by a tender letter from Annie: "It made me think you never had written so before," and she adds,

> I never felt before how hard it was to justify my right to love as since I was sick. . . . Sometimes I have a terror Annie that it will all disappear like a dream—that I will become indifferent to you all. I am foolish to speak in this way but I cannot help it.[29]

The next day she writes again,

> I wanted to write before only to say I loved you . . . but at first I was not able and now the doctor forbids the least reading or writing for fear of bringing back the trouble in my head. . . . These days have been so like the valley of the shadow of death, that I grow afraid of the end.

On the following day, she sent "The Wife's Story" (1864) to the *Atlantic*, explaining to Annie, "I am so much in the humour of these short sketches."[30]

There are strong autobiographical elements in the "The Wife's Story." Soon after her marriage to Clarke, a "sedentary reserved" man, she wrote Annie that she still felt a compulsion to write. "It is a necessity for me to write—well or ill—You know every animal has spirit and that is mine."[31] "The Wife's Story," which opens with the narrator's announcement, "I will tell you the story of my life" (112), was written during Davis's troubled first pregnancy. It is out of the emotional tumult of her marriage to a near stranger, the disruption of the move from her beloved mountains of West Virginia to Philadelphia, the economic pressures of urban life, the demanding intimacy of living as newlyweds with Clarke's family, her emotional collapse and enforced rest cure, that these stories of female ambivalence emerge.

With "The Wife's Story," the first major work to appear after her recovery, Davis launched a series of short stories that focus on women's isolated and frustrated lives. The finest of these are "The Story of A Song" (1864), "God Does Not Forget" (1866), "The Story of Christine" (1866), "At Bay" (1867), "The Harmonists" (1866), "In the Market" (1868), "Lois Platner" (1869), "Earthen Pitchers" (1873–1874), "Dolly" (1874), "Marcia" (1876), "A Day with Dr. Sarah" (1878), and "Anne" (1889). Engaging the most subversive elements of sentimentalism, these stories expose the painful consequences of an ethos that repressed women's independence and individuality.[32] They thus belong in the tradition of such widely popular novels as *The Wide, Wide World* (1850) by Susan Warner, *Ruth Hall* (1855) by Sara Willis Parton [Fanny Fern], *The Hidden Hand* (1859) by E. D. E. N. Southworth, and *Hitherto: A Story of Yesterdays* (1869) by A. D. T. Whitney, novels that portray the losses women suffer when they adhere to the "societal text" of feminine identity.

In delineating the subversive nature of "domestic narratives," Joanne Dobson extends Elaine Showalter's notion of "covert rebellion" and Helen Papashvily's judgment that domestic fiction is a veritable "witches' broth, a lethal draught brewed by women and used by women to destroy their common enemy, man."[33] On the one hand, writes Dobson, "In these novels marriage seems indeed to be the 'jumping-off place,' a sanctioned suicide of the uniqueness of the self. The heroine's progress is from individuality to self-renunciation, from energy to stasis."[34] On the other hand, Dobson also locates in these tales "a strong emotional undertow that pulls the reader in the opposite direction."[35] As Davis's female characters come to understand the economic realities and masculine tyrannies that shape their lives, they rebel, at least for a time, against their lack of property rights, the ideology surrounding divorce, and unequal educational and employment opportunities for women. Although her heroines of the 1860s may well reconcile themselves to the benefits of marriage, security, and an acceptable social identity, along the way they utter subversive expressions of reluctance and resistance. Often their gestures of rebellion are symbolic. As Papashvily observes, many an author of domestic fiction finds a way to "mutilate" her male characters —intellectually, morally, emotionally, and at times, physically.[36]

Resistance for Davis's heroines (as for the author herself) often takes artistic forms. As she describes women's attraction to creative lives, she rescripts the sentimental heroine's inevitable "progress" from autonomy to subservience, from independence to abjection, from initiative to stasis. Davis undercuts the obligatory paradigm of self-abnegation and uses her characters' newfound power and pain to sabotage her own plots, giving the lie along the way to her stories' endings of masculine superiority and social control. Profoundly ambivalent about the domestic contract in which women gain authority by redeeming men, she portrays the frustration women encounter when they pursue their own ambitions. In addition to acts of narrative subversion (which may not hold in the story's conclusion), Davis's ironic voice also lets us know how women's pursuit of art results in unearned punishment and unmerited self-doubt.

In these stories Davis also attacks the notion that a "separate female sphere" offers women a zone of refuge, community, culture, and, in a restricted sense, freedom. Ultimately, Davis's tales of mill girls, child prostitutes, female journalists, utopianists, opera singers, and circus performers question the possibility of any space, public or domestic, untouched by the marketplace. Not only do many of her working women inhabit both worlds; like Grey Gurney in "Paul Blecker," many of Davis's fictive wives and mothers come to understand that romance and the protective covenant of marriage are threatened by a public world of precarious economics, incompetent husbands, and vulnerable mortgages. Davis situates subjective experience and domestic life within the unstable economics of industrial capitalism.

The family—the sentimental metaphor for desire and the site of domestic sanctuary reenacts economic pressures and gender tensions. Femaleness is rarely a straightforward sign of either sanctuary or domestic authority. Nonetheless, while Davis continued to locate her domestic plots in authentic historical contexts, her narratives transform these political situations into psychological dilemmas and thereby reinforce the sentimental notion that resolution lies in the heart. Ultimately, social conflict emerges as personal history, at times returning us to the social plane in the end, at times persisting in concealing power in the domestic plots, subversive though they may be.

In "The Wife's Story," the theme of marriage as a woman's sanctuary is undermined by the heroine's discovery that family life results in intellectual suicide. The story is told by Hester Manning, Davis's most self-disclosing female narrator. Hester is a middle-aged New England woman who has recently married a widower with five children. Hester recounts how their early passionate and companionable relationship has fallen apart with the arrival of her husband's family. When Hester realizes that she is pregnant, she dreams of having a son to whom she can give the education she never had. To her dismay, she delivers a daughter, like herself, a "weazened-faced little mortal, crying night and day like any other animal. It was an animal, wearing out in me the strength needed by-and-by for its mental training" (121).

In an unusual portrait of postpartum depression, Hester describes how, suffering from weakness, nausea, and anxiety, she sent the colicky baby to live with a wet-nurse in the country. As she recounts her rejection of her daughter, Hester suddenly remembers, with "some latent, unconscious jar of thought" (191), a visit she had once made to the Paris studio of Rosa Bonheur, a well-known French painter and sculptor famed for her remarkable accuracy. Hester recalls the peculiar life that seemed to "impregnate" the studio: unlike her own recent experience, Bonheur had "her own precise niche and work in the world." She remembers Bonheur's observation, "Any woman can be a wife or mother, but this is my work alone" (121). Portending her flight into the world of the theater, however, Hester also recollects her impression that Bonheur's studio was a world of artifice: "the sharply managed lights, the skins, trappings, her disguises on the walls" (121).[37]

Soon Hester's husband, a hearty and passionate western doctor with a scanty beard, cheap wig, and slim economic sense, announces that his investments have failed, just as she learns that an opera she had written before her marriage and had kept secret from her husband has been accepted. To further complicate her wifely dilemma, she is offered a singing part in the premiere of her own composition. Facing middle-class poverty with an incompatible husband, Hester struggles with her own ambition. On the one hand, she asks, "What was there in the world good and pure for me but the man sitting yonder, and the thought that I was his wife?" (114). But because of her New England father's clique of transcendental friends, "Every meanest hint of a talent . . . had been nursed, every taste purged; . . . [her] unquiet brain, of moderate power . . . had been forced and harried and dragged into exertion every moment of [her] life, according to the custom with women in the States from which [she] came" (114). In "The Wife's Story," Hester's Promethean desire emerges as narcissistic and misconceived female ambition. Reversing the satiric thrust of *Margret Howth*, in "The Wife's Story" a woman's self-denying love of a man confronts her frustration and egotistical need to justify her ambition through the rhetoric of transcendental self-growth. In a parodic moment of philosophic cross-dressing, domestic values are posited as masculine, and individualistic goals are posited as feminine— only to condemn a bored and ambitious wife who suffers from the "egotistical sublime."

Once Hester equates artistic autonomy with transcendentalism, it becomes impossible for her to reconcile sentimental femininity with liberal individualism. Davis frames Hester's choice between her creative needs, her motherly duties, and her sexual attraction to her husband as a choice between Christian sympathy and transcendental egotism. Hester explains that she was raised on the New England dictum, "'The only object in life is to grow.' It was my father's,—Margaret Fuller's motto" (120). Rather than a feminist prerogative, however, Hester interprets Fuller's credo as a romantic imperative that she has been escaping since her marriage day.

Like Hawthorne's Hester Prynne, Davis's Hester must choose between transcendental idealism and domestic materialism, artifice and nature, the self and others. Davis, however, complicates romantic tensions by references to gender and class. Hester recalls that in her New England childhood intellectualism constantly fed upon itself because there was "more mental power than was needed for the work that was to be done" (115). By contrast, Dr.

Manning, her western husband, and his son seem "but clogs of flesh, the mere hands by which the manual work of the world's progress was to be accomplished" (115); they represent the industrial and masculine present. Further, Dr. Manning speaks in the rhetoric of realism, which Davis associates with the West and which further foretells her repudiation of transcendentalism.

> He had a curious epigrammatic way of talking that I have noticed . . . in many Western men: coming at the marrow and meaning of a scene or person in his narration with a sheer subtilized common-sense, a tough appreciation of fact beyond theory, and of its deeper, juster significance, and a dramatic aptness for expression. (117)

In contrast to Dr. Manning's "tough appreciation for fact beyond theory," Hester's need for "mental power" lapses into a self-indulgent career spree in a theatrical world of tawdry eroticism. The independent footsteps of Margaret Fuller lead her back to the dangerous egoism of her childhood. True female morality resides in social commitment, wifely martyrdom, and Dr. Manning's vocabulary of life in the commonplace, while the rhetoric of transcendentalism seduces her into feminist abstraction and sham creativity. Fed up with her colicky baby and bald husband, Hester decides to leave her family, "a mess of weakest pottage,—a little love, . . . petting and paltering such as other women's souls grew imbecile without" (121). Her marriage, she decides, is one between

> two middle-aged people, with inharmonious intellects: tastes and habits jarring at every step. . . . Better apart: . . . If I remained with Doctor Manning, my *rôle* was outlined plain to the end: years of cooking, stitching, scraping together of cents: it was the fate of thousands of married women without means, to grovel every year nearer the animal life. (122)

Rejecting the atavism of nature that defines her marriage—her western husband, childbearing, passion, the "animal life"—she sails for Manhattan to pursue a life of *"Vollmachtsbrief zum Glücke"* (121), the German romantics' "license for happiness." Her brief night at the opera, however, turns into a terrifying dream sequence of artifice, shame, abandonment, and death. The stage world of her opera, entitled "Life's Prophecy," emerges as a fake world of pasteboard castles, paper costumes, and false notes; one of the actresses tries to cover a mole on Hester's lip with a makeup called "Meen Fun." Her opera is a flop and Hester is hissed off the stage. Appalled to discover that her husband has been in the audience, she is guilt-stricken: "I wondered if my child would ever know it had a mother" (133). Running from the Broadway theater through back alleys, Hester suddenly comes upon the corpse of her husband, who had suffered a heart attack after witnessing her performance. In the mid-nineteenth century, as Glenn Hendler notes, the "real danger of theatricality is that, like sympathy, it encourages indiscriminate identification."[38] Believing that she has become the tawdry character she has portrayed on the stage, Hester concludes, "I had murdered him. I!" (134).

Hester's career, however, is only a bad dream. Awakening from the nightmare, she discovers that she never left for New York, but rather has been suffering from an acute nervous disease inherited from her transcendentalist father and brought on by her ambition.[39] She presses her face into her husband's breast and is metaphorically born again, cradled in her conjugal bed and nurtured into a new identity of wifely commitment, maternal passion, and economic security. Rather than representing repressed desire, the dream sequence in "The Wife's Story" reinforces Hester's guilt for even fantasizing about abandoning her family for an inadequate talent.[40] Only marriage, which she saw as the death of her unique self, offers her community and intimacy. Like the heroine Christie in Louisa May Alcott's novel *Work* (1873), who is also driven toward a career, Hester discovers that her real goal is to be initiated into the sympathetic community of the home;[41] her choice is not between career and marriage but between isolation and intimacy. In the end, seduced by familial sympathy, Hester finds solace by redefining issues of femininity and masculinity as issues of class and region, realism and transcendentalism. "The Wife's Story" fails to resolve the painful anxiety about female identity it has aroused.

Yet Davis was troubled by the conclusion that a woman should live solely for marriage, a romantic relationship that, as Simone de Beauvoir later argued, offers only vicarious access to transcendence. At best, the family to Davis signifies a communal alternative to the romantic and masculine notion of the self as separate, bounded, and autonomous. Shortly after Davis moved to Philadelphia in 1863, she became intrigued with the celibate experimental community established by the visionary George Rapp in Economy, Pennsylvania. "The Harmonists," published two years after "The Wife's Story," extends Davis's attack on romanticism as solipsistic, individualistic, and hostile to women's real needs.[42] An early critique of utopianism, "The Harmonists" shows how Economy has perpetuated industrial alienation and, along the way, repressed female subjectivity through a sexual exchange that promises women economic security under the benevolent patronage of male authority.

Written during the time when the author was intensely involved in raising her active and winsome two-year-old son, Richard, "The Harmonists" focuses on parenting as the central metaphor for the debate over social organization. Anticipating Charlotte Perkins Gilman's *Herland* (1915) by fifty years, Davis draws on a materialist conception of family life to picture the home not only as the site of tiring and unpaid labor, but also as the site of patriarchal forms of child rearing. Davis shows how the male followers of George Rapp have sought purity by defining themselves as not just against industrial society but also against women and children, even their own. As Davis continues her lifelong exploration of the relationship between society and the female self, she satirizes a community that purports to idealize women while ignoring the realities of domestic labor, motherhood, and female passion. Utopia represents a sexual exchange in which women do not achieve political power and yet lose their traditional authority over domestic life. In this, the Rappites mirrored the American Owenite communities of the 1820s, where women were "wives of members" rather than members in their own right, where unmarried women simply were not "members" at all, where women could vote only on domestic matters or only in the "female department."[43] Davis marks the ways in which utopian fantasies in the nineteenth century legitimized separate spheres.

In "The Harmonists," Knowles (the namesake of the utopian socialist in *Margret Howth*) parodies the romantic man on the run from civilization, still marked as women's space.[44] A single father, Knowles travels with his four-year-old son from Pittsburgh to the Rappite community just west of the city. He says, "We will go there together, shut out the trade-world, and devote ourselves with these lofty enthusiasts to a life of purity, celibacy, meditation" (169). Knowles, in essence, seeks a sentimental utopia; his scheme "professed to go back to the old patriarchal form for its mode of government, establishing under that, however, a complete community of interest" (170). But Davis not only questions the option of shutting out the world of trade; she also questions the possibility of a community of interest for men and women in a society that is hierarchical, celibate, and hostile to children.

Unlike the traveler in utopian tales that would become popular later in the century, Davis pictures Knowles, the male initiate, in female terms. The story is narrated by Zachary Humphreys, his misfit companion from the world of trade. When Knowles declares his scorn for "family affection," Zachary reminds Knowles of his tenderness toward his little son: "One night you carried the little chap, as he was sound asleep. . . . I saw you sit by the pond yonder, thinking no one saw you, caressing him, kissing his face, his soiled little hands, his very feet, as fierce and tender as a woman" (169). And Knowles is "like a woman in other ways, nervous, given to sudden heats of passion,—was leaky with his own secrets" (169). But Davis is not simply suggesting that women are garrulous, hysterical, and overly devoted to their children. Like Hugh Wolfe in "Life in the Iron-Mills," Knowles is a feminized seeker whose "gross animal body had been tortured nigh to death" (170) when his wife left him. Now he pursues emotional disengagement in utopia, where he hopes to replace his intense love for his child with a diffused communitarian spirit: "Why should my son be more to me than any other man's son, but for extended selfishness?" (168–69). Vowing, "I know no child, no wife, nor any brother, except my brother-man" (169), he gives his cherished son to the community. Knowles is seeking the promised space of romanticism, "a sphere of infinite freedom" (171), "a home where a man can stand alone"(171–72). This is not a sphere, as Davis was well aware, that can include a young child. As her harried letters to Annie Fields reveal, Davis, like most women in the nineteenth century, did not conceive of the home, practically or ideologically, as a sphere of one's own.

Humphreys and Knowles soon discover that Economy has reproduced the mercantile consciousness, emotional repression, and female oppression of the "great market" society they have tried to leave behind. If Pittsburgh is merely "a great property-exchanging machine, where everything has its weight and value" (166), the same is true of Economy. According to its elders, "it is chiefly an association to make money: the amount contributed by each new-comer ought, in justice, to bear some proportion to the advantage he obtains" (177). Utopia offers a prosperous version of the commercial and competitive mentality of industrial capitalism.

In contrast to the fat and wealthy utopian burghers, the Harmonite women are old, "dried-up," and "withered" (174), and they mourn the lost children, husbands, and lovers they accompanied to utopia. To fulfill their repressed yearnings, they cook and eat five meals a day. The celibate Rappite women, with "shrivelled" (174) breasts, tell the travelers of the murder of lovers who refused to submit to the community's decrees and describe their longings for husbands assigned to live in impersonal "families" of seven. Mostly, they mourn the children they never bore. At the least, the story confirms Davis's pleasure in the postwar safety of her marriage, the birth of her son, as well as her abiding sympathy for the plight of unmarried and barren women.

Davis depicts the present perfect to challenge a patriarchal paradigm as an ideal social model. Elsewhere I have used the term *apologue* to describe utopian tales in which internal literary structures point to a normative statement about historical process and political prediction. Such tales evoke "estrangement" because they constantly ask the reader to reinterpret experiences outside the textual world.[45] Jane Tompkins uses the phrase *typological narrative* to describe sentimental plots that "do not unfold according to Aristotelian standards of probability, but in keeping with the logic of a preordained design . . . which every incident is intended, in one way or another, to enforce."[46] In "The Harmonists," the apologic or typological design embodied in the utopian critique of industrial consciousness engages the sentimental critique of individualism.

"The Harmonists" appears to attack the notion of utopianism itself. Rapp, the community's spiritual and temporal head, "not by election of the people, but [having] assumed it as by Divine commission, as Moses and Aaron held theirs" (170), has designed a peasant despotism. He presumes a utopian vision that collapses history in a seamless and timeless reproduction of hierarchical authority, ordained and hence natural—a discourse about political place contests a discourse about domestic space.

The travelers enter utopia accompanied by transporting images of repose and sleep, a traditional utopian convention suggesting surrender and dissociation. In "The Harmonists," however, Davis recasts this romantic trope as a metaphor for repression:

The quaint little hamlet literally slept on the river-bank; not a living creature was visible on the three grass-grown streets; many of the high-gabled brick houses . . . were closed and vacant, their inmates having dropped from the quiet of this life into an even deeper sleep. (172–73)

Utopia as a living cemetery ironically recalls the female communards' refrain for their children, "Dey is dead in Harmony" (175). Rather than serving as a route to a transcendent and imaginative unconscious, the image of sleep mirrors the numbing effect of life in the community.

The two controlling images in "The Harmonists" are the figure of the female breast and the figure of the child, both Knowles's child and the absent children of the celibate women. As the two travelers approach the village of Economy, the narrator looks forward to peaceful experience of renewal: "Nature was about to take me to her great mother's bosom" (172). But utopia is a sterile mother. And the breast, the visitor's projection of female desire as social teleology, is in fact empty. George Rapp had cast women in the role of temptresses and then rejected them. The Harmonite women join Davis's gallery of disfigured spinsters whose loneliness and hunger tacitly question the sentimental contract whereby women are granted protection in exchange for submission; their emptiness signifies partial revenge against the men whom they serve but will not please.

Even so, Davis was fascinated with the sexual arrangements in intentional communities. In "Paul Blecker," Paul suggests that if Grey will not divorce her absent husband, they might join a Fourierite phalanstery. In "Lois Platner" (1869), a misanthropic husband leads his desperate wife across the prairies because he is excited by the polygamous marriages in the Church of Latter-Day Saints.[47] In the nineteenth century, many intentional communities experimented with celibacy and other nontraditional sexual arrangements. The Rappites, the Shakers, the Oneida Perfectionists, and the Mormons rejected monogamy and affection as a way of defining social-sexual patterns and experimented with such alternate models as abstinence, group marriage, and polygamy. In some communities, celibacy, particularly when combined with communal child rearing for members who entered as families, contributed to female equality. Celibacy in Shaker communities no doubt stemmed from founder Ann Lee's tragic loss of her four children, her sexual traumas, and her eventual attack against men's carnal nature; yet celibacy also freed Shaker women's time, protected them from serious illness or death from childbirth, and allowed them to focus on their extended relationships within the community. In some utopian communities, celibacy allowed women to assume significant positions of leadership.[48] Hence, it deconstructed biology as a social determinant.

By contrast, celibacy in the Rappite communities stemmed from George Rapp's apocalyptic visions and represented the subjugation of personal desire in preparation for the return of Jesus Christ. Knowles, however, believes that sexual sublimation has fostered the Harmonists' obsessive work ethic. Rather than a testament to the egalitarian possibilities of celibacy, "The Harmonists" represents celibacy as women's loss of control over their reproductive capacity and social destiny. When Zachary, the narrator, asks a Harmonite woman if she prefers to "dwell in purer thoughts than early love," she responds that marriage "ist not gut, Father Rapp says. He knows" (176). She has exchanged desire for Rapp's social vision and has surrendered self-knowledge, the knowledge of her body—hence the power of the sexual and maternal female body—as she wistfully plays with Knowles's young son. Thus, while Economy protects its women from public and political decisions, it also deprives them of authority over the home, pictured as the loss of reproductive and sexual control of their bodies.

"The Harmonists," along with "The Yares of Black Mountain" (1875) is one of the few tales in which Davis focuses on motherhood. Like many female authors of her time, Davis tended to repress the figure of the mother, who in many of her stories is either absent, trivialized, ineffectual, devalued, silenced, or dead.[49] Critics have debated the fate of this powerful missing person in nineteenth-century women's fiction. Sandra Gilbert and Susan Gubar argue that motherlessness is a textual emblem for female disinheritance and powerlessness.[50] Maternal absence ignores the power of matriarchy for a daughter and denies her a role model that can facilitate her passage into womanhood. By contrast, Adrienne Rich argues that motherlessness frees the Victorian heroine from a model of female subservience; without her mother she can create and determine her own development.[51] The motherless women in "The Harmonists," however, expose the link between women's public oppression and sexual repression in male political fantasies.

Through the androgynous mother/father figure of Knowles, Davis rescripts the oedipal plot and explores the meaning of maternal identity, recovering both the unavailable industrial father and the self-divided ambivalent mother. Initially Knowles had refused to sleep with his child, announcing, "I have thrust away all arbitrary ties of family life" (169). But redeemed by "mother love," Knowles finally reclaims his son from the community, "growling caresses like a lioness who has recovered her whelp" (172). Maternal instinct takes precedence over political theory in defining social relationships. As the travelers decide to return to Pittsburgh, Knowles concludes, "'It is as well not to live altogether outside of the market; nor—to escape from this,' lifting Tony up on his knee" (179). Knowles not only rejects utopia because it has reified gender roles at the expense of his natural maternal self; he also rejects autonomy, the very telos of the patriarchal utopia, in favor of the community of family.

The concept of female dependency and sympathy that emerges in Davis's "Paul Blecker," "The Wife's Story," and "The Harmonists" originates in the ideology of gender spheres, a cultural fantasy that organizes social obligations along segregated and idealized gender lines. While politics, business, and labor belong in man's purview, domestic life, circumscribed but highly valued, is the woman's sphere. In the home femaleness, albeit delineated and contained, is a socializing moral force. The power of salvation through motherly love gives women a central position of authority. Contact with the mother, rather than repudiation of the mother, holds forth the promise that people can free themselves of the status distinctions and attitudes that have organized the old society. Thus, through sentiment, men realize a new social identity. But Davis is also suspicious of the notion that domestic culture can transcend or restrain political and economic hegemony. On the one hand, she finds that by intensifying gender distinctions, sentiment offers nothing new: it is an idealized order that still gives men authority over women, even in the domestic sphere. On the other hand, she uses images of the family and the utopian topos to expose the tensions of the larger culture in which men define the future.

In showing how a father and son have restored their intimacy through a visit to the sterile village of Economy, Davis calls into question the idea, linked to industrial culture, that male individuality emerges from a young boy's need to realize his sexual identity by repudiating his early identification with his mother—the powerful, primary love object of the other sex. But to whom can he turn? As work moved outside the home in industrial societies, fathers became increasingly unavailable. A son's double loss, of mother and father, Nancy Chodorow argues, leads to an idea of individuality and identity that is based on a denial of intimacy.[52] Rather than reflect a balance of separation and intimacy, independence seems to exclude connection. Jessica Benjamin notes that boys' denial of dependency often leads to domination:

> Since the child continues to need the mother, since man continues to need woman, the absolute assertion of independence requires possessing and controlling the needed object. The intention is not to do without her but to make sure that her alien otherness is either assimilated or controlled, that her own subjectivity nowhere asserts itself in a way that could make his dependency upon her a conscious insult to his sense of freedom.[53]

In "The Harmonists" Davis finds that when Rapp designed his utopia, he reproduced this masculine idealization of independence. In this she anticipates modern feminist psychoanalysts, such as Chodorow, Luce Irigary, and Marianne Hirsch, who observe that because girls do not have to relinquish maternal dependency they may presume that intimacy is healthy.[54]

In "The Harmonists," Davis also exposes the segregation of spheres as a paradigm of male dominance.[55] In contrast to the sentimental notion of a sympathetic community, Economy has reified the view that genuine difference is inseparable from autonomy and control. Feminist psychoanalysts suggest that the situation of separate-but-unequal arises as the son resolves the conflict with his mother by turning to his father, who appears to be the agent, the subject of his own will and desire. Seemingly independent, the father represents the world. In their identification with this rigid father figure, the followers of George Rapp repudiate women as reproductive and sexual beings. Davis challenges the tendency of the community—a paradoxical tendency, to be sure—to make dominance and separateness the route, the goal, and the structure of utopia. Thus "The Harmonists" extends her attack on romanticism as individualistic and hostile to women's real needs.

Unlike most Victorian novelists, Davis bestows on mothers subjectivity, agency, and initiative. In this she joins Louisa May Alcott, whose "Transcendental Wild Oats" (1876) parodies her father's transcendental utopia, "Fruitlands"), and Mary E. Bradley Lane, whose *Mizora* (1889) appears to be the first matriarchal utopian novel written in the United States. What Davis and Alcott saw as they surveyed the communities of George Rapp or Bronson Alcott is that when men construct utopian spaces, they monopolize the authority of the father to represent or to define power and desire. Because Davis and Alcott refused to portray woman's social desire through her status as an object—her ability to attract or repel—they reject the dualism of subject versus object that hinges on repudiating the mother as the road to identity and power. Davis and Alcott both assert that unless the utopian woman is a political, maternal, and sexual *subject* rather than a political, maternal and sexual *object*, we have dystopia.

In Davis's view, Economy fails because it has reified gender roles at the expense of the natural self. A healthy society (although not necessarily a utopian society) must acknowledge and reflect the role of subjectivity and sexuality. The story ends not with a marriage but with an androgynous mother-man crooning old nursery songs to lull his child to sleep. Like Hester Manning in "The Wife's Story," Knowles ultimately rejects autonomy, the telos of the patriarchal utopia. In "The Harmonists" Davis again transforms a political debate into a psychological condition and recasts political distinctions as gender differences. Anticipating such twentieth-century critiques of utopia as Ursula LeGuin's *The Dispossessed* (1974) and Marge Piercy's *Woman on the Edge of Time* (1976), Davis suggests that economic rearrangements alone cannot free women from the distinctions of gender. In contrast to the fears of the Rappite utopians, Davis shows the mother figure to be neither menacing or engulfing. Utopian space need not involve her repudiation. As in *Margret Howth*, Davis is suspicious of social formulas in which the dreams of one man shape the community as a whole. Instead, Davis would seek philosophies forged through dependence, conflicted though it may be.

Davis's depiction of misogyny is probably at its most bitter in "The Story of Christine" (1866).[56] As a young and ingenuous girl in Amsterdam, Christine is kidnapped by a frustrated suitor, a wealthy ship's captain who tempts her aboard his vessel and sails with her to America. Finally reaching Philadelphia, filthy, terrified, and abused, he sells Christine as a redemptioner, or indentured servant, to a farmer with whom she must remain until she works off the cost of her passage. Although her employer learns that

Christine had been taken into servitude involuntarily, he purchases her bonds anyway and takes her to his remote farm. There she is put to work in a hot dirty kitchen, along with ex-slaves who (ironically) cannot find work except as indentured servants.[57] Desperate for her freedom, Christine runs away with a ship's surgeon who sails with her around the world and then abandons her in New Orleans. Desperate and alone, she makes her way back to the farm, where the farmer's wife, profoundly guilty for the abusive actions of her husband, sets Christine up in a tiny cottage where she lives as an outcast and survives by sewing carpets, dyeing old dresses, and selling herbs. Quarantined with a misdiagnosed case of leprosy and cared for only by the farmer's granddaughter, who had always been intrigued by this mysterious and lonely woman, Christine eventually dies. Again the diseased female body suggests her stigmatized social condition.

With the announcement that this is a true story, Davis makes "The Story of Christine" one of her most explicit studies of sexual and economic jeopardy. Written in 1866, a year after the passage of the Thirteenth Amendment, rhetorics of slavery signify a white woman's contingent status. As an example, the story opens with the narrator's comment: "'Dutch Christine' . . . is one of the properties of my childhood" (181); "Christine belonged to us" (183), she explains; Christine's return to the farm "smacked of the blind submission of a slave to his master" (183). Always a precise historian, Davis places the story in a time "nearly a century ago" when the system of indentured servitude enjoyed a brief rebirth in Pennsylvania. Large landholders who owned slaves become desperate for cheap labor when they were forced to comply with Pennsylvania's Gradual Abolition Act of 1780, the first anti-slavery statute in the United States. The story explains the situation of redemptioners in considerable detail. For example, the farmer explains to the sea captain why he is purchasing Christine:

> Our law forbids our holding such negroes as are yet slaves in Pennsylvania, after the age of twenty-eight; and by this law I lose, next year, both house and field hands, and, of course, must supply their place. That of redemptioners are the next most available service I could command. (189–90)

The narrator observes that such transactions, which usually involved bonds of four to seven years, seemed to be fair and just until people considered that the unfortunate wretches were publicly sold to the highest bidder, with no choice of their own as to the purchaser; that being sold, it was permissible for their owner to transfer them, at his own option, to whomsoever he pleased; that the ignorance even of the language of his new country, placed the serf entirely in the power of the master in the condition of absolute slavery. (190)

The situation was worse for female redemptioners because their terms were extended for several years if any "bound" time were lost to pregnancy and childbirth.[58]

Davis apparently wrote "The Story of Christine" while composing the first draft of *Waiting for the Verdict*, her powerful attack on slavery, the failures of Reconstruction, and the hypocrisies of northern racism. Though written decades after the demise of the system of indentured servitude, the story recalls the history of slavery in the North while it invokes the voice of a female victim to indict the bogus morality of an era that purported to protect women. To Davis, the abduction, rape, and sale of Christine signifies the coercive nature of male-female relationships; the false diagnosis of leprosy is a punitive mark of Christine's unmarried worldliness that calls into question the line delineating pure from impure women.

By the time of "The Story of Christine," Davis's relationship with the *Atlantic Monthly* was drawing to a close as a result of James Fields's reaction to Davis's decision to publish *Waiting for the Verdict* in *Galaxy*. Henceforth, Davis worked to free her prose from the domestic ideology of sentimentalism and to experiment with literary forms—characters, plots, and figurative language—that more directly refracted the historical tensions she wanted to portray. By the end of this productive decade, it is the radical and subversive elements within sentimentalism that endure in Davis's writing and shape a realistic discourse that resolves the dissonance between graphic exhibitions of women's repression and sentimental justifications for female subservience.

Davis's anger over the commodification of women is most explicit in a story published in 1868 for *Peterson's Magazine*.[59] "In the Market" is a study of the limited options open to four sisters of a poor but genteel family. As the story opens, Clara is playing a game of chess with her suitor, John Bohme. But he suddenly announces that he is leaving, not to return: "Check, and—mate! You will have no chance for revenge, either, Miss Porter, I am going west to-morrow" (198). Clara believes that he has authority, power, and autonomy on his side, while she has no route to adulthood but marriage. But with Bohme's departure, she had "missed her chance" (201). Despite their poverty, the mother, trapped by class pretensions, scorns her daughters' working for a living: "Surely a daughter of mine is not driven to manual labor—that is, outside of her father's roof" (203). Observing that because the West has "drained the eastern States of young men," her girls have little choice. "They must marry as they can" (203).

But while their brother is angry at being forced to work in his father's shop to keep his sisters in "idleness and plenty" (202), the sisters bemoan their object status. Dressed in tawdry finery for a dance, Clara declares, "I am on exhibition—in the market!" (203). Meanwhile, the sisters suffer from "unused brain or nerve-power . . . [that often] escaped (for it will escape) in perpetual headaches and hysterics" (204). Returning to the industrial metaphor, the narrator observes, "Had they been machines, some expert would have pronounced that the rust and decay came from want of use" (203–04). Panicked at a proposal of marriage from a mill owner who had bestowed unwanted "petting" on her since her childhood, Clara tells her mother that she thinks she is going mad and pleads to become a teacher or a seamstress. Her mother responds, "The country is overrun with female teachers," and, as for the needle trade, "You've no right to lower the position of your sisters. No one of our class would marry a sempstress." Although Clara sees that her friends have entered loveless marriages and "endure in legal prostitution" (207), she submits to unhappy wedlock with "a short, obese man of about fifty" (206).

By contrast, Clara's sister Margaret is prepared to defy her family by earning her own living. She is convinced that "the world is full of pleasure and comfort to be had for money; and God did not put the power into woman's head to make the money for no use" (208–09). Enduring her family's anger, shame, and embarrassment, as well as insinuations from the townspeople that she is a witch—"if she'd put in a broomstick it'd grow" (212), Margaret delays marriage in order to launch a successful business raising and selling medicinal herbs to doctors and pharmaceutical companies. Once married and mother of a family, she makes sure that each of her daughters learns a trade or a profession, concluding that there are "worse ways of unsexing a woman" (214) than by making her self-sufficient and prosperous.

Lydia Maria Child observed that all women come "within a hair's breadth of being the other."[60] Davis's stories speak to this unsteady perch. Written in the era of Civil War and postbellum economic expansion, geographical restlessness, demands for racial equality, and a new wave of women's activism, Davis extended her image of the "soul starvation" of the korl woman and Margret Howth and told of the various shapes of women's feelings of intense loss, intellectual longing, painful silences, and domestic confinement. In the decade during which Davis married and had two children, her stories describe how women's economic, aesthetic, and emotional hunger are not to be satisfied by marriage.

For Davis, women's inner life is always shaped by economic, ethnic, and political history. Although domesticity offers an image of fulfilled desire, it is still the locus of male authority and of female anxiety. Because the home reflects rather than resolves economic loss and sexual inequality, the patriarchal family is frequently lonely, repressive, and abusive for women. At best, the matriarchal family offers limited female authority, a modicum of affectionate responsibility, and romantic love. Davis's stories from the sixties reveal her concern that even with the end of the Civil War and the new opportunities that came with industrialization, women were still illiterate, uneducated, unemployed, lonely, impoverished, and dependent on frequently ineffectual men. Working through the seditious currents in sentimentalism, in this decade Davis comes to question the ideology that perpetuates women's powerlessness and ignorance. She experiments with literary topics and tropes that free her discourse of the commonplace from sentiment, a convention of accommodation, as she explores narrative forms that express rather than undermine the complex relationship she sees between the female self, industrial society, and literary tradition.

6 ❦ Race, Reconstruction, and
the Discourse of Sentiment

Waiting for the Verdict

In 1867 REBECCA HARDING DAVIS wrote and quickly serialized *Waiting for the Verdict* in *Galaxy Magazine*.[1] A fictional study of prejudice set for the most part during the Civil War, *Waiting for the Verdict* is an epic narrative of three families, white and black, whose lives mirror each other's in terms of poverty, illegitimacy, prejudice, and social exclusion. *Waiting for the Verdict* goes beyond freedom—the ending of most slave narratives—and considers the meaning of the freedom that has already been gained, using the novel's conventions empirically to explore the difficult future of race relations in the North. During 1867, as Davis wrote the novel for serial publication, the many implications of the North's victory and the shape of reunification were still in doubt. Within days of Lee's surrender in 1865, Abraham Lincoln was assassinated. His successor, Andrew Johnson, a southerner and former slaveholder, had tried to return the southern states to the Union with congressional representation based on the white electorate of 1860. However, because the states of the former Confederacy refused to give freedmen the vote, in December 1865 Congress refused to seat the new southern members.

After the Thirteenth Amendment abolishing slavery was ratified in 1865 (without the blessing of Mississippi), antislavery activists proceeded to seek the vote for newly liberated slaves. However, between 1865 and 1868, Wisconsin, Minnesota, Connecticut, Nebraska, New Jersey, Ohio, Michigan, and Pennsylvania all rejected bills granting suffrage to freed black males, and New Yorkers twice rejected propositions to remove a $250 property qualification for African Americans who wanted to vote.[2] In April 1866, convinced that reform needed to be initiated at the federal level, both Houses of Congress overrode Johnson's veto and passed the first Civil Rights Act, which conferred citizenship and civil rights, though not specifically suffrage, on African Americans.

During 1867, Reconstruction shaped the electoral debate, redefined the powers of the presidency, and prompted three Reconstruction Acts that in law, if not in practice, gave black men the vote. (Black and white women would wait another fifty-three years for suffrage.) By the end of 1867, local southern governments, biracial but primarily white, attempted to establish democracy in the South by launching plans for public education and lasting constitutions. But implementation was tenuous; grandfather clauses, literacy requirements, and poll taxes soon undermined the Fourteenth Amendment and then the Fifteenth (ratified in 1870), which guaranteed black males the right to vote. In less than a decade, with the retirement of Radical Republicans from Congress, granting of amnesty to former Confederate soldiers, the desire on the part of northern businesses to recapitalize the South, the return of plantations occupied by freedmen to their former owners, the rise of terrorism in the shape of organizations like the Ku Klux Klan, and, finally, President Hayes's withdrawal of federal troops from the South in 1877, Reconstruction was over.

Waiting for the Verdict depicts the national vacillation about the freedom of African Americans, while it exposes Davis's own lifelong ambivalence over race. Two main figures, Garrick Randolph, a plantation owner, and Dr. John Broderip, a prominent Philadelphia surgeon who is a mulatto passing as white, link the black and white families in the novel. Garrick, obsessed with blood lines and racial purity, has fallen in love with Rosslyn Burley, the illegitimate daughter of a slaveowner. Broderip, who had been raised by a Quaker woman who bought him out of slavery as a child and had him educated in Europe, falls in love with Margaret Conrad, the daughter of a Methodist preacher.

The lives of the white and black families are braided together with the appearance of Broderip's brother Nathan, a fugitive slave, and their father, Hugh, a slave still owned by Randolph. Nathan and his wife Anny have spent the war years searching for each other—they were separated in a sale—and for Hugh. Instead of freeing Hugh, as his father had wished, Randolph sells him to the Confederate Army to protect his illegitimate claim to the plantation. The covert manner whereby Randolph seeks to inherit the plantation is meant to parody the image of Dr. Broderip's "inheritance" of a few drops of "black blood."

In the romance between John Broderip and Margaret Conrad, Davis squarely addresses white anxiety over liaisons between black men and white women. In *Waiting for the Verdict*, sentimental trappings of lost children, lost inheritance, errant men, and frustrated love are all shaped by racial prejudice. By merging the fates of these families, Davis again calls into question the sentimental formula that makes the family the ultimate source of protection and identity; race rather than family establishes one's status and one's selfhood—an intimation of the "verdict": the failure of Reconstruction. Initially the narrative poses a parallel between Rosslyn, a white girl of illegitimate birth who sells herbs in the marketplace, and Broderip, a former slave—both of whom, in the course of the novel, rise through their own determination, moral scruples, wit, and the help of loving adults. The imperatives of race, however, pictured through the vocabulary of inheritance, property, and family, repeatedly dismantle the analogy between white and black alienation.[3] Instead, commonality between blacks and whites resides in their shared rights and responsibilities as citizens and family members. *Waiting for the Verdict* quells the alarm in postwar discourse about the erotic equation between political equality and black manhood—revealed, for example, in discussions by and about the Ku Klux Klan's obsession with black men's purported sexual violation of white women.[4]

The story opens on a Pennsylvania ferry where young Rosslyn first meets Broderip, a slave child known only as Sap, traveling with his master, Strebling, a member of Congress from Alabama. As Rosslyn watches Sap play with his dog, Davis indicates the shape that bigotry will take in the novel:

> The dirty yellow skin of the mulatto made her sick, she was sure; it was the
> same as if a toad or snake had stood upright, to see his grimaces and mon-

key tricks of delight at being kindly spoken to. She wished he was dead . . . was sure that, if she had been a boy, she would have thrown the yellow grinning thing into the water. (10)

Sap's unscrupulous master recognizes Rosslyn as his lost illegitimate daughter, but mistakes her poverty as a condition similar to slavery: "And you sit in the market? Selling herbs, and radishes—yes? My black people sit in the market" (11). To make up for his guilt, Strebling gives Rosslyn Sap's dog. At first Rosslyn was "glad that she was white, and stronger than this yellow monster of a boy; except a pet fox of her grandfather's . . . she never had hated anything so much before" (11–12). To taunt Sap, she puts her foot on the dog's neck, "determined that the beast should know that she was stronger than he. When she thought that he knew it, and lay with his jaws between his fore paws on her knees, she patted his neck and put her arms about it" (10). As she realizes that she is starting to love the dog because she can dominate him, Rosslyn discovers the meaning of ownership. Explaining to Strebling that the dog was not his to bestow, she returns it to Sap. The boy immediately kills the dog, observing, "He wur all I had" (13). This act recalls the murder in *Uncle Tom's Cabin* (1852) by Cassy, who kills her only remaining son rather than allow him to grow up in slavery. This opening scene prefigures both the articulated themes and the unwitting tropes of Davis's most extensive exploration of race—deprivation, domination, restitution, projection, and profound ambivalence.

With the brutality of the dog's murder, the analogy between the white working-class girl and the slave boy falls apart. That night Rosslyn discovers her own illegitimacy and decides to take her dead mother's name as her own, proclaiming proudly: "My mother's name's good enough for me. . . . I'll just go as I am, shame and all" (28). By contrast, there seems to be no mother (or surname) in the family tree of Nathan, Sap, or Hugh. Although *Waiting for the Verdict* suggests that women and slaves suffer a mutual status as human capital, the novel's detailed images of human bondage disrupt the sentimental analogy that rests on the shared powerlessness of women, children, animals, and slaves. The novel pictures a mulatto man's painful struggle to acknowledge his heritage with the same steadfast courage as a white girl, then exposes the rejection that he alone suffers when he tells the truth about his identity.

Waiting for the Verdict complicates the humanistic ideology of domestic fiction.[5] Davis, like many southerners, attacks the hypocrisy of antislavery Federalists who still nurture a deep contempt for black people.[6] Thereby she becomes ensnared both in the liberal argument that emphasizes the importance of environment in shaping individual capacity and in the contemporary racialized views of "instinct" and "blood." In each narrative episode, Davis insists that most whites misunderstand the dire implications of slavery. For instance, when Garrick Randolph, a southern pro-Unionist, secretly leaves his plantation to deliver a coded message to the Federal troops, one of his slaves observes to Margaret, a northern visitor, that in his excitement for adventure his master has forgotten the Union "cause": "*I* am de cause, an my wife—not Viney, but de one I lef on a Georgy rice-field—she am de cause, an my boy, Pont, who was hunted wid dogs in de swamp down dar, he am de cause." Margaret's reaction is "keen physical disgust in her blood to the black skin," a revulsion that is "as plain to his [the slave's] instinct, as if it had showed (which it did not) on her face" (43). The facts of northern bigotry, embedded in heroic adventure, insist on the pervasive power of prejudice.

In *Waiting for the Verdict*, Davis's portrait of the slaveowner Randolph serves as an allusion to the northern reader, well-intended but ambivalent and uninformed. Randolph's progress toward understanding slavery depends on Rosslyn, who helps him deliver his secret missive behind Federal lines and then arranges for his escape on a boat heading up the Ohio River—an image familiar at the time as a voyage toward freedom for African Americans. Randolph's change of views come from his sentimental encounter with a female artist and her Quaker chaperon who are active in the underground railroad. On the boat, a politically liminal space, Randolph finds himself separated from his designated identity. As it slowly and symbolically travels from south to north, under Rosslyn's tutelage he begins to sever his imagined connection with southern honor and masculinity—the culture of slavery. Responding one afternoon to his comment that she has only a northerner's knowledge of slavery, Rosslyn shows Randolph an engraving she has made in which two men stand by a packing box in an office. Half the box lid is off: "Within lay, bent double, the figure of a negro; an old and white-haired man; dead. There were the marks of the branding-iron on his forehead and back of his neck. The face was sketched with wonderful power; it told the whole history of a man who had starved and toiled to the end of the long voyage, and died in sight of land" (56). When Randolph calls the picture of the runaway slave a "fiction," Rosslyn replies, "There is room there, you see, for another figure. That was I" (57).

This abolitionist and self-referential image reconfigures Davis's representations of confinement—from the factory and prison in "Life in the Iron-Mills," to the mill in *Margret Howth*, to the guardhouse in "John Lamar." The author has both inscribed and erased a female artist, a witness who positions herself in and out of the frame. As Karen Sanchez-Eppler observes, in the intersecting discourses of feminism and abolition, the body "attains the status of a text." Abolitionists, she notes, transformed the body from early feminists' silent "site" of oppression into a "symbol of that oppression," and hence the body of the slave becomes a means of gaining rhetorical force.[7] Like the statue of the korl woman in "Life in the Iron-Mills," Davis uses an artist's rendering of a suffering body to make a political statement. However, by writing Rosslyn in and out of the engraving, Davis may be revealing her uncertainty about the relationship between politics and representation. The aesthetic objectification of pain in the image of a dead slave, suffocated in a packing crate, astonishes the slaveholder (and indirectly, the reader) who realizes that he is implicated in this oppression by his silence. The engraving that accompanied this passage in *Galaxy Magazine* was the only one that pictures an African-American character, and that from the back.

The urgency of prejudice in *Waiting for the Verdict* lies most compellingly in the tale of the African-American family. The romance between Broderip and Margaret Conrad, a white woman who does not know that he is passing for white, is set against Broderip's family's painful journeys toward freedom in the North—framed, in part, as a sentimental quest for reunion by Hugh, Nathan, and Annie. At the cost of denying his family and repressing his slave past, Broderip has become a wealthy surgeon, deflecting his needs for personal commitment by indulging himself in gambling, fanciful tastes in clothes, an exotic garden, and a fascination with purebred horses—a counterpart to Randolph's obsession with "unstained blood"—and by suffering bouts of depression. Although Davis represses links between race and sexuality, she suggests links between race and gender. Broderip, like Hugh Wolfe in "Life in the Iron-Mills," is another of Davis's feminized male heroes, a "womanly" man with a high voice and erratic moods. Broderip is stereotypically libidinous, irrational, untamed, just as both female and black characters were often presented; and as the author suggests in the eroticized scenes of his surgical operations, he is incipiently dangerous.

In the figure of this brilliant surgeon, Davis severs the conventional equations made between race and ability. By presenting the tragic octoroon, traditionally a female character, as a male (albeit a feminized one), Davis also represses the sexual vulnerability of the mulatta.[8] Through Broderip, Davis goes beyond the common theme in abolitionist fiction that attacks slavery as a form of sexual abuse and thus leads abolitionist narratives toward escape, suicide, or militant resistance. The fact that Hugh, a black slave, is Broderip's father means that the surgeon can accept his mixed heritage without identifying with a personal history of sexual violation. His story does not include the rape of a slave mother, the origin of most racially mixed slaves; both his parents were African-American. In fact, the source of Broderip's Caucasian ancestry remains obscure—Broderip insists that he is "pure." Thus racial mixing seems to have happened before the generations presented in the book; that is to say, it has happened offstage. Unlike George Harris in Stowe's *Uncle Tom's Cabin* or Archie Moore in Richard Hildreth's *The White Slave* (1836), both of whom are figured as autonomous and rebellious males in part because of their whiteness, Broderip achieves selfhood in female terms until Nathan insists that he must acknowledge him as his brother. At this point, Broderip also acknowledges his own black heritage, joins the Union Army, and (in Davis's view) acts like a man.

Davis's insistence in *Waiting for the Verdict* on the sexual purity of black women (as compared to Rosslyn's licentious white mother) also allows her to avoid depicting interracial romance or sexuality—erotic and racial taboos. Because of popular anxiety over race mixing, abolitionists were frequently attacked as hypersexual, sexless, and perverse.[9] It also allows her to suggest sentimental sisterly links between Anny and Rosslyn. The cultural proscription against miscegenation was more courageously handled by Lydia Maria Child in *A Romance of the Republic* (published in 1867, like *Waiting for the Verdict*) in which interracial marriages represent a route to racial integration.[10] In *Waiting for the Verdict*, by contrast, identity is grounded not in the figure of the sentimentalized mother but in the figure of the father—whether it is Rosslyn's loving grandfather, Burley, who raises her; her father, Strebling, who rejects her; or Nathan and Broderip's father, Hugh (the only father in the book who does not betray his children), who is lost to his sons through slave sales. Thus, the narrative puts forth a series of analogies between blacks and whites that it then bursts open. In a drama about fathers and their children, the sentimental identification with the mother breaks down.

Through his successful (if transient) embodiment of northern professionalism and racial denial, John Broderip, as a mulatto, disrupts the assumptions of black inferiority that countenance slavery. At the same time, his own ambivalence about his "drop" of African-American blood both insists on the common humanity of blacks and whites and mirrors the national confusion about the moral purpose of the Civil War. For Mary Dearborn, the figure of the mulatto resides in what Tvestan Todorov terms the "uncanny"—the boundaries between the conscious and unconscious mind where the lines dividing self and other waver, allowing repressed anxieties to surface. The mulatto, Dearborn observes, is "a kind of uncanny text about the coherence and limits of the self."[11] But Davis saw that these limits derived from cultural stereotypes. In *Waiting for the Verdict* graphic and accurate details of slavery and northern racism shape the mulatto's consciousness; throughout the novel she reiterates the fact that mulattoes are defined as blacks in all legal arenas.[12] Thus, Davis's references to the history of miscegenation undermines Broderip's status as a literary homology in which the sexual and the racial displace one another.[13]

Only a small handful of novels addressed the issue of miscegenation in postbellum America.[14] Indeed, the very depiction of a mulatto character challenged the view typified by a white supremacist, Henry Hughes, who insisted in 1860 that "impurity of races is against the law of nature. Mulattoes are monsters. . . . The same law that forbid consanguinous amalgamation forbids ethnical amalgamation. Both are incestuous. Amalgamation is incest." Thus, says Dearborn, the literary representation of a mulatto involved "naming of the taboo" and as such constituted a threat to cultural equilibrium.[15]

By severing Broderip from his white ancestry, Davis also severs him from the mulatto's conventional claim to patrician origin, the plantation owner as father. Blyden Jackson observes that mulattoes in fiction generally move from the top down, enacting the pretense that "Negroes are actually upper-class people who do the middle class a favor by identifying with it."[16] Broderip, by contrast, anticipates the mulatto character as depicted by such twentieth-century authors as Langston Hughes, Ann Petry, and Ralph Ellison, who rises into the stable middle class from the black masses. In depicting an ex-slave, Davis finds a way to talk about the possibilities and limits of freedom in America. Werner Sollars terms this racialized convention the conflict of consent and descent—a conflict Davis also depicts in her studies of women as divided selves.

Broderip thus undermines the contemporary assumption that the white man is the norm, while the black is other and subordinate. By making him a brilliant surgeon with a national reputation, Davis comes down on the side of environment rather than heredity in determining ability, undermining the popular theory, first put forward by Samuel Morton in 1839, of a multiple origin of the human species. Morton argued that blacks and whites evolved from different origins and hence, possessed innate differences—a theory that intensified the view that the "mixing" of races was "disharmonious." Broderip's medical achievement also counters the views of such theorists as John Buchanan, who argued for the existence of "hybrid degeneration"—the idea that mulattoes inherit the worst traits of both parents and pass on their inferior genetic makeup to future generations. During the Civil War, Louis Agassiz warned Lincoln that through a process of racial degeneration mulattoes would contaminate the "national blood," but he assured the president that lighter-skinned African Americans would die out and only a pure dark cluster would remain—in the southern states. Charles Darwin responded to such views with his monogenic theory of the origin of species, which ruled out the obvious falsehood that mulattoes are sterile and that blacks have diminished chances of survival. Darwin's theory, however, paradoxically encouraged the dangerous concept of "atavism," in which African Americans were thought to reverse the process of the "ascent of man."

In challenging these sham scientific positions that, taken as a whole, were invoked to justify the demise of Reconstruction (and later to defend manifest destiny), and in asserting the impact of society and education on a slave, Davis was an unusual white voice. John Broderip thus is a composite figure who offers a link between the world of slavery and white prejudice.[17] He speaks to the anxiety of alienation in a way that could touch Davis's mobile and fluid audience of *Galaxy* readers. Further, as a compassionate man who donates his wealth and services to many hospitals, he does not exist in and for himself—just like the best-behaved female character.

Broderip represents Davis's own grappling with the "verdict" of the war by pointing to the uncertain shape of personal relationships between blacks and northern whites and to the uncertain public future of African Americans in the North. When he visits the new black slums of Philadelphia, for example, Broderip sees unemployed freedmen and starving black veterans sleeping in gutters and discovers the terrible medical care provided to emancipated slaves who fought in the Union Army:

> He drew up his horse at the corner of Ninth and Mary's streets, and deliberately rode from one end to the other. . . . He missed nothing; the stench, the rancid, broken victuals exposed for sale, the swarms of drunken blacks lying on the pavements and gutters like flies in the sun. . . . He stopped again, looking back at these negroes as they had come out of the slave pens of the South, only to find in freedom a wider path to hell. (294–95)

The equation of slavery and northern poverty—the "wider path to hell" was a common southern equivocation. Davis continues,

> At any other time his fastidious white blood (and there were but few drops of any other in Broderip's veins) would have sickened here through every sense; but today a stronger emotion than disgust sharpened his face as he looked at the negroes, a sense of kinship and brotherhood, a fierce denial that his race must necessarily come to this. (295)

Thus, despite the pull of commonality, Broderip views his people through "bestial" stereotypes and still sees marriage to a white woman, the golden-haired Margaret Conrad, as his ultimate prize. Margaret Conrad, who recalls other women in Davis's work—stolid, inarticulate, and loyal to her blind father—is both intrigued by the inexplicable world of otherness that Broderip offers her and repelled by the temptations of romantic love, which Davis pictures as surrender and rape. Despite the respectful and playful friendship Davis depicts between Margaret and Broderip, she also pictures the possibility of interracial sex as violation of a white woman by a black man.

> She had felt day by day the magnetic, massive force of a stronger nature than her own pressing closer and closer to her. Her will, her opinions, her judgment,

gave way, she shrank back, step by step, paler and weaker daily, her secret hid in her breast, before the steady, entering hand that would have dragged it from her. (290)

The fact of Broderip's African-American heritage becomes unavoidable with the appearance of his brother Nathan, a fugitive slave. Nathan's arrival underscores the theme of the impending national "verdict." Wounded in the war, Nathan shows up at Broderip's hospital in Philadelphia and insists on their shared racial and family identity. Images of wounds and disease as victimizing symbols of national decay recall Deborah Wolfe's spinal deformity in "Life in the Iron-Mills" and Lois Yare's twisted legs and burn scars from the industrial fire in *Margret Howth*.

The repressed won't stay repressed. As Broderip operates on his wounded brother, he looks through a window of his surgical office and sees Margaret; on the one side is his injured family—metonymically, his injured race, and on the other the fulfillment of his dreams for status and security—pictured as a white woman. "All his recompense waiting with her; all the world of goodness, and culture, and beauty into which he had fought his way during these years, waited, it seemed to him, with her on that side of the thin glass barrier." However, concludes Broderip, "Let him acknowledge the mulatto as his brother, and he stood alone, shut out from every human relation with the world to which he belonged" (300). But this affiliation is a delusion. Although he is tempted to deceive Margaret and to murder Nathan on the operating table, Broderip decides to reveal his racial heritage. Margaret immediately confesses her "abhorrence to Negro blood" (313) and coolly rejects him, saying, "'I pray you to accept this disappointment with composure. We all have some cross of circumstance to bear. I would not whimper under mine,' with her old motion of putting her fingers on her blue, cold lips." Broderip proudly responds, "I have my brother, I have my own people!" Pushing her pitying hand away, he adds, "I would have married you if you had been a fiend from hell" (310)—a further suggestion of the phobia of miscegenation.

In 1867 Davis believed that miscegenation was not an inevitable consequence of freedom; all of the characters in *Waiting for the Verdict* who are close to Davis's voice repudiate it. For example, Rosslyn's grandfather—an elderly Union private and a loyal yeoman—observes, "The trouble is in reasonin' about niggers that the races is got so mixed down ther with you that you can't draw the line exact between nigger instinct and white feelin's. Now there's no danger of amalgamation with us. The antipathy's too strong between the colors" (346).[18] Anny, speaking from the perspective of a fugitive slave woman, sees "amalgamation" as a matter of rape and sexual oppression: "Dar's no danger of many marriages . . . an' as for mixin' de blood, it's been the fault ob de whites when dat eber was done. Dar'll be less of it when cullored women is larned to respect themselves. O, Missus! dat talk of marryin' is sech a fur-off shadder!" (355). By 1897, however, intermarriage was less of a "shadder," and Davis could describe with equanimity the public's reaction to an announcement of a racially mixed marriage:

> Last July, an educated mulatto in Philadelphia married a white woman, the daughter of a prominent journalist. The marriage was described in the morning papers as that of "two Philadelphians of high social position." I saw not a word of offensive comment. Thirty years ago they would have been in danger of a mob.[19]

Broderip's racial revelation allows him to separate his own self-concept from the image of himself that others, such as Margaret, have devised for him. As Judith Berzon observes, the moment when mulattoes reveal their whiteness transforms the mulatto character from a "thing in itself" to a "thing for itself."[20] Once Broderip establishes his identity as a subject, his actions rather than his body define his being. Rejected by Margaret and by most of his Philadelphia acquaintances, Broderip abandons his hospital. Determined to acknowledge his race, he volunteers and becomes a colonel in the first African-American regiment in the Union Army. Unlike such mulatto characters as William Wells Brown's heroine Clotel, Broderip does not return to the black world as an embittered exile from a higher station.[21] As he chooses to abandon his marginal position, he also abandons the self-hatred implied in his longing for a white identity.

In claiming his race, Broderip rejects the romanticization of the lone individual and emerges as a man who is "ancestrally" defined. His commitment to his true community undercuts his commitment to self—eroticized, powerful, and isolated. With references to Moses and Christ, Davis transforms Broderip into a black martyr and thereby contests atavism, the postbellum idea that the freed black will revert to a animalistic type. Urging his brother John to enlist, Nathan observes that although the slaves call Lincoln Moses, "Moses warn't a white man, an' a stranger. . . . He wur a chile ob de slave woman, an' he went an' stole all de learnin' ob his masters, an den come back an' took his people cross de riber inter freedom. *His own people*, suh" (314–15). As Broderip prepares to leave for war, he vacates his home and garden and gives away his expensive possessions, keeping only a painting of Christ, who is pictured as a "childless, wifeless, homeless man, of birth as poor, and skin as dark as his own, who had gone down into the dregs of the people, giving up a man's whole birthright to lead a great reform, to cleanse the souls of imbruted men and women" (325). Broderip's figurative association with Moses and Davis's description of a black Christ link the doctor to black pride—typical of Davis's view of the active Christ, the theology of the Social Gospel. Finally, in giving up his neo-African garden, Broderip abandons his attachment to the atavistic jungle in favor of political commitment to the "imbruted" man and the antislavery cause, shaped in *Waiting for the Verdict* as the nineteenth-century tradition of "racial uplift."

Thus Davis invoked what Werner Sollars terms the "typology of ethnicity," the assumption of reciprocal events that transform and elevate history into a biblical drama.[22] In the end, Broderip is shot on the march into Richmond and dies in the "rathole" of Andersonville Prison, rejoining the community of slaves through communal suffering. Yet unlike Stowe's Uncle Tom, Broderip's martyrdom has political rather than religious connotations. Broderip's death, a result of his courageous leadership of a black military regiment, transcends Uncle Tom's Christian martyrdom. Like sentimentalism's female orphan who is freed of a past that nonetheless returns to shape her future, Broderip has recovered his own people. In *Waiting for the Verdict* blackness also gives white men and women their identity: a white Union lieutenant reenlists to serve under Broderip, and Margaret becomes a teacher for children of former slaves who have migrated to Philadelphia.

Yet even within the sentimental paradigm, in which romantic love weakens patriarchal values as women become agents of active spirituality, the most unlikely aspect of *Waiting for the Verdict* is the romance between the abolitionist woman, Rosslyn, and the slaveholder, Randolph. Initially Randolph believes that as a member of the southern aristocracy he should serve as a model to the slave, whose "defects are inherent in his blood. . . . He is indolent, treacherous and sensual" (113). To save his patrimony for Rosslyn, Garrick Randolph has reneged on his father's promise to free his slave Hugh, because Hugh knows that his owner has usurped a cousin's rightful claim to the plantation. Unwilling to chance Kentucky law (which at the time did not accept Negro testimony in any case), Randolph sells the elderly slave to a Confederate contractor, hoping that Hugh will literally be worked to death—all on the pretext of southern honor. Randolph's sale of Hugh differs markedly from Rosslyn's identification with slaves: "I not only belonged by birth to the class which you place on a par with your slaves, but I worked with them. I was one of them. I believe in my soul I am one of them now" (230). Yet Rosslyn's romantic fusion of class and race is undermined by the passages describing Hugh's betrayal. Davis's powerful description of white violence, domestic poverty, and sexual brutality in the Randolph slave quarters, her details of the meager diet of beans and rice, and her discussion of the scars and welts on Anny's back intensify the painful irony when Hugh, believing that he is about to be freed, packs his few possessions, remembering, "I'se brought in hunderds a year to Mars Coyle, down in de mill dar. . . . An' I'se brought nuffin but dat yonder out wid my gray hairs to take to my boys." He concludes, "I'se neber bring anoder man child into de world to be a slave" (256).

As Hugh is sold to the Confederate trader, we follow the progress of his son Nathan (Dr. Broderip's brother). Nathan has run away to search for his "ole woman," Anny, who, he says, "wur not my wife, suh. But she will not marry any man but me" (264). Nathan is alluding to the fact that slave marriages had no legal status and hence, observes Claudia Tate, they seemed to exist outside of Western concepts of morality, civilization, and human progress.[23] Nathan loyally decides to risk his newfound freedom and remain in the South to search for his family and fight in the Union Army: "I'd like to hold a gun once in my hand to help my people" (265). With this phrase, uttered by the fugitive who will risk his own life to save a wounded Union soldier, Davis confronts the profound national fear of the armed slave or freedman. A sentimental tale of coincidences, near-misses, and broken families is, at all times, shaped by the pressures of slavery and the realities of war.

Meanwhile Anny (like Stowe's Eliza) also flees to the North, carrying her son, Tom, who, lacking shoes, can no longer walk on his bleeding feet; the presence of children inevitably made slave women's escapes more complex than those of slave men.[24] Anny's journey itself, with its ambiguous geography and confusing armies, also prophesies the confused destiny of freedom:

> How ken I tell which is de norf or which de souf? We's been trabellin . . . for many months, trough de mountains and cross ob de ribers, widout rest, night an' day. Once we wur put in de calaboose, and twice I was caught an' lashed. . . . Dar's one mountain passed and anudder risin' jest beyond, and dar's one army marchen today, an' anudder approachin' to-morrow, an' us hidin' an' hidin', an' no word comin' of dat which we seek. (269)

Like Nathan, Anny sees slavery and northward migration in economic as well as familial terms:

> They pay ther' for work. . . . The money that's bought them plantations and furnished them houses was made out of our sweat an' blood. *We* bought them; *we* paid for them. . . . If yer father an' me, an' them like us, hed been paid for our labor, we'd not have been the offscouring of the nation to-day, with scars on our backs in place of the wages that's bin our due. (271–72)

Nathan's absence on Anny's journey to freedom revises the conventional literary quest from a male's symbolic journey of growth to a historicized journey toward freedom for the black female. Anny's painful trek is one of the few representations of black migration in nineteenth-century literature outside of slave narratives, and even those, such as that of Frederick Douglass, frequently kept details to a minimum to protect the safety of the escape routes.

The discourse of realism contests the apologic nature of *Waiting for the Verdict.* Although Hazel Carby argues that in the literary representation of slavery, history is transformed into a series of moral lessons for the present, Nathan, Annie, and Broderip are not simply narrative voices that exemplify slavery's horrors. Rather, despite the racist stereotypes with which they are at times described, the African Americans in the novel behave and feel like full characters, produced and shaped by the realities of slavery. Slavery is the prehistory of this narrative and defines the options of all the black characters; their choices are plotted as historical positions within the confines of an enslaving nation. The brutality of slavery informs not only the text and context of the narrative of Reconstruction, but also its figurative language. For example, as she searches for Nathan among the corpses of a scorched battlefield, "'Nathan's not dead,' said Anny, loosening the collar that bound her like an iron band about the neck" (278).

In his review of *Waiting for the Verdict* in the *Nation*, Henry James argued that Davis had abandoned realism. Literary characters, he declared, "are worth reading about only so long as they are studied with a keen eye versed in the romance of human life. . . . Mrs. Davis's manner is in direct oppugnancy to this truth."[25] Instead,

> [Davis] drenches the whole field beforehand with a flood of lachrymose sentimentalism, and riots in the murky vapors that rise in consequence of the act. It is impossible to conceive of a method of looking at people and things less calculated to elicit the truth—less in the nature of a study or of intelligent inspection; . . . nothing is more trivial than that intellectual temper which, for ever dissolved in the melting mood, goes dripping and trickling over the face of humanity, washing its honest lineaments out of all recognition. It is enough to make one forswear for ever all decent reflections and honest compassion, and take refuge in cynical jollity and elegant pococurantism. . . . The reader, exhausted by the constant strain upon his moral sensibilities, cries aloud for the good, graceful old nullities of the "fashionable novel."[26]

Not only did James miss such turgid and controlled moments as the confrontation between Margaret and Broderip; apparently he did not consider Reconstruction an appropriate topic for art. His overdrawn attack on the novel in such gendered terms may have stemmed from his own silence on slavery and from the ambiguous wound that prevented his enlistment in a war, which he watched, he says, from an "almost ignobly safe stillness."[27] John De Forest went further than James in his discussion of the "Great American Novel" in the *Nation*:

> In reading [*Waiting for the Verdict*] we remember with wicked sympathy the expression of a bachelor friend, "I hate poor people's children," and we are tempted to add, "and poor people." . . . It is dreadful to have low, tattered, piebald, and stupid people so rubbed into one. The mild sermonizing twaddle of the "Hills of the Shatemuc" was better than this pernaceous exhibition of moral dwarfs, bearded women, Siamese twins, and headless calves.[28]

De Forest's catalogue is a telling list. The *Nation*'s damning reviews of Anna Dickinson, Elizabeth Stuart Phelps, and Harriet Beecher Stowe prompted

Stowe to organize rebuttals in the Boston press to James's "uncivil," "unmannerly," and "brutal" attacks on female authors, while the journal's exclusion of women authors prompted Henry Clapp (publisher of the *Saturday Press*) to suggest that its name be changed to the "Stag-Nation."[29]

The *Nation's* review of *Waiting for the Verdict*, along with its damning reviews of other novels that portrayed miscegenation, should be read in the context of that journal's attacks on proposed legislation banning interracial marriage. Launched in 1865, the *Nation* was to work "for the elevation of labor as a class and for the improvement of the Negro's lot" by monitoring the condition of freedmen, promoting popular education, and helping investors find openings in the destitute South. Its founder, E. L. Godkin, however, soon retreated from these progressive positions. Despite the large number of women on its subscription list, the *Nation* soon earned a reputation as a "masculine journal."[30]

In December 1867, a month after James's review of *Waiting for the Verdict*, in an editorial entitled "The Intermarriage Bugbear" the *Nation* argued that political equality did not guarantee social equality to blacks; rather, political equality might promote "a sense of absolute social *value*" that would be the "surest safeguard against that immorality from which the mixture of races so widely differing in physical and moral characteristics as the whites and blacks, mostly comes."[31] The author adds that miscegenation is a "bugbear" because "the whole standard of taste of the white race would have to be changed to make marriages between blacks and whites common, or even numerous. Nearly every white man and woman would have to recast one portion of his or her moral and physical constitution." Hence, although "a cross between the African race and the North American might turn out . . . a musical and industrious saint, . . . he might also turn out a lazy blackguard, in whose hands the country would run to weeds and civilization itself perish." Finally, the editorial writer concludes, "the white race on this continent is a very good race as it stands. We do not know of anything it needs that education and culture cannot supply without calling in the assistance of professional breeders." This apocalyptic attack on interracial marriage subsumes the discourses of eugenics, racial atavism, and white supremacy.

Clearly, *Waiting for the Verdict* is ambivalent in its racial politics. Despite the integrity and intelligence of her black characters, Davis frequently reverts to troubling stereotypes. Typical is the observation of the Quaker woman who buys young Sap out of slavery and pays for his medical education: "Ann Yates looked at the boy sharply. Nothing but an animal which a few dollars could buy or sell; shambling, undersized, loose-jointed, a puny, yellow face, out of which stared the treacherous melancholy eyes of his race." But her eye is caught by the child's "discontent, the appetite for something better than his brute life had yet known. 'Its the white blood in him!' she said aloud" (12). Uttered by an antislavery activist, this comment reflects Davis's warped notion of biological determinism.

Other flaws in the novel may derive from difficulties surrounding its publication. *Waiting for the Verdict* was published serially in the course of a turbulent year and written amidst considerable dispute with F. P. and William Church, editors of the *Galaxy,* who pressured Davis to finish the novel prematurely, in time for them to launch another serial. During the novel's serialization, the Churches changed the format of *Galaxy,* demanded a shorter text, and reneged on their contract with Davis.[32] Not surprisingly, the published novel was episodic and disjointed. Ultimately, Davis did not tidily account for over forty-five characters, a wide variety of settings—urban, rural, plantation—and midwestern, southern, and black dialects.

Nonetheless, Davis was evolving a literature of social realism, often in isolation. She was indeed aware that both in terms of content and form she was trying something new. In November 1866 she wrote to the Churches explaining that while she had completed a draft of the manuscript, she had decided "to entirely remodel and extend it." She writes, "The subject is one which has interested me more than any other, and I wish to put whatever strength I have into that book and make it, if possible, different from anything which I have yet been able to do."[33] In portraying people for whom De Forest sought total invisibility, Davis puts forward characters with endurance, commitment, and racial pride. While the eventual reunion of the slave family conforms to the literary stereotype of reunited families and generations that concludes the domestic novel, the convention is yet again transformed by Davis's insistence on its historical moment; the uncertainties of Reconstruction foreclose the possibility of family as finality. Her description of the painful separation of Nathan and Anny and their arduous search for each other on far distant plantations and civil war battlefields offers a tale of quest, adventure, and endurance shaped by graphic realism. The search for family also offers a fictional portrayal of this significant activity by runaway and freed slaves during and after the Civil War. Davis's tale of diaspora anticipates Frances Harper's *Iola Leroy* and Charles Chesnutt's "The Wife of His Youth."

By the end of the novel, Rosslyn has reformed Randolph, who learns to act like a northerner.[34] When Randolph first appeals to Dr. Broderip for help in getting a military commission, the surgeon tells him that he is unsuited for a soldier's life and arranges for the plantation owner to spend the war as a minor bureaucrat in Washington; as the representative southern man, Randolph is unable to fight or perform honorable labor. Typified by Randolph and Strebling, the southerner appears brutal, inconstant, guilt-ridden, and patriarchal. After the war and marriage to Rosslyn, Randolph returns to the South to arrange the reunion of the novel's black family.[35] Meanwhile, Rosslyn builds Nathan and Anny a small house on her Pennsylvania farm and allows them to work the land for their own profit. Davis believed in Jefferson's faith in agrarian redemption and the skills of black farmers. Davis wrote in "What About the Northern Negro?" (1889), "Go outside of New York. Wherever the African or mulatto has gone to work at farming with energy and steadiness, he has succeeded. . . . Farming is the work for which he has been trained, a bushel of potatoes being precisely the same price in the market whether sold by a white man or a black."[36] Nonetheless, Davis saw farming as a genetically transferred skill. After denouncing the prejudice of northern mill owners, mechanics, and trade union leaders, Davis goes on to observe that the Negro must not blame "white prejudice alone . . . for exclusion from trade; . . . the fact is, . . . the trading faculty does not belong to him as to the Jew or the New Englander."[37]

Thus, on the one hand, the conclusion to *Waiting for the Verdict* represents the sentimental confirmation of integrity, labor, and rural property; for Anny and Nathan in particular, agrarian domesticity replaces slavery as a form of social organization. In this household Anny and Rosslyn will, in effect, share the same master: Randolph. On the other hand, the marriage between Randolph and Rosslyn serves as a metaphor for national forgiveness and reunion, following the growth of southern consciousness—all taking place on Rosslyn's land. Even as the black family is reunited, the final union takes place between Anny and Rosslyn. Women are still responsible for and represent the community, and their domestic roles still define their relationship to citizenship. The verdict on Reconstruction is left to these two women, one a runaway slave, the other an abolitionist and a Union scout, who have acted heroically; the men are invisible, albeit powerful, on this integrated farm.

Although Anny's presence metaphorically grants Rosslyn access to political participation, Davis resists the temptation, common in antislavery fiction, to obliterate the blackness of her characters.[38] Rosslyn speaks optimistically of their shared birthright of "free air." She believes that the house she has built for Anny's family offers a domestic site of interracial sisterhood, and it will, in her view, make good the postwar promise of upward mobility. Anny, however, questions Rosslyn's optimism about her homey resolution that promises to annihilate the spatial distance between whites and blacks in a shared pastoral and domestic sphere; she understands that the house could keep the black family in a harmonious retreat. Unlike many white representations of black women as aggressive, unrestrained, and hypersexualized, Anny, like Harriet Jacobs, speaks from the perspective of black motherhood. She sees racial boundaries as dangerous and ongoing. She tells Rosslyn,

> Freedom and clo's, and a home of our own, is much. But it is not all. Forgive me. A mudder kerries her chile's life on her heart when he's a man, jes as before he was born. You know dat, I wondered what was my boy's birthright in dis country. . . . Dar's four millions of his people like him; waitin' for de whites to say which dey shall be—men or beasts. Waitin' for the verdict, madam. (354)

If, as Jane Tompkins observes, the great subject of sentimental fiction is always the nature of power,[39] here power—the verdict—still resides in the public sphere with "de whites." The national crisis of race emerges through the metaphor of Anny's deformed but clever son, Tom, who as a child typifies Davis's view of the future. "Dar's power in Tom's head, Missus, and dar's bad passions in his blood, and ef dar's no work given to de one, de oder has its work ready. He must be a man or a beast, an' dat soon" (354). Unlike Jim's tenuous freedom in *The Adventures of Huckleberry Finn* (1885), a novel written twenty years after passage of the Thirteenth Amendment but set before the Civil War, emancipation has occurred by the conclusion of *Waiting for the Verdict*, and the narrative confronts the implications of the social cataclysm.

Nonetheless, Davis's recurrent and troubling insistence on racial "instinct" and "blood" undermines the prescient vision of her novel. The conflicted representation of race in *Waiting for the Verdict* shaped the debate over the novel upon publication. Caroline Healey Dall, an author, reformer, and agent on the underground railroad, first praised the novel in the *National Anti-Slavery Standard*:

> Had the consciousness of the *needs* of the black race penetrated to the heart of the nation, as the utter hatred of slavery had begun to do when Uncle Tom was published, "Waiting for the Verdict" would have created a similar excitement, as it really deserves to work a wider reform.

Although Dall observes that the novel lacks characters who have the "airy grace" of the St. Clares in *Uncle Tom's Cabin*, she still remarks, "We have never seen any book which shows such familiarity with every aspect of our present problem as this. No other author has comprehended as well the various ways in which the curse still rests upon the people, white and black." Yet in her very praise Dall reproduces the essentialism of Davis's vision:

> In the character of Broderip many of the best traits of both races are brought out. It is the simple negro heart that anticipates so gaily the dawn of the day of festival, and demands that the whole world shall keep holiday with it. It is the Anglo Saxon blood that thrills when the coarse discourtesy of Margaret Conrad shakes the note which the negro woman brought . . . it was the loyal soul of the negro which made it cut [Broderip] to the heart to see *white men* giving their lives for *his* race.

Dall thus concludes, "How much more deeply slavery has harmed the white man than the black, is delicately indicated when the chivalrous honor of the Randolphs falls before the test which Broderip meets like a man."[40]

Davis's racial determinism prompted the African-American abolitionist, Charlotte Forten, to respond to Dall in the *Standard* two weeks later. While Forten praises Davis for being willing to "take up the vexed question of inter-marriage—that bugbear with which the enemies of the colored man are wont to terrify his timid friends," she ends, "How plain it is to see that she who wrote this book, despite her rare strength of mind, has not outgrown the prejudice against the outcast race." Quoting such passages as Rosslyn's revulsion at the mulatto boy, Sap, Forten comments,

Does it not seem that the child's repugnance is to be understood as *instinctive?*—an *intuitive* shrinking from a "yellow skin"? I can but think so. I would not do the author injustice; but it seems hardly possible to overstate her belief in the importance of "blood." "Anglo-Saxon blood," "negro blood," "the Burley blood," "the Randolph blood"—such expressions abound throughout the book, and one cannot help feeling that the author needs gently to be reminded that "God has made one blood of all the nations of the earth."

Forten's concern is to protest the idea that "pervades the book," that "prejudice against color is instinctive in and natural to the whites." Hence she observes, "Surely a Southern woman must know that Southern children, in the old slave days, did not shrink from the colored nurses in whose arms they slept, and from whom, often, their life drew its nourishment."[41] This is quite a different view from the natural "antipathy" between the races posed in the novel.

Along similar lines, Lydia Maria Child wrote to Forten, "I have not read 'Waiting for the Verdict. . . . [All Davis's] writings excite more or less antagonism in my mind. In her views of things she seems to me to drift about, without any rudder or compass of moral principles. It is a pity, for she has a powerful intellect. I have thought several times that she was confused in her ideas as to which was the *right* side, the U.S. or the Rebellion; a thing not to be wondered at, considering she is a Virginian."[42]

In the end, Anny is both the final subject and the context of *Waiting for the Verdict.* As in "John Lamar" and "Blind Tom," Rebecca Harding Davis presumes to speak for African Americans, to understand and to represent the slave and the freedman's point of view, to put their histories into words, to interpret through representation and projection. Rosslyn achieves freedom for herself by assisting in the freedom of a black woman—one who will remain dependent on her. Unlike many antislavery novels, however, Davis builds this analogy through economic as well as female similarities. Because of her early poverty and illegitimate birth, Rosslyn believes she can transcend the boundaries separating black and white.[43] The book ends with an interracial community. The slaves and the illegitimate daughter of a plantation owner, all wrenched from their pasts, have the possibility of a shared future in a liberated home—a home owned by a white woman.

Yet in *Waiting for the Verdict* Davis continues to extend the suasive purview of female ethics.[44] The movement toward the hearth is neither movement inward, nor movement away from the world, nor simple acquiescence in a community as imagined by Rosslyn. Anny insists that the facts of slavery and the uncertain future of Reconstruction mean that happiness in Rosslyn's home will not redeem or even change the world. Slavery has called into question the sentimental theory that social equality can be achieved through small acts of moral significance. Within the discourse of realism, Anny suggests that white women cannot run away from the pain of a troubled home; Rosslyn must reform Randolph, but Anny must face a bigoted world. Unlike Lois, the mulatta child in *Margret Howth*, Anny finds no pleasure in submission. Although Rosslyn has proved the reforming power of love, the open-ended "verdict" underscores the impossibility of this hope as the solution for the nation. Anny announces that the sentimental tools of patience, example, and passivity, and even the final discovery of long-lost parents, will not resolve the national problem.

In *Waiting for the Verdict*, Davis repudiates the Calvinist tendency in sentimentalism that views suffering as the effect of heavenly wrath. By externalizing suffering and representing it as historical, political, and institutional, and by violating the sentimental contract in which the arena of human action is defined not as the world but the human soul, Davis insisted on racism as a national crisis. Rather than offering the reassurance of a sentimental closure, Rosslyn's and Anny's agrarian home will continue to reflect the public concern. At the same time, unlike the melodramas about mulattos that appeared around the turn of the century and that reconstituted the black family through the figure of the black mother,[45] *Waiting for the Verdict* invokes an integrated and domestic utopia to represent the national capacity for racial harmony.[46]

There is no evidence that Davis ever became publicly involved in a political or social cause—abolition, suffrage, temperance. Indeed, her characterization of Rosslyn reflects a sentimentalized view of her friend Lucretia Mott, as well as her ambivalence about female reformers in general. In 1903 she wrote "A Peculiar People," drawn from her personal knowledge of abolitionists. This essay appeared in an era of racial hysteria, "Negrophobic" mob violence, the institutionalization of Jim Crow laws, and racial Darwinism. The essay's title itself harkens back to the southern euphemism for slavery, "the peculiar domestic institution of the South." Here Davis describes the male leaders of the antislavery campaign as Radical "good fellows," "chivalric reformers" touched by eccentricity: "Why, because the good folk wanted to free the slave, should they refuse to cut their beards, or to eat meat, or . . . run after new kinds of fantastic medicines or cookery?"[47] Unlike the female abolitionists whom Jean Fagan Yellin calls "routinely outrageous," and those whom President John Tyler called "the presiding genius over the councils of insurrection and discord,"[48] Davis describes the women involved in abolitionism as "honest of heart, sweet of face, soft of speech . . . as only your gentle, soft woman can be."[49] While Nancy Hewett finds that Quaker abolitionists "by-passed, for most of their lives, the basic elements of the new urban bourgeois gender system—the separation of spheres, the sex consciousness of domesticity, and the idea of female moral and spiritual superiority,"[50] in "Peculiar People" Davis insists that the power of her friend Lucretia Mott, the most important and inspiring Quaker lecturer on the abolitionist platform,

> came from the fact that she was one of the most womanly of women. She had pity and tenderness enough in her heart for the mother of mankind; . . . she might face a mob at night that threatened her life . . . but she never forgot in the morning to pick and shell the peas for dinner; . . . she knitted wonderful bed spreads and made gay rag-carpets as wedding gifts.[51]

Waiting for the Verdict appeared during the postwar period when slavery was romanticized in reborn plantation novels. Even Unionist publishers like Harper's or Ticknor and Fields readily reprinted earlier proslavery novels by southern women, including Caroline Lee Hentz's *The Planter's Northern Bride* (1853) and Maria McIntosh's *Two Pictures* (1863).[52] *Waiting for the Verdict* is an exception to the pattern described by James Kinney, who argues that during Reconstruction abolitionist authors were satisfied with the results of the war and hence ceased to write about miscegenation.[53] Unlike Harriet Beecher Stowe, moreover, Davis never resorted to pleas for the removal of freed slaves to a republic in Africa and continued until her death to call for economic and educational reforms to address the poverty and unemployment of former slaves. In *Waiting for the Verdict* may be found the seeds of her later admiration for Booker T. Washington. Davis felt that Washington shared her view that the progress of the "Negro . . . depends not on his affiliation, political, mercantile or social, with the whites, but on the development of his own people." To Davis, economic degradation was a form of prejudice.

> The prejudice against the Negro in the Northern states has been as unjust and cruel in its effects as was slavery. . . . We opened our schools and universities to him, and when he was ready and eager to earn his living we barred every way before him except those which led to the kitchen and the barbershop. . . . No merchant would dare to put behind his counters colored salesmen or women, however competent or courteous they might be. (419)

In *Waiting for the Verdict* Davis fictionalizes her belief in the role of environment in shaping ideas of human equality and possibility. Racial prejudice, she concludes, is neither a private nor a spiritual predicament, but a compelling economic and social problem that the North was trying to evade.

7 ❦ Nature, Nurture, and Nationalism

"A Faded Leaf of History"

THE VICTORY OF the North in the Civil War arrived under a banner of nationhood loosely stitched from the repression of sectional autonomy and united by emerging corporate industrialism and the new geographical links brought by the railroads.[1] To allow for white settlement in new territories, the federal government proceeded with the final stages of plans to eradicate Native Americans and to abolish their rights to traditional lands. The Homestead Act of 1862 was neither simply a democratizing gesture of land distribution for the American yeoman farmer nor a westward magnet for immigrants and the unemployed. Rather than "a safety valve to the great social steam engine," in the words of Edward Everett, a northern Whig, the Homestead Act was also a strategy to encourage agrarian development of Indian lands.[2] Viewed through the popular literary forms of the tall tale, the captivity narrative, and the dime novel, expansive nationhood seemed organic and hence inevitable.

America, it appeared, still suffered from what James Fenimore Cooper called our "greater want of finish."[3] In the decade following the Civil War, women, nature, and Native Americans still appeared in fiction and visual arts as interchangeable metonyms for incompletion. That is to say, women, nature, and Indians mutually anticipated and required civilization. In *Home Book of the Picturesque* (1851), an antebellum anthology that celebrated and defined the American landscape, Cooper likened the quality of American nature to the promise of American nationhood and to the immanence of American women and Indians; he said that unlike Italy's Lake Como and Lake Maggiore, Niagara Falls lacked "accessories, . . . for a union of art and nature can alone render scenery perfect." Even though "in the ways of the wild, the terrific, and the grand, nature is sufficient of herself . . . now men are become familiar with its mysteries, and penetrating into its very mists, by means of a small steamboat." Without such promising and penetrating signs of "the works of man," nature invokes the feminine. Cooper's phallic image of familiarity, conquest, and correction of Niagara Falls extends to the ejaculatory moment when "the waters of this mighty strait are poured into the bosom of the Ontario."[4]

In addition, observed Cooper, although American landscape lacks "that wild sublimity which ordinarily belongs to a granite formation" (that is, the rock-hard masculinity of the Alps), it does become attractive when "the peculiar blending of what may be termed the agricultural and the savage unite to produce landscapes of extraordinary beauty and grace." By "taming of the land" in the immanent presence and potentiality of the Indian, "beauty and grace," traditionally female attributes, may emerge. Cooper does not confuse civilization with domesticity, however: "A fence that looks as if it were covered with clothes hung out to dry does very little toward aiding the picturesque."[5] Along similar lines, Washington Irving in 1835 warned young American men not to "grow luxurious and effeminate in Europe" and instead encouraged them to take a tour of the American West to develop "manliness, simplicity, and self-dependence most in unison with our political institutions."[6] Thus, the civilized feminine—not to be confused with wet laundry—resides in the rational presence and control of autonomous white masculinity. In the 1860s and 1870s, representations of women, nature, and Native Americans would mutually participate in an affiliation with the tempting, if dangerous, wildness of the female eros, cohabiting in a marginal territory of immaturity analogous to, but not equal to, the American home. In the promise of nationalism, the discourse of domesticity subsumed the discourse of race.

By the 1870s pressures toward an ideology of nationhood prompted elegiac and wishful representations of American unity in such literary forms as regional fiction, the plantation novel, the domestic novel, the pastoral utopia, idealized tales of colonial revival, and stories about the inevitable eradication of the Indian. To confront emerging concepts of the nation as white, male, and industrial, Rebecca Harding Davis resuscitates an eroticized and politicized image of domesticity within nature. Her fiction of this period insistently questions the self-congratulatory tone of popular images of nationhood and reflects instead the profound national anxiety that accompanied the collapse of Reconstruction, the rise of European immigration, pressures for women's suffrage, and the genocide of Native Americans.

In "A Faded Leaf of History," published in 1873 in the *Atlantic Monthly*, Davis rewrites a well-known seventeenth-century captivity narrative from a woman's perspective—yet again embedding her political critique in an ambivalent dialogue with sentimentalism.[7] "A Faded Leaf" is in effect a palimpsest of Jonathan Dickinson's *God's Protecting Providence Man's Surest Help and Defence In the times of the greatest difficulty and most Imminent danger* (1699). In this popular narrative, reprinted fifteen times between 1700 and 1868, Dickinson describes the "Remarkable Deliverance of divers persons, From the Devouring Waves of the Sea, amongst which they Suffered Shipwreck, and Also From the more cruelly devouring jawes of the inhumane Cannibals of Florida."[8] This story of captivity is told from the perspective of Jonathan Dickinson, a wealthy Quaker slaveholder and owner of a vast plantation in Jamaica, who was shipwrecked with his family en route to Philadelphia, where he planned to pursue a career in international trade and local politics. In rewriting this text, Davis suggests that Dickinson's expansionist impulse derives from his nativist assumptions about cultures, his optimistic assumptions about providential nature, his imperialist assumptions about expansion, and his masculine assumptions about individualism and family. In "A Faded Leaf of History," the Quaker colonist's views of the conquest of nature, women, and Indians emerge as conflated and interchangeable symbols for the justification of manifest destiny.

From a woman's point of view, Davis retells the Quaker's "testimony" of God's protection of a group of travelers who sailed from Port Royal, Jamaica, on the barkentine *Reformation* on August 23, 1696. After being lost at sea for weeks, they were shipwrecked just off the Florida coast and captured by two Indian tribes before undertaking a dangerous northward trek through five hundred miles of swamps and barren coastal areas. The Dickinson party reached Charles Town, South Carolina, the day after Christmas, where they spent the winter, and finally sailed into Philadelphia in March, seven months after their departure. Among the castaways were Dickinson's wife, Mary, their six-month-old son, John, as well as Joseph Kirle, commander of the ship, Robert Barrow, a prominent and frail Quaker en route home after years of unsuccessful missionary work in the islands, and ten of Dickinson's slaves —including an Indian woman named Venus who died of seizures after a month at sea.

In his version, Dickinson describes how the *Reformation* became separated from its armed convoy during a storm. Trying to avoid both pirate ships and the French navy, yet fearful of Indians who beckoned toward the shore, the ship tacked between Cuba and Florida for several days until it foundered on a barrier reef about twenty miles north of what is now West Palm Beach. In chilling rain, with the ship sinking and the livestock washed away, Dickinson erected a tent on the barren beach for his family, using the ships's sails, while his slaves and the ship's crew unloaded his chests and sodden clothing from the wreck. Within a few hours, two Indians appeared, "running fiercely and foaming at the mouth having no weapons except their knives" (28). They seized two slaves, whom Dickinson easily ransomed for pipes and tobacco, and ran off to notify their "cassekey" or chief, who returned to capture the entire party. Despite Dickinson's fears that these "man-eaters" of foaming mouth and "dismal aspect" would cruelly murder him, within fifteen minutes, he reports, "it pleased the Lord to work wonderfully for our preservation and instantly all these savage men were struck dumb, and like men amazed" (30), a typological interpretation that marked Dickinson's Quaker faith in a beneficent and protecting God.

Reluctantly accepting the travelers' claim to be Spaniards (rather than the hated English), the Indians (whom Dickinson names the Jobese, from the nearby Rio Jobe), plundered the ship but left the travelers their foodstuffs and one remaining hog, despite their own intense suffering from a two-year famine. The Indians stripped them of most of their clothing and led the frightened travelers, now covered only in strips of sailcloth, on a five-mile trek, by foot and canoe, along the barren sand bar back to a wigwam village. There the Indians offered them water and boiled fish and built them wigwams of sticks and palmetto leaves. The chief's wife offered to suckle the starving baby, to which Mary reluctantly agreed. Clearly, the travelers were not strictly captives. Over the next two weeks, the tribal leaders urged the travelers to head south in order to avoid the territory of a neighboring tribe, where they would have their "throats and scalps cut and [would] be shot, burnt and eaten" (32).

Nonetheless, convinced that the Jobeses' warnings were a trap, Dickinson and his party set out on a perilous journey north, partly on foot, partly by longboat and canoe. Within two days, they were recaptured by a hostile tribe of Ais Indians,[9] who detained them for a month until their chief seized the travelers' goods, held by the Jobese. Interspersing his story with observations on God's mercies, Dickinson describes the struggling band, stretched over miles of marshes, swamps, and shallows, passing through famine-stricken Indian villages, sleeping briefly in canoes, and suffering intensely from exposure, hunger, and attacks by mosquitoes. Finally in mid-November, eighteen of the original twenty-five reached the Spanish fort of St. Augustine, only to find an unsupplied garrison that could not feed them for long. After two weeks' rest, pledging to repay the Spanish governor for supplies, they again moved on, now minimally equipped with blankets and enough canoes for the whole party. Delayed and lost in the labyrinthine marshes and fogs of coastal Florida, Georgia, and South Carolina, sleeping in abandoned wigwams, eating berries and fish, they finally reached the British settlement of Charles Town four months after their departure from Jamaica.

Although the Native American was an unusual topic for fiction in the *Atlantic Monthly*, in the decade following the Civil War Indians appeared frequently in the dime novel as tropes for primitivism and social anarchy, dangers that would surely recede before the vanguard of white society.[10] If Jonathan Dickinson's narrative, first published in 1699, was written for a growing Quaker community committed to economic expansion and Indian conversion, Davis's tale almost two centuries later addressed an expansionist nation attempting to eliminate the "Indian problem" through the eradication and removal of tribal peoples.[11] Most eastern tribes had been removed beyond the Mississippi by the 1830s; however, the opening of western lands after Louisiana Purchase in 1803 and the Treaty of Guadalupe-Hidalgo of 1848 brought another wave of struggles over Indian land that lasted throughout the Civil War.

By the time of "A Faded Leaf" (1873), Indians were engaged in armed resistance to policies that forced them to live, travel, and hunt within the boundaries of reservations and required thousands of Indian children to attend Christian boarding schools, learn manual skills, and spend summers with white families. As plains Indians found themselves caught between the forced migrations of other tribes, the advance of the mining frontier, and the expropriation of their land under the Homestead Acts, they began their "last stand." Although peace may have come to the plains less from military victories than from the ravages of the advancing railroad, new diseases, and General William Sherman's and General Philip Sheridan's deliberate destruction of buffalo herds between 1866 and 1870,[12] the warfare of the plains Indians—nomadic horse-mounted hunters—caught the attention of eastern readers. The Sioux warrior in particular emerged as the timeless Indian in the white imagination—noble if he died bravely, ignoble if he massacred pioneers.[13]

Davis dismantles both the popular geography and the characterization of the plains Indian in "A Faded Leaf," just when the plight of Native Americans in Florida and the Southeast was becoming prominent news. The people Dickinson called Jobese were probably a northern branch of powerful Tequesta Indians, whose numbers dwindled in the early eighteenth century under attacks by lower Creek tribes pushing southward under pressure from British expansion into South Carolina. Eventually, all the remaining Florida tribes would be termed Seminoles, the "wild people," those who held aloof from whites. Following their defeat in the brutal Seminole War of 1842, Seminoles who refused to move into the swamps of Florida's interior endured the infamous westward march to Oklahoma. After the Civil War, despite their loyalty to the Union, Seminoles were forced to confess to war guilt, cede 2 million acres to the government at fifteen cents an acre (land that Congress then bestowed on the railroads) and resettle on a 200,000-acre tract for which they paid fifty cents an acre to the government.[14] It is estimated that a population of Native Americans that totaled one million before contact with Europeans had fallen to approximately 237,000 by 1900, a decline of nearly 75 percent; the precolonial population of 150,000 south-eastern tribal people was reduced by 90 percent. By the time Davis wrote "A Faded Leaf," the Tequesta and Ais were extinct.[15]

Dickinson's colonial narrative reflects an optimistic Quaker testimony of a merciful God who operates through providential nature and human endurance and compassion. The Bible itself was useless to them, he admitted:

> We brought our great Bible . . . to this place. And being all stripped as naked as we were born, and endeavoring to hide our nakedness; these cannibals took the books, and tearing out the leaves would give each of us a leaf to cover us; . . . instantly another of them would snatch away what the other gave us, smiting and deriding us withal. (44)

Nonetheless, Dickinson explains, "It pleased God to order it so that we went on shore, as though there had been a lane made through the breakers" (42), and, similarly, "it pleased God to tender the hearts of some of them towards us" (44). Unlike Cotton Mather's appropriation of Hanna Dustin's tale of captivity, Dickinson's *God's Protecting Providence* is never a cautionary exhortation.

Davis, however, sees Dickinson's pamphlet itself as a fetish for a deathlike narrative of history. She finds the thin coffee-colored pages of the ragged pamphlet to be "like rotting leaves in the fall." Developing the image of decay, the pages "had grown clammy to the touch . . . from the grasp of so many dead years" (362). To Davis, as an artifact the book itself suggests contamination: as the narrator sits in "one of the oldest libraries in the country" (presumably, the Philadelphia Free Library, where Davis had a desk), she notices "a peculiar smell about the book which it had carried down from the days when young William Penn went up and down the clay-paths of his village of Philadelphia" (362). When she first discovered the pamphlet, she had expected to read another expansionist history, "some 'Report of the Condition of the Principalities of New Netherland, or New Sweden, for the Use of the Lord's High Proprietors thereof' (for of such precious dead dust this library is full)" (362). What she seeks from stories of conquest is a sense of historical subjectivity: "If only to find human interest in them, one would rather they had been devoured by inhuman cannibals than not" (362–63). Initially Dickinson's party seemed "only part of that endless caravan of ghosts that has been crossing the world since the beginning," she says, adding, "they never can be anything but ghosts to us" (362).

Within Dickinson's expansionist narrative, however, Davis's narrator suddenly "found, instead, wrapped in weighty sentences and backed by the gravest and most ponderous testimony, the story of a baby" (362). Undermining her image of the original pages as "rotting leaves" is her discovery that the pages of the "father's book" were "scribbled over with the name John . . . in a cramped, childish hand" (362), literalizing a sentimental intent. Through the act of writing, childlike and inept though it may be, another version of history announces itself.[16] In her revisionist history, Davis addresses the "sweet-tempered, gracious women," warm in their snow-covered homes in contemporary Philadelphia "with their children close about their knees," and tells them the story of "a baby and a boy and an aged man" (363). She intends in her version "to bring this little live baby back . . . out of the buried years where it has been hidden with dead people so long, and give it a place and home among us" (363). Davis's interpretation suggests that rather than a Quaker utopia, seventeenth-century Pennsylvania was "a most savage country"; "to this savage country our baby was bound" (363), a play on words suggesting a natural destination of constriction. The home will revise the narrative of colonization.

In Davis's tale, the voyage was undertaken because Jonathan Dickinson, "a wealthy planter, [was] on his way to increase his wealth in Penn's new settlement" (363). His rigidity and prejudice quickly imperiled the travelers:

> The captain held all the power and the Quaker all the money. . . . The captain, Kirle, debarred from fighting by cowardice, and the Quaker Dickenson, forbidden by principle, appear to have set out upon their perilous journey, resolved to defend themselves by suspicion, pure and simple. They looked for treachery behind every bush and billow; the only chance of safety lay, they maintained, in holding every white man to be an assassin and every red man a cannibal until they were proved otherwise. (363–64)

Dickinson's blindness to the informative, aesthetic, and redemptive power of nature further endangers his group. He was so obsessed with pirates and savages that he would not spare time to his "jealous eyes" to enjoy the beauty of the white-sailed fleet "scudding over the rolling green plain" or permit his sickly baby to prosper from the vitality of the sea air, but kept him smothered below deck, "in the finest of linens and the softest of paduasoy." (364).

Thus, in Davis's view, the shared ineptitude and racist paranoia of Dickinson and Captain Kirle caused the calamitous wreck. Omitting any mention of the storm that grounds the barkentine in the original text, Davis describes how the two men caused the ship to lose its way in the night and then aimlessly "beat about" for fifteen days without any aim but to "escape the enemies whom they hourly expected to leap out from behind the sky line" (364). When they saw "friendly signs" of people beckoning from the shore, Kirle and Dickinson, "seized with fresh fright, put about and made off as for their lives" (364). Yet when they saw signal lights from other ships, "doubtless from their own convoy," they presumed it to be the French navy and again tacked back. With the captain injured by a jib boom, "Dickenson brought his own terrors into command, and for two or three days whisked the unfortunate barkentine up and down the coast, afraid of both sea and shore, until finally, one night, he run her aground" (364), blaming the wreck on the "judgment of God."

As he watched his slaves and crew desperately unload his property from the sinking ship, Dickinson continued to assume the "universal treachery of his brother-man" (365). He awaited the tribal chief, prepared to "use his burly strength and small wit" (364) in what he saw as a contest of cultures: "Christianity was now to be brought face to face with heathenness" (365). Insufficiently armed, the party pretended they were Spaniards: "It is curious to observe how these early Christians met the Indians with the same weapons of distrust and fraud that have proved so effective with us in civilizing them since" (365). As "the good Quaker" prayed that God's wrathful punishment would rain upon these "pagan robbers," he ordered his slaves to bury his money on the beach, "quite blind to the poetic justice of the burial, as the money had been made on land stolen from the savages" (365). Unlike Dickinson, Davis's narrator is a cultural relativist who observes that because of the famine, "in all probability these cannibals returned thanks to whatever God they had for this windfall of food and clothes devoutly as our forefathers were doing at the other end of the country for the homes which they had taken by force" (366).

In contrast to Dickinson's interpretive paradigm of "God's Protecting

Providence," Davis shapes the historical narrative through the paradigm of sentimentality; the travelers' survival is evidence of the redemptive powers of Indian motherhood and female community. Yet because Davis represents history *through* but not solely *as* a psychological dilemma, the political context—power that is white, masculine, and wealthy—endures as an real presence. Although historical conflict affects personal history, "A Faded Leaf" remains in the public realm; the rescue of Mary and the baby underscores the capacity of sympathy to change the reader's views of Indians. Thus, unlike Dickinson's text, which operates through vivid descriptions of physical hardships inevitably ameliorated by a beneficent God, Davis's text returns to the vocabulary of feelings to shape our perception of Anglo-Indian contact. If in Dickinson's poignant version the traumas appear ongoing and inexorable, calling forth the utmost in the travelers' endurance and faith, Davis's story centers on Mary and the baby, whose perils are exacerbated by the blind egotism of Jonathan. It is the melodrama of maternal plight that prompts observations on colonialism and misogyny.

According to Davis, Jonathan's racism and expansionist hunger continually made his family vulnerable. Despite the sexual contract of domesticity, rather than offer a woman sanctuary, patriarchy puts a wife at risk. Comparing the dangerous sea voyage from the male and female perspective, Davis's narrator notes that the sailors had "chosen a life of peril," Dickinson enjoyed a "tough courage" (367), and the old prophet had the comfort of access to the divine word. Mary Dickinson, however, "was only a gentle, commonplace woman . . . whose highest ambition was to take care of her snug little house, and all of whose brighter thoughts of romance or passion began and ended in this staid Quaker and the baby that was a part of them both" (367). Unlike the Promethean egoism of Jonathan's quest, domestic life, inscribed in the language of physical passion, represents Mary's image of fulfilled desire. In a story of female adventure, Mary has no power over the course of the journey, but rather she collaborates in images of her own confinement.

Unique in Davis's writings, however, is the focus on a baby (rather than a wife) as a totem both for maternal martyrdom and imminent female community. Further, only in "A Faded Leaf" does Davis so fully represent the "bonds of womanhood," as Mary finds refuge in the enduring sensibility of female dependence. Davis develops this perspective through the primal trope of food and orality, which contrasts with Jonathan's obsessive fear of cannibalism. Hence, while the white woman forged a community with the Indian women through the hungry baby and found food and friendship in the tribal community, Jonathan, despite the generosity of the Jobese, "was sure of the worst designs on the part of the cannibal, from a strange glance which he fixed upon the baby as he drove them before him to his village" (366). As soon as the shipwrecked travelers reached the Jobese village, the cassekey took them to the wigwam of his wife, who put aside her own child to suckle the infant. In Dickinson's text, Mary tried to resist this gesture, but in Davis's version, the baby, "born tired into the world, and [who] had gone moaning its weak life out ever since," was now "warmed and fed. [It] stretched its little arms and legs out on the savage breast comfortably and fell into a happy sleep, while its mother sat apart and looked on" (367–68).

By feeding the white child with her own milk (also a recurrent motif in slave narratives), the lactating Indian mother appears closer to nature, tied to preindustrial life, while the arid and alienated white mother, feeling intense loss over her one area of power, observes the rebirth of her child, an image of regeneration that the reader understands through the conduit of the white female gaze. Because the Jobese woman's maternal act rejuvenates the white family, on the imagistic level it participates in the defeat of the view of the Indian as defiant. Thus, Mary's role as witness to a performance that preempts Jonathan's masculine duty to engage in violence on her behalf serves to co-opt the Indian and the white female at the same time.[17] As Richard Slotkin notes, the cultural litmus test of nineteenth-century Indians is how they respond to whites.[18]

The sentimental metaphor of orality—hunger, nursing, famine, provision—shapes Davis's critique of romantic male egoism, and, in turn, defines Jonathan's racism. In Dickinson's version, as the Jobese chief led the travelers to the village he said "with a treacherous laugh, that after they had gone there for a purpose he had, they might go." His "purpose," however, was to feed the travelers. Davis describes the emaciation and hunger of travelers and Indians alike, observing that Jonathan Dickinson, trapped in "his suspicious bigotry," was convinced that every warming fire "has death in the pot" (368)—that is, the Jobese intend to cook and consume him and his party.

Throughout, according to Davis, Dickinson refused to acknowledge the "kind treatment of the chief, who appears to have shared all that he had with them" (368).

Davis uses the metaphor of cannibalism, a trope with long colonialist associations, to expose Jonathan's stereotyped assumptions about the Indian threat. Images of cannibalism fulfill what Michel de Certeau terms "a colonization of the body by the discourse of power. This is *writing that conquers.* It will use the New World as if it were a blank, 'savage' page on which Western desire will be written."[19] Louis Montrose describes Amerigo Vespucci's sixteenth-century personification of America as a nude female Indian performing cannibalistic fellatio, an oral fantasy of female insatiability and male dismemberment that forged a powerful conjunction of the savage and the feminine.[20] Captivity narratives, from the seventeenth through the nineteenth centuries, involving tribes ranging from New England, the Great Lakes, the plains, and the Southwest, recorded incidents of cannibalism, but rarely was it interpreted in tribal terms as a ritual that bonded victor and vanquished, capturing the courage and strength of the enemy.[21] Women's captivity narratives virtually never recorded incidents of ritualized cannibalistic slaughter, although they did include accounts of captives eating human flesh to avoid death from starvation.[22]

Indicative of what psychoanalytic theorist Jessica Benjamin sees as the relationship between domination and the denial of connection, Davis's Jonathan defends himself from what he takes to be the alien otherness of the Jobese. Repudiating the maternal metaphor and locked in his racial stereotypes, he persists in denying the Indians' generosity. Davis's narrator observes that "the shipwrecked people, instead of being killed and eaten, went to sleep just as the moon rose" while the Indians sing of welcome or worship, a chant that Dickinson, in his narrative, calls "a Consert of hideous Noises" (368). By contrast, because Mary, as a woman, does not have to forgo dependency, she may forge relationships with the other Indian women and children—connections that appear to deny the role of race.[23] In "A Faded Leaf" the ideology of sentimentality conflates white women, children, and Indians in a sympathetic community in which all but the white men partake. Davis arrives at this unity by the eradication of difference and the cultural assimilation of the Indians. While Jonathan insists on his role as the agent of his own desire and destiny, and while he persists in the dangerous myth of endangered white independence and power, the narrator, who is identified with Mary, sees the Jobese chief as "this friend in the wilderness" (368).

When the Jobese chief understands that Dickinson, still suspecting treachery, is resolved to lead his party northward, he retrieves the longboat from the wreck, along with barrels of butter, sugar, wine, and chocolate, which he presents to Dickinson. Themes of female vulnerability and communalism shape Davis's version of the journey north. With Barrow, Mary, the baby, and two sick members of the crew traveling by canoe, and the rest of the members of the party walking on foot, they begin the long trek, suffering from extreme cold, sand flies, and mosquitoes. Soon they encounter the Ais ("Jece") Indians, the "fiercer savages of whom the chief had warned them," and again the travelers pretend they are Spaniards. Davis's narrator sardonically observes, "By this time, one would suppose, even Dickenson's dull eyes would have seen the fatal idiocy of the lie" (368). Interestingly, when she pictures Indian brutality Davis quotes Dickinson directly: "'They rushed upon us, rending the few Cloathes from us that we had; they took all from my Wife, even tearing her Hair out, to get at the Lace, wherewith it was knotted'" (368). Davis continues to read through Dickinson to stress aspects of this attack that endanger Mary and the baby, who is also stripped of his garments "while one savage filed its mouth with sand" (369). Yet while the purported sexual threat of the Indians undermines community, the Ais chief's wife also comes to Mary's rescue, "protects her from the sight of all" (that is, covers her nudity), and cleans the sand out of the baby's mouth, "whereon the mass of savages fell back, muttering and angry" (369). Even in a fierce tribe, a woman has the authority to nurture and protect orality.

Thus in "A Faded Leaf" the reformative power of gender triumphs over the dangerous essentialism of race. The Ais woman brings "poor naked" Mary to her own wigwam and shows her how to cover herself with deerskins. Davis observes that the Ais were also suffering from famine and had little to share but scarce fish and palmetto berries: "Their emaciated and hunger-bitten faces gave fiercer light to their gloomy, treacherous eyes" (369). Speaking from the viewpoint of one whose duty is to provide food, the narrator observes that nothing could have been more unwelcome to the tribe than this hungry "crowd of whites." Even so, by the second day, the chief "looked pleasantly" upon Mary and the baby, and "instead of fish entrails and the filthy water in which the fish had been cooked . . . he brought clams to Mary, and kneeling in the sand showed her how to roast them" (369). The native male enters the domestic sphere. The Ais women soon realize that Mary has no breast milk, and, like the Jobese, they pass her baby around to nurse, "putting away their own children that they might give it their food" (369). The redemptive power of mother and child and the profound maternal identification of Mary and the Indian women not only deprive Dickinson of power, and hence, of masculinity, but again deemphasize the difference between whites and Indians.

Nonetheless, by focusing on lactation, food, and famine, "A Faded Leaf" participates in what Lora Romero calls a transformation of native Americans into vanishing Americans by "incorporating the racial other as an earlier and now irretrievably lost version of the self."[24] In these primal passages, moreover, the famine suggests the inevitable demise of the Indians; the feeding of the white infant alludes to the ultimate survival of the white race at the expense of their own. After the baby is nursed by the Indian women, whose own children are dying of famine, Davis notes, "The child, that, when it had been wrapped in fine flannel and embroidery had been always nigh to death, began to grow fat and rosy, to crow and laugh as it had never done before, and kick its little legs sturdily about under a bit of raw skin covering" (369). The restoration of social equilibrium for the whites fixes native activity in domesticity and involves the colonization of the Indian woman's body and the white son's assumed right to possess her breast. The appropriation of the Indian woman's breast similarly constructs a dominant subject position for the (presumably white) reader of the *Atlantic;* through the discourse of sentimentality, the female reader becomes complicit in this objectification. Davis, I suggest, hints at the link between the narrative of the feminization of power and racial genocide, the geopolitics of the conflation of the body and the state. As Romero astutely points out, such micro narratives of individuals usually appear oblivious to the politics of the nineteenth-century macro narrative of modernization, which involved the massive destruction of populations.

Expansionism, writes Amy Kaplan, regarding later novels of empire, makes the colony a site for recuperating a primitive corporeal virility.[25] In "A Faded Leaf," this recuperation is achieved through a feminized view of the Indians and an Indianized view of Mary. In Kaplan's theory, any feminized view of colonized people makes it hard to represent them as subjects taking action on their own accord.[26] Yet Davis's conflation of race and gender is somewhat more complicated. In neither Dickinson's nor Davis's version does Mary rage against her predicament, nor does she attempt any act of survival on her own behalf. By concluding with the successful return to Philadelphia and the home, Davis reidentifies Mary with Jonathan; the wife's experience is recuperated, as is the narrator's. Indeed, Mary's journey affirms her commitment to the home and to the colony. Annette Kolodny observes that "westering" nineteenth-century women shared their husband's and father's motives of economic expansion; women too dreamed of transforming the wilderness. Even though massive exploitation and alteration of the continent were not part of most women's fantasies, through an extensive reading of frontier women's diaries and letters, Kolodny establishes that they also planned to build a home on the frontier—even if they imagined a "cultivated garden" rather than a privatized space of erotic mastery or infantile regression.[27]

Davis's maternal figure, however, powerfully aware of the extensiveness of the famine and the arrogance of her husband, refuses to accept the "disappearance of the primal wild" with equanimity.[28] For Davis, the domestic images of nurturance and community function as the ethical core of nationhood. Yet, by reconstructing a domestic and Indian utopia in the wilderness, Davis puts forward a totalizing cultural imposition on the wilderness, one that reflects Mary's dream of domesticity and Davis's fantasy of racial harmony. At a time of racial genocide, "A Faded Leaf" perpetuates a representation of America that dates back to the earliest engravings depicting explorers: an image of the New World as a voluptuous Indian woman.[29] But rather than invoke this popular trope in order to legitimize possession, Davis dialogically inscribes this sentimental figure in an anti-imperialist voice—ambivalent though it may be.

In "A Faded Leaf" Davis's representation of nature contests the traditional motif of a journey as a ritualized passage toward power, understanding, and growth. Her images of Florida's scorched beaches and humid swamps subvert Mary's regressive fantasy of pre-oedipal nurturance and intimacy, as well as Jonathan's masculine dream of patriarchal authority in the wilderness. Images of decay shape a premodernist wasteland that portends the false consciousness of Dickinson's vision of control. From the first, the land, seen from Mary's perspective, is hostile to their expansionist enterprise:

> It was a bleak, chilly afternoon as they toiled mile after mile along the beach, the Quaker woman far behind the others with her baby in her arms, carrying it, as she thought, to its death. Overhead, flocks of dark-winged grakles swooped across the lowering sky, uttering from time to time their harsh foreboding cry; shoreward, as far as the eye could see, the sand stretched in interminable yellow ridges, blackened here and there by tufts of dead palmetto-trees; while on the other side the sea had wrapped itself in a threatening silence and darkness. A line of white foam crept out of it from horizon to horizon, dumb and treacherous, and licked the mother's feet as she dragged herself heavily after the others. (366)

In effect, the mother and child enter the wilderness alone, figuratively behind the group of men. Suggestive of the forsaken wilderness of Exodus, the hot beach and the distant birds also mark the end of romantic exuberance. The inexorable sand and the dead palmettos, the source of food and of sheltering fronds to the Indians, serve as a pathetic fallacy suggestive of the bigoted inner life of the travelers and their public preoccupations. Framed by the narrator's promise of a story of "a baby and a boy and an aged man" (363), the trek along the hot sand marks the beginning of a pilgrimage; but when a woman undertakes such a life journey, she makes it not alone but in the company of a child. The perspectives of the female heroine and female narrator thus displace the conventional allegory of a voyage. Absent intimations of infinity in a Burkean sublime, Mary is a dwarfed and abandoned female figure who never aspires to transcendence.

Without the providential interpretations from Dickinson's original text, Davis's representation of nature suggests a Darwinian struggle for survival in the most bleak landscape to be found in all her oeuvre, a landscape that insists that nature will frustrate economic enterprise. The image of the abandoned woman on the barren beach, with the foreboding grackles flying overhead, mocks what David Miller terms the conservative "aesthetic desiderata" of the picturesque: unity, hierarchy, and collective continuity with the past.[30] Instead, Davis's image of migrating birds parodies the journey of the straggling travelers below. Unlike the picturesque, which promised the harmony of nature's parts in the presence of human associations, a facsimile of social and political harmony, the reemergence of the primal swamp on the travelers' flight from the Ais Indians suggests the political and psychic degeneration of their endeavor: "Once a tidal wave swept down into a vast marsh where they had built their fire, and air and ground slowly darkened with the swarming living creatures, whirring, creeping about them through the night, and uttering gloomy, dissonant cries" (370). The swamp, which resists the civilizing campfire, displaces the patriarchal urge to control or suppress a "female," "savage," or precivilized nature, traditionally the source of heretical and potentially anarchic meaning.[31] Nature, once the fruitful mother, turns into the withholding mother who threatens the hero with annihilation if he tries to establish his independence.[32] Thus, unlike the popular visual images of distant prospects of vastness and changing lights in paintings of the Hudson River School, controlled by the gaze of a viewer at the pictorial edge, Davis's travelers move through mysterious wet and dark swamps, by tradition dangerous and infected female spaces that challenge the sentimental quest for purity and the flight from death.

Richard Slotkin notes that even as captives tried to maintain their racial and cultural integrity in the wilderness, they sought to seize the power they believed was immanent in nature in order to renew themselves and the civilization they left behind.[33] Thus Dickinson reads the famine and desolation as a typological narrative—the dangerous swamps and the Native Americans who inhabit them offer him further opportunity to impose his preconceived interpretation of a redeeming God. Davis, by contrast, although still committed to inscribing accurate regional details, reads nature as an engendered political projection that frustrates Dickinson's interpretive paradigm. She inverts the regressive pattern of captivity narratives in which, typically, a man or woman unwillingly leaves society to enter what they believe to be a primitive world. In "A Faded Leaf," nature is no longer a place to recover childhood in the absence of history. Instead, nature condemns rather than redeems the present, undercutting Thoreau's vision of transcendental progress that subsumes the wilderness in an optimistic vision of unity. Davis finds no enduring regeneration in pastoralism—either for the individual or the state. This story calls into question the view of Barbara Novak, who argues that while Americans were coming to believe that Darwinian "savageries" could threaten the dream of an American paradise, they still believed that the national destiny could keep such "natural" energies at bay.[34]

As Davis feminizes the wilderness, and thereby renders nature valuable, vulnerable, and menacing (all at the same time), so too she feminizes the Native American—both man and woman. By identifying the Indian both with nature and with a female culture of nurturance and community, Davis's story of captivity offered the post–Civil War reader, whose country was engaged in the brutal slaughter and expulsion of Indians, an image of national identity that incorporates the Native American at a most fundamental ideological level.[35] Unlike captivity narratives of adaptation to Indian life, such as those by Mary Rowlandson and Frances Kelly, or of militant resistance to Indian violence, such as Hanna Dustin's or Mrs. Jemison's, "A Faded Leaf" fuses Mary's subject position as both colonial and colonizer. Through the sentimental vocabulary of gender, Davis positions the Indian as redemptive and hence culturally valuable. Thus in "A Faded Leaf," sentiment's insurgent voice parries with its complicitous voice in a complex story of difference and assimilation.

By consolidating the wilderness and the Native American as mutually engendered sites of exploration, exploitation, and conquest, Davis inscribes rather than effaces a narrative of cultural destruction. As the baby, now full of milk, kicks its legs under a bit of raw deerskin, the narrator comments, "Mother Nature had taken the child home, that was all, and was breathing new lusty life into it, out of the bare ground and open sky, the sun and wind, and the breasts of these her children" (369). Davis's domesticated image of mother earth–mother Indian recalls Thoreau's rejection of that common metaphor when he climbed Ktaadn Mountain:

> "Perhaps I most fully realized that this was primeval, untamed and forever untameable *Nature*. . . . Nature was here something savage and awful. . . . Man was not to be associated with it. . . . not his Mother Earth that we have heard of, not for him to tread on or be buried in,—no, it were being too familiar even to let his bones lie there. . . . It was a place for heathenism and superstitious rite,—to be inhabited by men nearer of kin to the rocks and to wild animals than we.[36]

Whereas Thoreau embraces a gendered image of nature as a witch (unworthy to tread on) in order to free himself from civilization, Davis pictures maternal primitivism as a return to the sanctuary of domesticity and community. Thus she challenges the midcentury view of the relationship between nature, nationalism, and the Native American, typified in Toqueville's "honest citizens" who announce, "This world here belongs to us. . . . God, in refusing the first inhabitants the capacity to become civilised, has destined them in advance to inevitable destruction. The true owners of this continent are those who know how to take advantage of its riches."[37] In feminizing the Native American, Davis, by contrast, confronts the tenet of manifest destiny that constructs the Indian as degenerate in order to view expansion as providential. As she parodies Dickinson's image of himself as a member of the chosen people of a superior race, an identity that served to disguise his economic goals, she points to the contradiction of an expanding democratic society that denies democracy to those who lived on its newly conquered lands.

William Truettner states that rarely do visual images of national expansion "openly advocate territorial expansion, commercial opportunity, or dispossession of native races. . . . Instead, they turn back the clock and present their arguments as part of a distant past, in which they gain time-honored legitimacy." To penetrate this "deceptive patina," he argues, the viewer must "doubt the authority of the past as well as the legitimacy of a political experiment held aloft as the premier American virtue."[38] In appropriating Dickinson's popular colonial captivity narrative and rescripting history from the point of view of the white woman and, allegedly, the Indian, Davis doubts the authority of the past so that she may question postbellum policies of expansionism. By writing through the early colonial perspective, she need not presume the victory of European civilization in the New World. Instead, Davis can question the "authority of history" by retelling the history of Native Americans through female icons; shelter, domesticity, orality, and the female breast emerge as fetishes in her revised rhetorics of expansion.

Davis's recurrent figure of a Native American woman nursing a baby summons a familiar image from paintings of expansion. In Peter Rothermel's *De Soto Discovering the Mississippi* (1843), for example, an Indian woman's naked breast, surrounded by light, is at the very center of the field of vision; the woman, bare to the waist, sits against an Indian man who gestures with an open arm, offering the land behind him to the explorers who tower over him. In Victor Nehlig's *Pocahontas and John Smith* (1870), the youthful breasts of a very pubescent Pocahontas again draw attention to the center of the painting, where the naked princess is interceding with an Indian who is about to club Smith to death, suggesting the conflation of the female body with the female power of rectitude and redemption. Rarely do we see brutality figured in a native woman. Instead, as in Emanuel Leutze's painting, *The Founding of Maryland* (1860), while the Indian and white men ratify a treaty on one side of the canvas, on the other side Indian women, still naked from the waist up, present trays of fruits and oysters to the colonizers. While an English woman reluctantly accepts a fruit, another naked Indian woman at the bottom of the frame points to a pile of dead game, an offering visually affiliated with the buxom and fecund native women—a graphic script analogous to "A Faded Leaf." As early as Benjamin West's *Penn's Treaty with the Indians* (1771–1772), as Penn presents cloth to the Indian men (whose arrows lie ignored at their feet), an Indian woman nurses her baby in the foreground. As in later paintings, unfinished houses occupy the background; the inevitability of civilization is conceptualized as a female trope, the house in the garden. Thus, domesticity shapes narratives of expansion by appropriating the ideology of female primitivism.

"A Faded Leaf of History" is a palimpsest, a revisionist captivity narrative that engages in an ambivalent dialogue with the genre's traditional conclusions about nature, nurture, and nationalism. By the 1860s and 1870s the captivity narrative had reemerged as a tremendously popular genre; Edward Ellis's *Seth Jones's or the Captives of the Frontier* (1860), for example, quickly sold 400,000 copies.[39] Yet the captivity narrative's recurrent motifs of confinement, separation, contamination, adaptation for survival, the breakup of a family, ambivalence about adoption, and female survival and adventure were tropes inherited from the domestic novel. Interestingly, these are the same literary strategies that shape the slave narrative. In contrast to such popular masculine texts, in "A Faded Leaf" two female voices, that of Mary's passive endurance and the narrator's articulate skepticism, put forward a decentered female subjectivity that refuses to be forged in opposition to the Native American man.

By repudiating Dickinson's popular text, Davis revokes Mary's symbolic function as the innocent victim of barbarous savagery—a trope also found in dime novel stories of Indian captivity, abuse, and rape popular in the 1870s, which strengthened the white male hero at the expense of a frail, childlike, and sexually vulnerable female captive.[40] "A Faded Leaf" calls into question familiar portraits of female victims who were viewed by Francis Parkman and George Bancroft as sacrificial "bit players" in the drama of conquest and progress.[41] In contrast to tales of rape in captivity narratives such as those of Caroline Harris and Clarissa Plummer in the 1830s, as well as popular contemporary tales of Moccasin Bill (1873), which titillated white audiences and played upon postwar fears of miscegenation, Davis refuses to portray Indian men as sexually dangerous. Of the two thousand captivity narratives that document the hardships of tens of thousands of white and Mexican captives, few directly address the issue of sexuality.[42] Recent scholarship has uncovered some instances of Indian rape, gang rape, and enslavement of white women, but scholars have found it difficult to establish just how common such acts were.[43] Anglo women were reticent about discussing sexual violation, and eastern tribal men generally showed little sexual interest in their female captives—apparently owing to ritual sexual abstinence in times of war, lack of interest in white women, and incest taboos in case a white woman were to be adopted into the tribe.[44]

Davis's representation of the Indian also differs from other mid-nineteenth-century captivity narratives in her treatment of violence. While Jonathan Dickinson was obsessed with his fears of cannibalism and Indian assault, Davis represents the Indians as nurturing and very concerned with feeding the castaways. Indeed, Davis omits the most violent episode in Dickinson's text, when the Jobese first encounter the shipwrecked party on the beach. Dickinson records that he was convinced that he had fallen "amongst a Barbarous people, such as were generally accounted *Man-Eaters.*" He recalls,

> These bloody minded Creatures placed themselves each behind one; . . . the *Casseekey* had placed himself behind me, standing on the Chest which I sat upon, they all having their Arms extended with their knives in their hands, ready to execute their bloody design, some taking hold of some of us by the heads with their knees set against our shoulders. (30)

Because the Lord fortuitously intervened, the "savages" fell silent, forgot about white scalps, and became involved in ransacking the trunks from the boat. Davis's omission of this passage questions the popular narrative's tendency to gothicize, to control the reader by stimulating fear.

Davis's title itself, "A Faded Leaf of History," is a self-deprecating comment on the ancient text that her narrator has discovered. Seen through the experience of the baby, the tale culminates in the refugees' final passage northward. If in Cooper's tales the Indian is the occasion for moral growth of the white man, here it is the baby who transforms all fellow travelers. "Savage or slave or beast were his friends alike, his laugh and outstretched hands were ready for them all" (370). Through his totemizing power as sentimental innocent, the baby transforms the Indians, the slaves, and the local animals into one homogenized and safe *other*. Reiterating the conflation of gender and race, Davis's narrator observes, speaking for the first time as a mother,

> It makes a mother's heart ache even now to read how these coarse, famished men, often fighting like wild animals with each other, staggering under weakness and bodily pain, carried the heavy baby, never complaining of its weight, thinking, it may be, of some child of their own whom they would never see or touch again. (370)

Contact with the baby, rather than the experience of captivity and wilderness, transforms all men:

> A gentler, kindlier spirit seemed to come from the presence of the baby and its mother to the crew; so that, while at first they had cursed and fought their way along, they grew at the last helpful and tender with each other. (371)

In other words, the baby makes the men act like women.

Nonetheless, in the end, the discourse of sentiment and the ideology it espouses cannot thwart the corrupt inevitability of patriarchy and imperialism, pictured in the figure of the unredeemed father whose beliefs will triumph in the construction of American nationhood. The lost band is finally tracked by a Spanish scout from St. Augustine, who has heard of the infant in the shipwrecked party. Hence "through the baby that deliverance came to them at last" (371). Recalling that along the way all the men have been willing to give their lives for the baby, the narrator discovers that she can now "understand better the mystery of that Divine Childhood that was once in the world" (371). In April 1697, the family sailed into the raw settlement town of Philadelphia in an arrival that suggests the restoration of patriarchy and the inevitability of civilization. Reminiscent of midcentury paintings of conquest in which Indian wigwams abut colonists' houses under construction, the Dickinsons find that many settlers in Pennsylvania are still living in caves, but the village's "one or two streets of mud-huts and curious low stone houses" (373) will soon frame and contain the wilderness.

At home in Philadelphia, according to Davis, Jonathan Dickinson "closed his righteous gates thereafter on aught that was alien or savage." He "became a power in the new principality," remembered mainly for his "strict rule as mayor, his stately equipages and vast estates" (373). Mary, whose breast milk returns once she is back in civilization, is restored to her previous domestic status and her limited capacity to act; in her new home she "nursed her baby, and clothed him in soft fooleries again." Yet the narrator refuses to investigate what happened to the baby and decides to atrophy him in eternal infancy. Insisting on his divine role, she concludes: "I will not believe that he ever grew to be a man, or died. He will always be to us simply a baby; a live, laughing baby, sent by his Master to the desolate places of the earth with the old message of Divine love and universal brotherhood to his children" (373). The images of maternalism and childlike natives and the anticipation of white civilization eclipse the narrative of the Indian; nonetheless, Davis refuses to let the baby become a civilized adult, complicitous with the reign of a powerful father.

Gayatri Spivak writes that "the discourse of man is in the metaphor of woman."[45] In rewriting Dickinson's popular captivity narrative, Davis appropriates a central masculine paradigm of contemporary westward expansion in order to question both its public and private ideologies. At the same time, she reiterates the convention that romanticized colonial space; Indian land is still a utopian site that projects the fantasies and needs of colonizers. This invented landscape permits the fulfillment of a desire to possess land and people, which become one. Like other Euro-American women, Davis presumed, in Caroll Smith-Rosenberg's phrase, "the right to write" the story of conquest, and thus inevitably she too appropriated the right to "represent a white America," assuming the "dominant male discourses of imperialism and social order."[46]

The white captive appropriates the role of mediator between native and white civilization; as a female, she presumes an affiliation with both worlds. Yet even though "A Faded Leaf" ends in a utopian moment of redemptive

Christianity, a metaphor that allows for a humanist belief in the realization of progress, it recasts the narrative of colonial captivity and conquest in relation to patterns of history that Davis views as ongoing. The autobiographical nature of the captivity narrative gave Davis a form that made the private world public, just as it positioned white men as agents of history which they fail to understand. In this story of colonization, Davis again tells a sentimental story of involuntary enclosure. Like her earlier stories, "A Faded Leaf of History" describes how a female subject—whether slave, woman writer, or abandoned mother—attempts to fantasize community. Thus, the power of Davis's story derives from her reworking of the heroic conventions of the captivity narrative in terms of her assumption that women exist both inside and outside public history. By rescripting the captivity narrative as a story of female–Native American dispossession, Davis questions the legitimacy of the narrative perspective within the form itself. Through a parody of the genre, Davis repudiates the activities that prompt it. "A Faded Leaf of History" questions the captivity narrative's very act of claiming historicity.

8 ❦ The Politics of Nature

"The Yares of Black Mountain"

By 1875 it was clear that radical Reconstruction was coming to an end. To justify abandoning the post–Civil War goal of political equality for freed slaves, the North needed to reinvent southern history, indeed, to reinvent the South. Revised cultural representations of southerners—in plantation novels, vernacular fiction, and minstrelsy—provided northern readers one way to ignore lynchings and racist voting restrictions, and to sanction the withdrawal of northern troops from the South. Another way was through modifed representations of the South itself. Depictions of the American landscape have always been a trope for cultural nationalism.[1] In the mid-nineteenth century, images of nature, writes Angela Miller, "proffered a sense of national identity in the absence of shared race history."[2] But traditionally the invented harmonious landscape is devoid of artifacts of human life, human labor, and human history. And any landscape that appears "empty" allows for social definition, invites political intervention, and promises passivity.

In "The Yares of Black Mountain" (1875),[3] however, Rebecca Harding Davis populates and politicizes the southern landscape, exposing aesthetic constructs that invited either hegemonic or solipsistic reactions to the South. The story concerns a young Civil War widow from New York City who travels to the Blue Ridge Mountains of North Carolina in hopes of healing her sickly baby in the high pine forests, only to discover, once there, a matriarchal family of Civil War resistance fighters. In this story Davis suggests that, like the widow, the industrial North depends on the rural South for healing and political renewal. Davis's literary strategy works, however, only because she has erased slavery as the source of American sectionalism. Reunion and reconciliation, she suggests, will arise from a new understanding of southern place and from a recognition of southern women as rebellious, matriarchal, communitarian, natural, and pro-North.

The story begins as a group of northern tourists arrive at the end of a railroad line thirty miles from Asheville, North Carolina. "Civilization stops here, it appears" (292), remarks an industrialist from Detroit. This is a false appearance, however, as the travelers are immediately welcomed into a hospitable rural community. Even so, most of the tourists are disappointed by what they see. The mountains, they find, offer neither inspiration nor industry—the "cloud-effects" lack "the element of grandeur" (292–93) of the White Mountains, and a speculator from Detroit—a postlapsarian industrialist, to be sure—finds the balsam lumber so spongy that "a snake couldn't get his living out of ten acres of it" (292). Even the travelers' fantasy of venison cooked over an open campfire is frustrated by the "civilized beastliness" of greasy fried food in a local barroom, where "a fly-blown print of the 'Death of Robert E. Lee'" hangs on the wall (293); insistently, the Civil War brackets this study of the sylvan picturesque.

In "The Yares of Black Mountain" Davis explores cultural archetypes that convert the wilderness into economic and cultural raw material. One of the tourists, a female journalist mockingly named Miss Cook, has come to the southern highlands to collect material for her book, *The Causes of Decadence in the Old South*. Miss Cook represents Davis's pointed (and perhaps self-reflexive) critique of the female local colorist, an outsider who reduces the complexity of southern history to the sketch or tall tale. In Asheville, after Miss Cook has made a quick tour of the four local "emporiums," the village jail, the "quaint decaying houses, the swarming blacks" (299), she purchases a package of photographic postcards from which to draw the sketches for her book. Echoing the sentiment of James Fenimore Cooper and others who bemoaned the absence of the American picturesque, Miss Cook concludes

that the villagers "would be picturesque, dirt and all, under a Norman peasant's coif and red umbrella, but in a dirty calico wrapper—bah!" (295).
Satisfied that in one morning she has "done the mountains and moun-
taineers" (299) and has found nothing to write about, she announces that
she is moving on to Georgia. Through this figure of a female author, Davis
writes about the act of writing about nature. Unlike Davis, whose works
present closely observed and well-researched details of the geological, botanical, and social life of the southern mountains, the fictional journalist claims,
"I can evolve the whole state of society from half a dozen items. I have the
faculty of generalizing, you see" (299).[4] There is no doubt that Miss Cook
will produce a manufactured and mythologized landscape that conforms to
popular aesthetic conventions—partly because, as she confesses, she has quite
forgotten to ask the local inhabitants about their views on the Civil War, a
portentous omission.

Interestingly, none of these middle-class visitors has come south to in-
dulge in the conspicuous consumption of landscape for its own sake, what
Robert Bredeson calls the era's aesthetic "badge of status,"[5] because, as Davis
notes in her own southern travel studies, "By-Paths in the Mountains" and
"Here and There In the Old South,"[6] the postwar southern landscape had
not gained the status of other emerging tourist destinations. Yosemite, for
example, was "discovered" in 1851 after the Mariposa Battalion pursued a
group of Miwok and Piute Native Americans into the valley. Sensing the
commercial possibilities in its "wild and sublime grandeur," writer and publisher James Mason Hutchings quickly recruited artist Thomas Ayres and
photographer Charles Leander Weed to attract groups of tourists. Hutchings
promptly published their conditioned observations, such as "'What! . . .
have we come to the end of all things? . . . Can this be the opening of the
Seventh Seal?'"[7] "The Yares of Black Mountain" was the first of a series of
studies in which Davis calls attention to the economic and tourist possibilities of the South.

Davis sought to recapture the aesthetic and moral sympathies of northern readers by describing a northern woman's discovery of the power of
southern female voice and female activity. For Davis, the allure of the Appalachians is not the enchantment of the sublime. Mrs. Denby, the young widow,
rejects the voyeuristic gaze of the overwhelmed tourists as she locates the

social in the natural, a cultural recovery that emphasizes human actions over spiritual resolutions. Dismissing the fearful rumor repeated by Miss Cook that the Ku Klux Klan is terrorizing the area and her warning that the "mountains are inaccessible to women" (292), the widow leaves the village of Asheville to go deeper into the mountains in the oxcart of a trapper named Jonathan Yare. Parodying the lone male traveler of literary convention who leaves civilization (read *women*) in his quest for adventure in an eroticized frontier, Mrs. Denby also enters the high wilderness with a guide; and Jonathan, true to mythic convention, turns out to be more than what he seems. However, unlike a panoramist, who looks at nature from a high place in order to "take in a large stretch of open country and remain outside of nature, master of what he observes,"[8] Mrs. Denby sees herself as a domestic intruder: "She had come unbidden into Nature's household and interrupted the inmates talking together" (301). Rejecting the perspective of a master or hunter, she discovers that nature is a site of verbal domesticity.

As Mrs. Denby and her baby travel by oxcart higher into the mountains, Davis explores a series of cultural tropes: romantic perceptions of nature as the eroticized female, sublime and masculine visions of nature's dangerous wildness, and ultimately, allegorical images of nature as a female sanctuary. Leaving the village behind, the widow first sees the mountains as a beckoning virgin: "The very earth seemed to blush. . . . The tupelo thrust its white fingers out of the shadow like a maiden's hand" (301), the flowers reminiscent of the sensual orchids and hummingbirds of contemporary colorist Martin Johnson Heade. These erotic tupelo flowers mark the sensual appeal of southern flora as female. But as Mrs. Denby "penetrates" (302) the higher summits of the Appalachians, nature as seductress evolves into nature as a mother figure; the enticing heights become the "the nursery or breeding-place" of all the mountains that wall the eastern coast (302). And at midday Jonathan, the rugged trapper, finds fresh milk for the baby by catching and milking a wild cow because the city-bred mother's milk has run dry.

Paralleling the shift in Mrs. Denby's perception from nature as sexual to nature as maternal, enclosing, and protective, is the deconstructive shift from images of nature as luminous and sublime to those representing nature as companionable and familiar.[9] Initially, the widow sees that "the sun was out of sight in a covered, foreboding sky, and black ragged fragments of cloud from some approaching thunderstorm were driven now and then across the horizon" (301). The sublime, quite typically, dislocates Mrs. Denby from her worldly affiliation, defamiliarizes her, and makes her receptive to a female story of the symbiosis of land and politics. Yet Davis immediately subverts the romantic sublimity of panoramic vistas characteristic of painters such as Thomas Cole, Frederick E. Church, and Albert Bierstadt. In the tradition of Washington Irving and James Fenimore Cooper, many contemporary artists depicted the sublime as a frightening lesson in cosmic moralism—what Howard Mumford Jones calls "the majesty of deity, the wildness of nature, the littleness of man":

> How was pygmy man not merely to subdue the wilderness but also found an enduring republic? Landscape could teach him that he might be, and frequently was, at the mercy of great natural forces, yet if he would but penetrate into the beauty and harmony of the whole, if he would set himself to understand the dynamism of the world, all, under God, might go well.[10]

Davis usurps the high romantic iconography of the sublime landscape to feminize it:

> The road, if road you chose to call it, crept along beside the little crystal-clear Swannanoa River, and persisted in staying beside it, sliding over hills of boulders, fording rushing mountain-streams and dank snaky swamps, digging its way along the side of sheer precipices, rather than desert its companion. The baby's mother suddenly became conscious that the river was a companion to whom she had been talking and listening for an hour or two. (301)

Mrs. Denby, the figure in the foreground, repudiates the overwhelming wrath of the Burkean sublime that conventionally emphasizes the terror of nature, the helplessness of humanity, and the precariousness of civilization in a world in which traditional meanings are jeopardized.[11] The widow's trip up the mountain involves not a male quest for absolute meaning but a female quest for a communal animism that is both material and psychological.[12] In this more mundane view of nature, Davis is closer to the realism of Winslow Homer's paintings, which frequently depict a large central female figure at work in the wilderness, than to the immense canvasses of Frederic Church, which typically picture a tiny male viewer, dwarfed at the pictorial edge of a magnificent, sublime, and symbolic wildness.

Through Mrs. Denby's trip into the higher peaks of the Appalachians, Davis punctures a romantic moment of awe and melancholy to rescript the oedipal plot, to foreshadow the movement from isolation to maternal community, from solitary adulthood to childlike dependence, from loneliness to intimacy—hence, from a male to a female way of viewing nature. During the 1870s, contemporary landscape emphasized the distant prospect, with a natural hierarchy of elements moving *from* an inhabited foreground *to* heaven,[13] signifying either a topos of harmony (the picturesque) or an expression of divinely instituted authority (the sublime). By contrast, through the image of the loquacious river, Davis deconstructs the figure of the lone tourist dwarfed by the glorious silence of nature. The companionable river, traditionally a feminized symbol in any case, leads Mrs. Denby to a filthy and rugged hut, the home of Jonathan's mother, who warmly welcomes the widow and her baby. The widow's voyage into the wilderness is in essence a trip home, back to mother and her landscape of gendered political resistance.

At this point, Mistress Yare takes over the narration to tell Mrs. Denby the real story behind the legend, the "terrible history" of the Yare family. The linearity and chronology of Mrs. Denby's quest and her false assumption that "human nature could reach no lower depths of squalor and ignorance" (303) than she first perceives in the filthy cabin, collapses as Mistress Yare (rather like Mrs. Todd, the narrator of Sara Orne Jewett's "The Foreigner," 1900), relates the family saga. While old Mr. Yare tells Mrs. Denby stories of bear and panther hunts—that is, tales of his own heroism, Mistress Yare tells of a mountain woman's courageous loyalty to the North during the Civil War. The Yare sons, she explains, had refused to join the Army of the Confederacy. Along with her daughter Nancy, they spent the war years serving as mountain guides, leading both southern deserters and Union soldiers who had escaped from the brutal prisons at Andersonville and Salisbury across icy mountain gorges to the safety of the Federal lines in Tennessee. Northern readers would vividly remember the brutality of Andersonville and Salisbury, the Confederate prison in North Carolina where, by 1864, 10,000 destitute prisoners huddled in tents or burrowed into the earth in mud huts, and where, between October 1864 and February 1865, 3,500 prisoners died.

As Nancy participated in the liberation of northern soldiers, one of whom could have been Mrs. Denby's late husband, she took on the traditionally male capacity to move widely in geographical space. Yet these deeds were not performed at the expense of her traditionally domestic role, as she also worked with her mother to maintain the Yare hut as a refuge for Confederate deserters headed North. Most heroically, when one of her brothers was wounded on the mountain, Nancy evaded the Confederate soldiers and, on her own, built a log cabin to hide and shelter him in the frozen woods— thereby reappropriating the image of the house as a political space. Eventually Nancy was captured and jailed in Asheville (ironically, in the jail Miss Cook plans to expose in her writing), where the Rebels threatened to hang her unless she disclosed her brother's whereabouts. She was saved only by the announcement of General Lee's surrender and the end of the war.

Through the story of Nancy Yare, Davis liberates nature from the discourses of the ideal, the discourses of northern domination, and the discourses of female irrationality. By appropriating nature as a sign of female resistance and orality, Davis peoples and historicizes the southern landscape. "The Yares of Black Mountain" resists the inference, noted by Howard Mumford Jones, "that American writing cannot be rich and full because the American landscape lacks historical, feudal, medieval . . . or family associations."[14] In "The Yares of Black Mountain" the vernacular is no longer a "metonomy for a folk culture,"[15] in Sandra Zagarell's phrase, but rather a realistic, accurate, and detailed construction of a particularized moment of national reconciliation situated domestically and geographically.

In the end, overwhelmed by the Yares' rural poverty and the story of their postwar ostracism, Mrs. Denby urges the family to move to the North, where they will be rewarded for their loyalty and service to the northern cause. Mrs. Yare, however, refuses: "It must be powerful lonesome in them flat countries, with nothing but people about you. The mountings is company always, you see" (309). Thus Mrs. Denby discovers that the true intimacy of nature transcends social relations. She has also come to understand that nature and female speech transcend class: "These were the first human beings whom she had ever met between whom and herself there came absolutely no bar of accident—no circumstance of social position or clothes or education: they were the first who could go straight to something in her beneath all these things" (304).

Yet for Davis, nature cannot transcend racial difference. Unlike her anti-slavery stories from the 1860s, such as "John Lamar," "Blind Tom," and her early Reconstruction novel *Waiting for the Verdict* (1867), "The Yares of Black Mountain," written during the decline of Reconstruction in the 1870s, shows that the telos of community hinges on the repudiation of race. While Mrs. Denby, "a violent abolitionist in her day," insists that the Yare sons should have joined the Federal Army to help free the slaves, Mistress Yare explains that her sons simply could not "turn agen the old flag" (304). She then adds, "We never put much vally on the blacks, that's the truth. We couldn't argy or jedge whether slavery war wholesomest for them or not. It was out of our sight" (305). Such racial invisibility would soon allow the demise of Reconstruction in the North. Indeed, given the enduring political and economic inequality of African Americans in the South, this erasure of racial awareness became one of the unspoken terms on which national reconciliation would proceed.

Through the figures of Jenny and Nancy, Davis reconfigures the romantic hero. As Harold Bloom notes, although the intent of a quest is to widen consciousness as well as to intensify it, a romantic journey is inevitably "shadowed by a spirit that tends to narrow consciousness to an acute preoccupation with self."[16] In the conventional romantic resolution, the Promethean hero finally stands "quite alone, upon a tower that is only himself, and his stance is all the fire there is."[17] Mrs. Denby, by contrast, in forging political, female, and verbal reconciliation, locates the unity of the self and the social. Ending her story inside a female house rather than upon a phallic tower, Davis claims that engagement rather than isolation forges identity.

Like many women authors writing in the mid-nineteenth century, Rebecca Harding Davis inherited from her literary models a sentimental critique of America's passage from a decentralized agrarian life to life under industrial capitalism. Davis, however, rejects sentiment's generalized and nostalgic view, a view aligned with contemporary romanticism, that the preindustrial or nonindustrial world offers a natural home in an earlier moment of economic development. Unlike popular domestic images that sever rural life from urban life, Davis's fiction deconstructs evocations of nature as a place where women can find meaning and where men can avoid society. Nature is not the safe spot that Annette Kolodny finds in the fictions of

Alice Cary, where Eve may cultivate her New England garden.[18] Instead, Davis pictures the dangers of rural life that are disguised in ideologies of nostalgia, be they romantic, sentimental, or southern: the growth of industries in mountain towns in West Virginia, hardships in fishing villages on the Jersey coast, or the brutal mountain battles of the Civil War.

Davis's stories of isolated Delaware fishermen, of "wrakers" who scrounge for the salvage from wrecked sailing ships, of impoverished women in coastal villages compelled to take in rude tourists as boarders, suggest that life close to nature promises neither nurture, abundance, nor unalienated labor. At times, her lonely female characters succumb to the fantasies Kolodny locates in women's journals, records of visions of a harmonious natural space where they might find a maternal and feminine presence, an enclosing receptive environment that will offer painless satisfaction.[19] But for the most part, Davis deconstructs images of nature as a female respite from adult responsibility, and she questions voyages that recapture the primal warmth of womb or breast in an abundant, tempting, if vulnerable, landscape of filial homage and erotic desire.[20] Nature is not a simple pastoral "home" for Davis; nor are her rural women unauthorized presences in landscapes to which they do not belong.[21]

In the famous conclusion to "Nature," Emerson exhorts, "Know then, that the world exists for you."[22] Davis, by contrast, rejects the masculinity of transcendentalism, which sees nature as an occasion for the individual mind to discover a reflection of itself, and ultimately, God. She also rejects the mechanistic masculinity of the Enlightenment that sees the wilderness as a repugnant space wherein human beings live mean and savage lives, a primitive space needing urban intervention and control.[23] Instead, Davis sees in nature the dialectic of matter and consciousness, the dialectic of matter and social history. In "The Yares of Black Mountain," she distrusts the modernist task, the Protestant duty, and the rational responsibility to understand and harness nature, to transform the wilderness, in particular the southern wilderness—into another industrialized northern civilization from which Mrs. Denby has so recently fled. Questioning the mountains as a topos for aesthetic reassurance or psychological domination, Davis confronts the era's profound homocentrism, stimulated on the one hand by transcendentalism and on the other by the discoveries and demands of industrial capitalism.[24]

Emerging ideologies of territorial and economic conquest encouraged northerners to think that nature had a duty to satisfy their financial aspirations,
political disillusion, and aesthetic hunger. If New York is the place where, as
Mrs. Denby observes, "we came strangers, and were always strangers" (297),
Black Mountain, read through the hermeneutics of female community and
pictured through the acts of female storytelling, reveals nature as a space of
female interdependence, communication, and balanced reciprocity, rather
than as a site for man's dominion over all living things.

In "Life in the Iron-Mills," the narrator, a middle-class spinster, remarks,
"The dream of green fields and sunshine is a very old dream—almost worn
out, I think."[25] Almost. The narrator identifies her arid intellectual and sexual life with the suffocation of urban poverty in a raw factory town. To condemn a culture of urban and male individualism, she blends a sentimental
appeal to feminine sympathy with images of industrial pollution. After Deb,
a hunchback spinner in a textile mill, serves three years in jail for theft, she
flees into the hills to live with the Quakers, "pure and meek . . . more silent
than they, more humble, more loving" (33). Like the lonely narrator, Deb
ends up "waiting: with her eyes turned to hills higher and purer than these
on which she lives" (33). A silent woman dressed in gray, she suggests the ultimate failure of industrial desire. In one sense, rural life implies ascetic self-
denial to these two women, both figures of female endurance; it subsumes
the story's political thrust by emerging as a metaphor for eternal life. On the
one hand, nature is regenerative and available as a fantasized abandonment of
urban history. On the other, because Davis so often praised the Quakers as
engaged social activists in the movements for abolition and prison reform
and wrote of their rural communities as stations on the underground railroad, the ending of "Life in the Iron-Mills" anticipates Davis's suggestion in
"The Yares of Black Mountain" that a life lived in nature offers the possibility of attachment, continuity, and fusion. From the outset of her literary
career, Davis saw the environment as a determining and feminist element in
her social vision. Region—its botanical features, weather, local history, landscape, dialect, dress, and the economics of place—joins social class and gender to shape character and consciousness in her fiction.

Other compelling stories of rural life, mostly written in the 1870s, also
challenge the romantic idea that through intuition and reflection, one can

participate in an organic encounter with nature. Davis's knowledge of country life was rooted in her childhood in the mountains of West Virginia, her frequent trips to a farm in Manasquan on the barren New Jersey coast, and in her travels in the South. Her informed intelligence about botany, geology, and climate does not lead to descriptions of plants or storms, for example, that exemplify Emersonian universals. Instead, her stories are much closer in intention to the writing of Henry David Thoreau, who argued that a "true man of science . . . will know nature better by his finer organization; he will smell, taste, see, hear, feel, better than other men. His will be a deeper and finer experience."[26] Davis similarly sought to reintegrate industrial consciousness through contact with the knowable natural world. Informed yet unmediated experiences in nature encourage social and political understanding. And feminist understanding. For Davis, the urban visitor to the wilderness is neither scientist, naturalist, proto-Indian, nor aesthete, but one who learns to understand that the cultural impositions on the natural world are polluting, hegemonic, homocentric, masculinist, and ultimately, antisocial.

Thus Davis refused to divorce nature from society and explored the economic and technological links between the country and the city, always grounding her rural tales in local history. In "David Gaunt" she pictures the ravishment of the land during the Civil War; in "Out of the Sea" she refers to the immoral role of insurance companies in shipwrecks; in *Dallas Galbraith* she describes how mining has ravished the land; in "Earthen Pitchers" she sees land as a female property right and also as a dangerous symbol of desire that women must conquer and domesticate; in "The House on the Beach" (1876) she describes financial pressures to build lighthouses along the Jersey shore and explains how inventions for predicting the weather united rural communities across the country; and in her late study, "In the Grey Cabins of New England" she describes how men have abandoned the barren land, leaving the women similarly forsaken.

Davis rejected the metaphor in which nature is to culture as female is to male[27] because she believed that the female telos resides in the cultural as well as in the natural world. In this she anticipates and shapes American regionalism. Nature to Davis is neither presocial or oceanic. Rather, her images of the city and the country, civilization and wilderness, mind and body, expose how culture has shaped our perception of nature as simple, static, and continuous. Political, economic, and cultural relationships between city and country do signify relationships between men and women, but Davis resists the essentialist view that nature and woman are mutually vulnerable and available to human intervention, control, or even definition.

As L. J. Jordanova reminds us, any distinction that poses woman as natural and man as cultural inevitably appeals to ideas about female biology.[28] Davis's stories of rural life challenge an essentialist analogy whereby women and nature are both seen as fertile, backward, ignorant, and innocent. Neither woman nor nature is a repository of morality. Not even a rural woman, such as Mistress Yare, can completely transcend or escape culture. Nonetheless, because for Davis civilization is rational, exploitative, dominating, and competitive, it is often her metaphor for masculinity. As early as "Life in the Iron-Mills," the struggle between the sexes took on a historical dimension; the power and pollution of the industrial North exemplified the rise of American civilization through domination of nature and, at the same time, represented the realization of masculine ways of being that women should resist.[29]

Thus Davis's stories undermine the widespread view in American literary criticism that women's regional writings of the late nineteenth century were emasculated tales produced by "'New England spinsters . . . driven to extremes of nostalgic fantasy' about 'imaginary pasts.'"[30] Caroline Gebhard shows that as early as 1919, the *Nation* announced that women's local color stories revealed a "triviality of observation . . . connected with [a] strongly, often stiflingly domestic atmosphere,"[31] immured, Santayana would add, from the "rough passions of life."[32] Wallace Stegner similarly notes, "As a group, [female local colorists] avoided the commonplace, concerned themselves chiefly with the unusual, were incurably romantic, obsessed with the picturesque, and accurate only to the superficial aspects of their chosen materials."[33] Annette Kolodny argues that if a woman writer who lived on or visited the frontier saw it as the metaphorical landscape of someone else's imagination, she could not locate herself in nature.[34] To feminize the frontier, she would confine herself to an "innocent amusement of a garden's narrow space" and welcome with equanimity the disappearance of primal wild spaces.[35] Ann Douglas likewise finds women local colorists to be "paranoid and claustrophobic."[36]

Rebecca Harding Davis, however, projected onto nature a vast imagined territory, a fantasized landscape of gendered values. She seems to have avoided not only the colonizing female tropes that Kolodny identifies, but also several recurrent male constructions of nature—as the place of a brutal exodus to an unpromising land, as the eroticized site of violent conquest, and as a source of guilt for its destruction. Surely she holds a unique position in the tradition of female regionalists, who were urged on by a succession of editors of the *Atlantic* who between 1857 and 1898 promoted a realist aesthetic that could depict authentic local details. Men such as Davis's early mentor, James Fields, and later James Russell Lowell, William Dean Howells, Thomas Bailey Aldrich, and Horace Scudder, sought an American literature that would debunk overgeneralized descriptions, essentialist characterizations, and the pastoral nostalgia of sentiment,[37] and they called this new prose local color. Among the authors of this emerging literature, Davis shares the grim antipatriarchal indictments of Rose Terry Cooke, the ironic ambivalence about matriarchal pastoralism of Mary E. Wilkins Freeman, the early class consciousness of Elizabeth Stuart Phelps, and the close observation of southern botany, geology, and dialect found in later regional writers such as Mary Murphy and Constance Fenimore Woolson.

As a realist, Davis alters the pastoral landscape—which is not to say, as Roger Stein wryly reminds us, that nature doesn't still "mean."[38] She repopulates arcadia with intelligent and competent female figures, empiricists who survive through their knowledge of tides, herbs, clouds, rock formations, and the dangers of storms, quicksand, and rural marriage. Abandoning the traditional female narrative of seduction and betrayal, romance and marriage, Davis describes the realities of rural family life centered around shared projects of agrarian and domestic work. With their survival itself imperiled by droughts, blizzards, war, and an encroaching industrial culture, Davis's rural women are frequently impoverished, lonely, sexually repressed, and intellectually frustrated.

In order to portray rural life and nature itself as a female community, Davis recasts the rhetorics of romanticism. In her stories situated on the Jersey shore, in the Appalachian Mountains, and on barren New England farms, nature emerges through images of dependence rather than autonomy, intimacy rather than isolation, speech rather than the silent awe of the sublime. The female traveler cannot remain a voyeur or outsider and finds, through whatever natural epiphany the plot provides, an organicism in nature. She also finds a voice. To the degree that Davis pictures nature as maternal, it motivates her heroines not through a quest for conquest but through a quest for transcendent recognition of their own identity.

In Simone de Beauvoir's words, "For the woman [writer] who has not fully abdicated, nature represents what woman herself represents for man: herself and her negation, a kingdom and a place of exile: the whole in the guise of the other."[39] It is in this feminist sense of transcendence that Davis builds on the narcissism of romanticism. By submission to natural law and the growth of a friendship with a rural woman, Mrs. Denby, a city dweller, recognizes the possibility of intimacy and allows the dissolution of ego.

Thus, through the voice of Mistress Yare, Davis shifts the story of "The Yares of Black Mountain" from an emblematic to a realist social narrative, undercutting Mrs. Denby's early impressions that equate women with nature. While in the narrator's text, she identifies with nature as female, immanent, communal, and available, in Mistress Yare's text nature refuses to become an object of tourist enjoyment, moral instruction, isolation, or even inspiration. Nancy emerges as an autonomous rural subject who lives within and works on nature to shape her rebellious deeds. In this matriarchal text, nature is populated and politicized. Mistress Yare's narrative thus signifies the mediation of a woman rather than the representation of a woman as nature. Although at first Mrs. Denby assumes that contemporary southerners are still "churlish and bitter" (298) as a result of their defeat in the war, ultimately, it is Mistress Yare's story, as much as the balsam air, that heals the female traveler and promises national reconciliation.

The "Yares of Black Mountain" opens as the northern travelers debate how to experience and interpret nature—for amusement, profit, instruction, inspiration, or healing. Mocking the taste for the picturesque through her portrait of Miss Cook, and then deconstructing the magnificent subjectivity of the sublime in Mrs. Denby's oxcart ride up the mountain, Davis suggests that the real meaning of nature lies in its connection with history and its role in forming true communities. Mistress Yare debunks the rumors of the untold tale of the "terrible history of the Yares" and tells Mrs. Denby a story of the complex actions of rural people who are defined in and through the land as political territory. A romantic attachment between the widow and one of the rugged mountain sons is never an issue. Instead, Mrs. Denby is rewarded with the female grail, an intimate relationship with a mother figure who can tell a great story. Her passage into the southern mountains from in her lonely apartment in New York City suggests a daughter's return. However, Black Mountain would not qualify as a "female pastoral" as defined by Gail David: "a place out of time associated with recollections of edenic childhood and fantasies of eternal paradise . . . nurturant, festive, and leisurely."[40] Instead, Mrs. Denby's quest for healing has led her to sympathetic engagement with a woman who teaches her the priority of history over allegory, struggle over escape, and the intimacy of women's narrative. Hence, the telos of her quest into the wilderness is not the inscription of the heroic and indomitable self,[41] but the discovery of female community achieved through female au/orality that is, in itself, about community.

In "The Yares of Black Mountain," Davis describes the disjunction between the perceived images and the historical meanings of the South. As a geographical metaphor for the realization of freedom, she replaces the nation's traditional cultural movement from east to west with a movement from north to south. Through her representation of the southern wilderness, of rural communities in North Carolina, and, in particular, of southern womanhood, Davis erodes the patriarchal-industrial assumption that nature, like the South itself, is primitive, knowable, and separate from culture. "The Yares of Black Mountain" repudiates the emerging view whereby the North sentimentalizes southern history in order to force a premature reconciliation between the defeated Confederacy and the industrializing Union. By including the story of wartime resistance on Black Mountain, the southern Appalachians join the Connecticut River and Hudson River Valleys as natural sites that characterize America.[42] "The Yares of Black Mountain" thereby resists the literary politics of appeasement currently emerging in such journals as *Lippincott's, Harper's,* and the *Atlantic Monthly.*

In this story, the radical role of nature thus counters the hegemonic view of landscape that one sees, for example, in Frederic Church's *Rainy Season in the Tropics* (1866), a painting described by Angela Miller as "adamantly national, employing an imagery of plunging spaces, grandly scaled distances, and scenery aglow with the light of the spirit, [whose] central event is the rainbow, symbol of the renewed national covenant interrupted by the war."[43]

In contrast to Church's archetypal conventions, Davis roots her narrative of reconciliation in detailed particularities of place and region. In "The Yares of Black Mountain," nature suggests neither the utopian telos of Church's national covenant, nor the pastoral regression of William Dean Howells's anti-industrial Altruria.

For Davis, nature belongs in the discourse of realism. If we compare the titles of Emerson's "Nature," Thoreau's *Walden,* and Davis's "The Yares of Black Mountain," they themselves bespeak the progression I am delineating: from the abstract to the particular to the communal. Rather like Winslow Homer's representations of fisherwomen, Davis's story deconstructs the American sublime by inserting the feminized hut and inscribing the rebellious story of Nancy Yare. Yet, paradoxically, Davis's representation of nature also supports those cultural representations—humorous tales, local color stories, sentimental fictions, plantation novels, and transcendental landscapes that offered justifications for abandoning radical Reconstruction and restoring the national bond between North and South. In a story written as radical Reconstruction was about to fall apart, Davis's unifying cultural symbol is the figure of the southern mother. Reconciliation need not hinge on repression, nostalgia, romanticism, or the collapse of localism. Nor need it rely on accepting racial equality. Instead, nature will provide a realm of power that can, through female sympathy and orality, stimulate affection, nationalism, and social responsibility.

9 ❧ To Be, to Do, and to Suffer

The New Woman

By the late 1860s, the marriage within sentimentalism that brought together a democratic rhetoric about social change and an evangelical claim about female nature had disintegrated in the writings of Rebecca Harding Davis. In stories such as "A Second Life" and "Paul Blecker," Davis had explored how home is a literary space that reveres but ultimately excludes men, a place that assures women neither financial security, emotional repose, nor passion. Her increasing awareness of women's economic and creative frustrations leads her to expose the contradictions in domesticity's promise of the home as a finale. As Davis observes in "In the Market," domestic sentiment simply leaves women with "unused brain or nerve-power" (204). Searching for a rhetoric to depict women's dormant capabilities, she had found that romanticism failed to represent women's Promethean hunger. If the romantic individualist and original genius is male, if the sentimental man of feeling feels mainly for himself, and if the sentimental woman of feeling hides herself away in her own interior space, how then to represent the female relationship to the world? Over the next twenty years, Davis would try to find a mimetic aesthetic that could replace sentiment and inscribe her concerns for women's life in the commonplace.

In the 1870s, Davis wrote her last body of historical fiction, struggling to find a form to portray the lives of women troubled by their lack of freedom.[1] But Davis was unable to imagine resolutions through which their freedom might be realized; she was unwilling to release them from the cult of true womanhood and unable to adequately reconfigure its literary discourse. Her problems were literary and political: How to represent women as they set forth into the world of work? What constitutes narrative if the telos is not family and romance? How to reconceptualize the dialectic between a female character and a public environment? How to represent women's impact on the polis and embed that in narrative?

Davis's characters from the 1870s anticipate the "new woman" of the 1880s and 1890s, not only in her professional, marital, and political energies, but also in her ambivalent conceptualization. Ann Ardis observes that the rhetoric of new womanhood "was aimed not at characters in novels but at real women, women whose violations of the social code were viewed as a serious threat to bourgeois culture's hegemony."[2] In other words, the new woman is accused of as many ills as she implicates others in. As Davis locates the occupational and marital dilemmas of her female characters in particular historical crises, she suggests that the troubled situation of the working woman is not a literary convention. By situating her characters in the professional and psychological complications of work, suffrage, and divorce, Davis confirms the relationship of literature to life and lands herself in the middle of a cultural debate that became central to discussions of the new woman later in the century.[3] Davis was a pioneer in the depiction of the new woman as a person who inhabits spaces that are both domestic and public, female and male. By depicting the pain, confusion, and humiliation suffered by the new woman as she participated in the public world, Davis both acknowledged and subverted the hegemonic power of the bourgeois ideology of separate spheres. These stories defuse the caricatures of the new woman, popular in the weeklies, as anarchic and promiscuous.

Davis's portraits of women actively engaged in the world are infused with her awareness of the potency of domesticity—the guilt, anger, and ambivalence of women who often collude in their sentimental identity, attracted to feeling more than reason and emotions more than work. As Mary Wollstonecraft wrote a century earlier, "Women, subject by ignorance to their sensations and only taught to look for happiness in love, refine on sensual feelings and adopt metaphysical notions respecting that passion, which lead them shamefully to neglect the duties of life."[4] By structuring narratives around sensations and sensual feelings, domestic fiction had contributed to the notion that a woman's emotions are excessive and aberrant; consequently the superiority of the rational over the sensible became a fundamental element of liberal feminism.[5] Nineteenth-century fiction, however, offered few traditions through which to represent the female "rational"—that is, to depict the dilemmas and activities of women who are enthusiastically involved in the "duties of life." Women with a public identity had yet to take their place in the American epic. In the 1870s, Davis sought to represent this divisible, disempowered, ambivalent, and public female figure.

At a time of a radical disjunction between historical change and literary tradition, to write of women's worldly activities and explore the painful tensions created by the pull between public and private life, Davis needed to reconcile historical content and literary form. In such works as *Dallas Galbraith* (1868), "Two Women" (1870), "Clement Moore's Vocation" (1870), "Berrytown" (1873), *John Andross* (1873–1874), and "A Day with Dr. Sarah" (1878), she was able to emplot the profound difficulty women had in interpreting their limited choices. Long before modernists challenged "the representability of the sensible" and tried "to stop the dialectic and end history," as Suzanne Clark puts it,[6] a group of feminist realists explored ways to represent women who challenged the split between public and private life. Sara Parton [Fanny Fern] and Rebecca Harding Davis, and later Elizabeth S. Phelps, Harriet Wilson, Kate Chopin, and Sara Orne Jewett, created characters who placed themselves both in the world and in the matrix of feelings and who explored the painful tensions of these ever conflicting demands. Pioneering with this theme in a series of stories about working women, Davis countered the view that a woman's emotional and economic need for creative and productive work—that is, her "soul starvation"—would cause her masculinization.

What is also notable in these stories is what is missing. Davis never spoke of suffrage, although her stories make it clear that, for the first time in many years, the definition of women's citizenship—votes for women—was on the political agenda.[7] Despite Davis's literary fascination with the situation of women who were unemployed, undereducated, and trying to find their way in the world of publishers, merchants, medical schools, prisons, courts, and Congress, her characters remain disengaged from the public forum that surrounded Davis in Philadelphia, as the Fifteenth Amendment divided women's suffrage advocates, fragmented the women's rights movement, and sundered ties that had been forged between black and white women during the abolitionist movement and the Civil War. While Lucy Stone, Henry Blackwell, and Frederick Douglass argued that the hour belonged to the Negro, Elizabeth Cady Stanton, Susan B. Anthony, and Sojourner Truth expressed dismay that the Fourteenth Amendment (giving slaves citizenship status) was limited to men. They predicted that if the Fifteenth Amendment passed (assuring men the right to vote regardless of race or color), the opportunity for universal suffrage for both sexes would disappear. Stanton and Anthony went on to tour the country seeking to defeat the Fifteenth Amendment.[8]

Two other contemporary issues shape Davis's fiction of the 1870s. Davis believed that consumption of alcohol encouraged men to abuse women. During the economic depression in 1873, the issue of temperance—an issue for over forty years—reappeared as an expression of anxiety about the disruption of communities and families. On one level, alcohol abuse became a further manifestation of women's economic and physical vulnerability; on another it was a more generalized cultural referent to middle-class fears about the new demographics of nationhood and class. As Elizabeth Cady Stanton described the immigrant Irish women who lived nearby, "Alas! Alas! who can measure the mountain of sorrow and suffering endured in unwelcome motherhood in the abodes . . . where terror-stricken women and children are the victims of strong men frenzied with passion and intoxicating drink?"[9] The discourse of the Women's Christian Temperance Union mirrored that of Davis in asserting that women's values should shape public policy—a discourse that would soon emerge again in the rhetoric of populism.

The 1870s also witnessed the dramatic rise and fall of the Knights of Labor, an organization that began in Philadelphia in 1869 with a small group of blacklisted garment workers. The Knights absorbed both republican and religious traditions to create an alternative vision to industrial capitalism[10] through "assemblies" (locals) of female clerks, teachers, and waitresses, as well as workers in textile mills and other factories. In the South, women joined assemblies of servants, laundresses, and cooks—groups traditionally difficult to organize because they worked in separate places and often lived in their employers' houses. In Arkansas, the Knights even established an assembly of women farmers. Nonetheless, although these issues and these groups of people were topics of Davis's fiction, she remains virtually silent about their public articulations in the Gilded Age.[11]

Davis also does not speak to the new vision of a maternal commonwealth, an ideology about the public importance of domestic values that emerged in particular in women's higher education, even though education for women was an issue of pressing concern in Davis's social fiction.[12] It appears that Davis never embedded in her stories such relevant activities as the founding of women's colleges—Vassar in the 1860s, Smith and Wellesley in the 1870s—the rise of coeducation in state colleges and universities, the feminization of the teaching profession, and the opening of nursing schools.

Unlike the sentimentalists, Davis believed that women's "savage reality" would be solved only by "more work and more wages." In an early essay, "Men's Rights" (1869), Davis anticipates Freud in her male persona's question:

> What is it they want? What is it they do *not* want? . . . Suffrage, they cry; emancipation from a bondage as old as the world; equal wages and property-rights; work to save them from prostitution; and—God help us!—food for them and their children.[13]

Women respond, Davis writes, "Suffrage, or work, any of the popular cries among us, are but so many expressions of this same mental hunger or unused power. Unused, and therefore unwholesome power" (346). In industrial cities and rural areas alike, Davis saw a large surplus of women who, lacking masculine financial support, eked out a meager existence as seamstresses or teachers. Although Davis generally supported women's suffrage, in "Men's Rights" she insists that only financial independence will give women enough confidence either to remain single or to choose an appropriate husband. Women's "urgent and immediate necessity" is work; suffrage and property law reform are secondary.

It is through this economic lens that Davis understands the behavior of the "silly madonna" and coquette who live solely for men and who believe that only in marriage can they find their "being" (352). Nearly thirty years in advance of Charlotte Perkins Gilman's *Women and Economics,* in "Men's Rights" Davis describes the financial pressures that determine what Gilman would later call women's oversexualization. Her portrait of women who degrade themselves in their effort to find men—by wearing revealing clothing or permitting unwanted sexual contact—is an astute view of the relationship between economics, sexual objectification, and the loss of women's self-esteem. In "Men's Rights," Davis observes that although a man condemns a woman for her expensive and revealing clothes, he will nonetheless "lean against doorways, criticising the paces of the delicate young girls who are whirled past, as a trader might the slaves in the market" (348).

This commodified woman, a "pink-and-white doll," stands in the way of the woman who is "clear-eyed, large-brained, large-hearted, fitted by nature and training to be either seeress, orator, sea-captain, or clerk in a cooperative grocery" (352). In contrast to her stories that picture the painful limits on women's professional lives, in "Men's Rights" Davis blithely observes,

> There have been women-judges, soldiers, merchants, in every country and in every time; women who were leaders in the state or in war or in trade; and the readiness with which their ground was ceded to them, the applause with which their slightest merit was welcomed, prove how easily climbed was the path they trod, and how accessible to every woman, if she had chosen to climb it. (350)

This was an easy climb never apparent to her fictional women. The "great stumbling block" is the "domestic woman":

> She promulgates the idea that you, who talk of Woman's Rights, belong to a class of long-haired men and Bloomer-trousered women, who have lost all faith in God or George Washington, and are bent on forcing her into a cold-water pack, and marrying her daughter to the first convenient mulatto. (352)

Only in the context of *Waiting for the Verdict,* which describes the painful frustration of interracial romance, can we place this derogatory comment within Davis's attack on the narrow confines of domestic ideology. The "Domestic Woman," Davis argues, will continue to spring up, like "many-headed" sweet clover, because men prefer her and because tired women so envy her that they too may seek this form of "legal prostitution" (354). Unlike Gilman, however, Davis avoids the political implications of the portraits she has drawn. Through her sardonic title, she leaves the solution up to the individual woman who, Davis proposes, should begin humbly, find a trade, and quietly learn printing, stenography, beekeeping, or paper hanging while she "waits" for the arrival of suffrage and women's colleges. However, as Davis counters the male voice in "Men's Rights" with the women's voices and expectations in her stories, we witness Davis's own struggle to come to terms with this "state of transition with women" (344).

Davis's conflict about the choices a new woman faces between family and creative life appears in "Clement Moore's Vocation" (1870), a story of an impassioned young sculptress named Clement (an androgynous name), who wears a man's loose-fitting corduroy coat and has a "red-hot energy" that makes her "intolerable and aggressive to others of her sex."[14] Despite her own recent professional success and her contented marriage to a man who respected her writing (Davis met Clarke after he sent her a fan letter for "Life in the Iron-Mills"), Davis returns again and again to a gender paradigm that conceives of creativity as a masculine tendency. Clement's choice is either to acknowledge that she is "unlike all other women she had known" and accept an offer to go to Rome to study art or to marry an elderly rural judge, a widower with four sons, who invites her, "Come into that filthy den yonder, to spend [your] life in kitchen and housework, slaving for my boys, because I am fool enough to love [you]" (58). Typically, Davis's ending fails to resolve the painful dilemma of identity that she has raised. As Clement opts for marriage over sculpture, the narrator lamely comments, "Let us be rational as we will about the work of woman, and the fields suited for that work, but when love comes in, the best laid schemes will 'gang aft agley'" (59). But the overwhelming task of being a mother in the judge's household and the description of Clement's significant talent not only undercut the marital ending, but also, early in the tradition of American realism, point to the problems for professional women in the romance plot.

By 1870, a decade into her career as a successful writer and after seven years of an apparently happy marriage, Davis was becoming increasingly bitter about the enduring power of the angel in the house and the pressure toward female conformity imposed by both mothers and suitors. In "Two Women" (1870), a southern farmer falls in love with two young women—

Alice, an impoverished orphan who is devoted to his motherless son, and Charlotte, a strong-willed but bored heiress who wishes her fortune would disappear so that she "might do something to justify [her] right to live."[15] Lachrymose Alice spends her days curling the hair of the farmer's son: "She slily sewed on missing buttons, or darned tears in his trowsers . . . the always ready tears coming to her eyes at the thoughts of how neglected Tom's clothes . . . must be who had no woman to love them" (806). But perhaps Alice is really crying because her mother has refused to let her get a job even as a seamstress, claiming she would "unfit herself by doing men's work" (804). According to Alice's mother, the idea of a woman working for a wage is just an "ism" comparable to "spirit-rappings, Indiana divorces, and infidelity" (805).

Charlotte, by contrast, remarks that the happiest time in her life was when she served as a Confederate spy, hiding military maps in her chignon or boot heels as she sneaked across the Federal lines: "Then I lived! Like a man" (805). Hearing that her suitor has risked his life to attend coal miners stricken with yellow fever, Charlotte dresses in man's clothing to help in his desperate mission. When her lover discovers her disguise, however, he is choked with dismay and gasps: "What *will* people say?" (812). Somewhat chagrined, Charlotte demands, "Are men only to be heroic?" (813) When she is rejected by this man who believes that "men-women" such as she do not even have hearts to break, she leaves town. Quickly the villagers forget this scandalous woman "in watching the sorrows of the gentle Ophelia" (815). Identifying Alice with Ophelia, Davis links the angel in the house with female grief, revealing how debilitating she found the ideology of domesticity to be.

"Earthen Pitchers" (1873–1874) is Davis's most sustained exploration of women torn between a feminine world of nature and a masculine world of culture.[16] Framed by a plot about female disinheritance and property rights, this is the story of two young women who struggle with the meaning of "earthen pitchers," the teleological image of women as nature's vessels. Jenny, a Philadelphia journalist, lives by writing book notices, women's columns, and portraits of country life. An adventurous sort, she has gone on expeditions to "Indian country" to get material for her articles, but despite her talent and ambition, Jenny suffers from the poverty and isolation of the single career woman. Barely able to get by, she tries to insinuate herself into the bohemian society of Philadelphia by throwing literary soirees, only to be seen as a sharp woman pushing into a man's place. One of her visitors observes,

"American ladies are all oppressively clever, you know. 'Have you read my last tragedy?' says one. Another thinks it more a woman's work to dissect babies than to suckle them. The very school-girls attack you with their views of John Stuart Mill; and this Miss Derby . . . lives alone, and has her 'Saturday evenings.'" (216)

Jenny lives at the edge of a literary world controlled by men such as the publisher who "advertised himself into a fortune" with his "one smile, affable, patronizing, aggressively innocent" (219). He has come to Jenny's party to "buy" some authors "on as easy terms as possible" (221). This commodification has led to the masculinization of the woman artist, whom men flatter by speaking of the "strength of her articles; 'quite as masculine as if they had been done by a man'" (228).

Another damaging result of the merchandizing of culture by men is that nature has become a fashionable artistic trend—a source of "pretty effects" for writers and engravers commissioned by the weekly papers. Yosemite, the Rocky Mountains, the Maryland countryside, and Indian country are merely attractive new settings to replace Europe, the Nile, and Australia, which Dickens, Kingsley, and their followers have exhausted as interesting "backgrounds." Thus, the economics of publishing and the pressures of literary convention have given Jenny a utilitarian view of rural life and a diminished sense of her own talent. She cannot afford to write her poetry, even though "it tells," and instead produces streams of "shop-work." Rather than develop her style or struggle to elaborate an idea, she spends her time scouring the countryside for "ideas and facts as capital" (226).

Jenny is in love with Neil Goddard, an effete landscape artist whom she longs to marry and protect. Clever, incompetent, and parasitic, Neil has gone to a fishing village on the Delaware shore to pursue a legacy of a peach farm that Jenny knows properly belongs to her. There he encounters Audrey (whose name evokes a pastoral shepherdess), an impoverished young woman who survives through her knowledge of the sea—harpooning fish and catching crabs. Jealous at Neil's interest in Audrey and prepared to reveal her rightful ownership of the farm, Jenny follows him to Delaware. In a story colored with images of cross-dressing, mistaken gender identities, and hints at homoeroticism, nature becomes the trope through which Davis explores the confused relationship between gender, culture, and female aesthetics.

Disoriented by the silence of the land and the roar of the ocean when she arrives at the coast, Jenny, the urban new woman, is relieved to see a boy catching blue mackerel in the surf, using a squid as bait:

> The lad, who had a curiously free, lithe movement, paced slowly along the beach, as he rolled the line into a coil on one arm, then darted breast-high into the breaker. The glittering lead was thrown like a lasso far out into the still water; then he walked backward with head thrown back, and high, quick steps up the beach, drawing in the cord, hand over hand. At the end flapped a large shining fish. (235)

When Jenny discovers that the "fisherman" is in fact Audrey, she is captivated by the woman's power and autonomy: "What a magnificent build and freedom of action she has for a woman!" (236). To Neil, by contrast, Audrey represents natural wisdom and instinctual female creativity—all healing to his tired masculine and urban spirit. "To be with her is for any man to breathe a new and alien air" (234).

Audrey also represents the indeterminate aspect of nature that resists the tourist's hegemonic gaze: Neil says of Audrey, "How can I tell what she is to me? Say that you go out and see the sea and the mountains for the first time, can you map and paint and label them out for your parlor at home? I cannot map out Audrey Swenson for you" (234). However, because she is identified with nature, Audrey is available to anyone's definition. To the visitors from the city, she suggests the pastoral promise of woman as primal, maternal, a vanished Eve living in indolent harmony with nature, an aesthetic but uncreative vessel for their repressed urban desire. While Neil sees Jenny as a "scribbler for the press who lives by her wits" (243), he sees Audrey as a primitive "oracle, through whom the divine message [comes]" even though she lacks any "special shrewdness of her own" (237). Neil presumes that Audrey, who understands the tides and the sand dunes and who knows the local legends of the Barnegat pirates, is a dangerous and layered symbol of a woman's unconscious, a romantic unity that he, as the agent of society, pressures her to conquer and domesticate. What Audrey well understands, however, is that nature is not a site of plenty and ease: "No fish, no supper" (236), she explains. She also realizes that Neil's and Jenny's romantic projections will not help her get a job as a singer.

"Earthen Pitchers" is among the most formless, modernist, and, to my mind, difficult of Davis's stories. The landscape of Lewes, Delaware, like the landscape of Jewett's "Dunnet's Landing" or Constance Fenimore Woolson's "St. Clair Flats," is a watery indeterminate place where an outsider such as Jenny can lose her bearings in the shifting dunes and where rural characters blend indistinguishably into the landscape. One night, for example, Jenny falls into a bog of quicksand and is nearly suffocated. In a moment of romantic dissolution of the self, she relinquishes her masculine and urban need to control, permits Audrey to rescue her, and prepares to lose Neil. Unlike the detached narrator in "Life in the Iron-Mills," Jenny is literally immersed in the world of Lewes, forced by nature to melt, if only for a time, the barriers between subject and object. Yet the romantic discourse yields to realism, structured by precise geographical and botanical details that Davis knew well, particulars of the transitions of the coastal economy from fishing to farming to tourism, and an accurate rendering of the Eastern Shore dialect. Economic progress and marriage conquer Jenny's threatened romantic diffusion of self, which endures only as traditional female deference for others. Marriage emerges as betrayal and loss: Jenny trades literature for a husband and creative autonomy for the illusion of domestic authority. She thinks she has exchanged the individualistic and competitive values of the town for the coastal legend, related by Audrey, which promises "that the sea stretches out its hands to punish selfishness. Sand or wave creeps over every man's life who lives for himself alone" (247). But in fact the waves threaten every *woman's* life; Jenny and Audrey will live for others, but Neil will live "for himself alone."

Like Sara Orne Jewett, Davis invokes place to examine how women yearn for a full identity that is at once bound and free. At the end of "Earthen Pitchers," both women sacrifice their artistic ambitions in order to provide for their husbands. Jenny marries Neil, letting him believe the farm is his by rights. She becomes a competent peach farmer, living simply so that Neil can spend his winters in the Philadelphia libraries or in Europe with his lover, ironically a "noted painter of *la nature morte*" (284). In one sense, Jenny has exchanged identities with Audrey; she has become the urban version of nature and, as such, is betrayed, despondent, and cast off. In another sense, Jenny, the journalist, has become an abject and humiliated wife, just as nature has succumbed to farming; matriarchal nature is an unsatisfactory exchange even for the vagaries of female professionalism in cultural world controlled by effete and untalented men. In the end, Audrey marries a local farmer, a blind man, and wastes her voice by constantly reading to him—a fate that marks the inevitability of women's artistic sacrifice. The farms, marriages, and children in the story become middle borders for incomplete women who wander isolation and identity, nature and civilization. The only triumphant woman is the adulterous woman artist who paints the "death" of nature. Ultimately, the sentimental paradigm is quite at odds with Davis's ironic narrative stance, the imagery of nature, and the representation of men who continue to abuse and betray their wives—the realization of civilization that Davis portends in "A Faded Leaf of History."

Davis's subsequent stories about women who seek a vocation as actresses, artists, authors, or performers revisit themes from her earlier critique of romanticism: From whence comes a woman's drive to create? Is creativity innate or trained? What is the role of self-expression in a married woman's life? If women claim "authority as subjects possessing . . . an expertise in empathy," as Susan Kirkpatrick defines the sentimental view of the female self, must they draw upon this authority only to produce images of their lives?[17] Or could this empathic reaction, this specialization in subjectivity, help women find new ways of imaging the relationship of the self to the world? Davis refused to separate the aesthetic self from history; her fiction is always about the relationship between public and private identity. The aesthetic self is never separate from the economic and public self; at the very least, the aesthetic self always needs money.

Davis continued to write of women's ambivalence about needing both intellectual activity and family life. In "Berrytown," serialized in *Lippincott's Magazine* in 1873, the heroine must decide whether or not to marry the founder of a nearby utopian community, if only to escape an overbearing mother and her tedious life in a rural village.[18] Kitty's need for self-expression and her right to political authority mirror the debate within utopian socialism about women's roles. For Davis, the utopian community literalizes notions of civilized progress:

> Berrytown was the Utopia in actual laths, orchards and bushel-measures of the advance-guard of the reform party of the United States. It was the capital of Progress, where social systems and raspberries grew miraculously together. (401).

Locked in its own paradox, Berrytown undermines the nihilism of Thomas More's pun: *eutopia*, the good place; *utopia*, nowhere. The community purports to actualize an ideal future for women and answer their demands: "Suffrage, Free Love, spiritualism . . . had there food and shelter" (401).

Yet, through the socialist women, Davis questions not only the particular "progressive" rearrangements in the community but also the very notion of femaleness itself. From the first, the image of utopian progress is sterile—particularly for women. Unlike the natural fecundity that surrounds Kitty's house, "old walnut trees growing close to its back and front, young walnut trees thrusting themselves unhindered through beet and tomato patches" (400)—in Berrytown "not a tree stood between her and the sky-line. Row after row of cottages replete with white paint and the modern conveniences; . . . the great Improved Canning-houses for fruit flanking the town on one side, [the] Reformatory for boys on the other" (401). The town and the era, like Kitty herself, are squeezed into a "landscape which, from horizon to horizon, Reform swept with the newest of brooms" (402). The name Berrytown is a satire on Bronson Alcott's Fruitlands, which his daughter, Louisa May Alcott, had recently parodied in "Transcendental Wild Oats" (1872). Fruitlands, a transcendentalist "consociate family" of visionaries who believed in cold showers, linen togas, and a rigid diet of fruit, bread, and water, endured only a few months until Louisa's mother fled with her children, bankrupt and angry at the impractical and authoritarian experiment in which she alone had done nearly all the domestic and agricultural work.

Kitty's choice is defined through images of domestic confinement: "Outside lay emancipated Berrytown, to unemancipated Kitty only a dumb panorama: inside, her meals, her lessons and perpetual consultations with her mother on bias folds and gussets while they made their dresses or sewed for the Indian missions" (402). Berrytown women, by contrast, share in the community's physical work—cooking in the cannery, packing grapes for shipping—aware that the profits support teachers in the freedman's schools set up during Reconstruction. Berrytown also seeks to bridge the divide between intellectual and physical work; Kitty learns that one of the female cannery workers is studying to become a shorthand reporter, and another is writing a lecture on Shakespeare's women.

In contrast to Kitty is Maria Muller, the community's doctor and a well-known lecturer on women's suffrage; she is also, to Kitty's surprise, pretty and frail, with a "very genuine" look and voice. At first, Maria urges Kitty to marry Berrytown's founder and work in the boy's reformatory: "You're very young; you've dreamed a good deal, most likely: this wakening to the fact that there is work in the world besides marrying and nursing babies revolts and shocks most young girls. Yet here it is" (408). Although Kitty has no special feeling for the founder, she finds a "terrible grinding power" in Maria's words (408). Davis remarks, like "every wide-awake young woman among our readers . . . [Kitty] knows the closing-in process by which society, expediency, propinquity, even moral obligations, hedge many a man and woman, and drive them into marriage" (411), and she accepts his proposal.

For Kitty, however, utopia is like marriage, a "closing in process." Berrytown offers a false promise of maturity and growth, emblemized by the reformatory where Kitty is to work. She sees the boys mechanically respond to her future husband: when he claps once, the children immediately raise their hands, twice they fold them, three times they "rattle off" the Lord's Prayer, a rote gesture of obedience. The reformatory suggests her impending marriage, whose "gates . . . were about to close on her" (698). Contemplating her wedding, Kitty realizes that even if "she lived to be gray-headed, he alone owned her, mind and body. 'If I were dead in my coffin, he would put his mild, fat little hand on me, and look forward to owning me in heaven'" (35). With this bitter and angry line, which could never have been written by Stowe or Alcott, Kitty reveals her knowledge that as wifely property, she would always be sexually available; deciding that she would belong to no man, socialist or not, she breaks off her engagement, only to return to her sewing and cooking and an oppressive relationship with a difficult mother.

By contrast, Maria's choice to become a doctor required a campaign, by "strategy or assault," to persuade medical professors to let her attend their lectures and clinics. Her struggle mirrors that of Elizabeth Blackwell (1821–1910), the first female graduate of an American medical college, who was admitted to Geneva Medical School (now Hobart College) only as a joke and who had to fight to attend courses in physiology and anatomy, presumably inappropriate topics for a modest woman.[19] When one of Maria's patients addresses her as "Miss Muller" rather than "Dr. Muller," she rebukes him, "I earned my right to the title of physician too hardly to give it up for that which belongs to every simpering school-girl; . . . Besides, the sooner we doctors sink the fact that we are women the better for the cause—and for us" (707). According to Davis, however, a sorry consequence of Maria's professional ordeal is that she has "taught herself to think and talk like a man" (707)—alluding again to the masculinization of the professional woman. In "Berrytown," the debate about utopian feminism turns on a debate about female nature.

In the end, Kitty decides to marry a local widower and forget about Berrytown. She will become "a good-natured little woman, with no opinions of her own. A bit too fond of dress perhaps, and a silly doting mother" who can rule only her husband "and the house and their lives absolutely, with but little regard for justice" (48). But even domestic authority is a myth: Kitty's husband never "suspects" that she has any power, even over him; indeed, she "hardly knows herself that she does" (48). Besides, he finds her domestic obsessions attractive. Maria, on the other hand, remains a lonely spinster, obsessed with "nursing her dog as if it were a baby" (48). Even so, shaped by the critique of a socialist utopia, Kitty's decision to reject a life, whether in marriage or in utopia, where she would be an equal partner emerges as an option rather than an inexorable moment in political development. Like marriage itself, to Davis "Berrytown" is a dystopia, an extended literary metaphor about the precarious course of social equality. The novel anticipates by over a decade Anna Bowman Dodd's *The Republic of the Future: or, Socialism a Reality* (1887), which mocks the utopian conjunction of socialism, feminism, and technology in a dangerous and repressive futuristic state, as well as Charles Elliot Niswonger's *The Isle of Feminine* (1893), which parodies feminism on an imaginary Caribbean island ruled by women. "Berrytown" calls into question the wish-fulfillment aspect of utopian narratives and speaks to Davis's ambivalence about the conflict of women's needs.

As Sharon Harris shows, the early 1870s was a time of "major artistic transition" for Davis. In this period she published two novels and one novella, serialized four others, and began to write for both the *New York Tribune* and the *Independent*. During this prolific decade, which also witnessed the birth of her third child, her daughter Nora, she also published more than 140 articles and short stories in sixteen periodicals, including literary journals, children's periodicals, and religious magazines.[20] However, I disagree with Harris's contention that Davis resented "what she perceived as the new woman's corruption of history" and thus continued to sympathize with the sentimentalists. Clearly, as Harris proves, Davis never took "that final step of advocacy."[21] Nonetheless, in my view, her fiction from this last creative era confirms her profound critique of sentimentalism and the ideology of domesticity that it inscribes.

In "Dolly," published in 1874 in *Scribner's Monthly Magazine*, a young painter named George Fanning becomes obsessed by a beautiful young Moravian woman while on a sketching tour of the Allegheny Mountains. The Moravians were a devout Protestant sect who lived in their own communities, with separate living quarters for men and women. George is fascinated by the fortress-like "sister houses," where females lived, and he sketches Dolly framed by a "deep-arched" door, "a young girl looking back with a laughing good-bye before she disappeared in the darkness," apparently intrigued by the idea of female imprisonment and celibacy.[22] Although George thinks of Dolly as "one of Correggio's Madonnas" (288), to the scornful narrator Dolly is "much less insipid than any of those virgins, who, surely, were only immaculate from the sheer lack of ideas" and observes that he is reading Dolly's history "like a story in a cheap magazine" (288). Clearly Davis is contemptuous of the domesticated woman and the men who idealize her. While George continues to fantasize about marriage to this immaculate and picturesque madonna, Dolly shocks her admirer by taking a job as a servant in a country inn; "nauseated" by the loss of his "dead illusions," the painter flees.

But it gets worse for George. Two winters later, George attends a hippodrome (an indoor horse race) at P. T. Barnum's circus in Philadelphia, where he sees Dolly, in spangled robe, standing on a gilt chariot and driving three horses abreast at a frightful speed: "It was for the moment Boanerges rushing to victory" (290). The patent pleasure in Dolly's flashing eyes and burning cheeks make it clear to the narrator that this joyful performer is not a madonna at all, but rather an unrepentant Magdalene. It turns out that she has joined the circus so that she and her husband can afford to buy a farm in Nebraska: her rebellious energy is bracketed by marriage. Nonetheless, throughout his life George continues to paint Dolly as a faded old woman in the Moravian sister house and wistfully describes his eternal subject as an old "instrument of marvelous sweetness that lay buried there until it crumbled to pieces—'died with all its music in it'" (291). Better, in his eyes, for

Dolly to have been constricted, restricted, and repressed; George's *belle ideal* is a subject denied subjectivity.

In "Marcia" (1876), Rebecca Harding Davis tells a story of sentiment and silence, of publishers, husbands, and a literary tradition that conspired to mute women.[23] In this powerful story about telling stories, Davis projects her ambivalence about ambition onto Marcia, a young woman writer who desperately tries to challenge the powerful literary province of sentimentalism. Reversing the compromises that Davis had earlier made in some of her own fiction, "Marcia" tells of a female author who suffers for her refusal to become a "literary domestic." "I think I have something to say, if people only would hear it," exclaims Marcia Barr, who has come to Philadelphia from her family's decaying plantation in Mississippi, "vowing herself to literature." Marcia's vow is a play on the marriage metaphor made by a young woman who has chosen the "business" of authorship over the "business" of marriage. Seeking to attach literary realism to political activism, Marcia has resolved to use her writing to "assist in the Progress of humanity" (310). Northern publishers, however, have rejected her regional tales about slimy reptiles in stagnant ponds, the unbearable heat and poverty, the "dirt and dreary monotony" of her dreary southern home, a decrepit plantation on the Yazoo River (312). Although the narrator, a male publisher, finds that Marcia's stories linger in his mind as "strong and vivid as a desert by Gérôme or a moor by Broughton" (312), he advises her to "put away pen and ink" and study other literary styles. The magazine trade, he believes, is unprepared for realism.

Davis, however, grounds her story in the material realities of a woman writer. Marcia has refused to produce the "usual talk of countesses, heather, larks, or emotions of which she knew nothing" (312). That is to say, she has refused to join Nathaniel Hawthorne's "damned mob of scribbling women" and now must figure out how to survive in Philadelphia as a writer. This was a crisis with which Davis herself struggled when she decided to write for women's magazines such as *Peterson's* and for children's magazines such as *Youth's Companion*, which appealed to mass audiences and offered her several times more money than the *Atlantic*. While many "feminine writers" succumbed to economic pressures and "responded gallantly to the call, and turned out such works in staggering numbers to the polite applause of their reviewers, who complacently praised their piety, lack of energy and resolute disregard of conflict," Marcia resists.[24] These authors produced children's literature, books on child care and household management, and "works of sensibility steeped in depoliticized and lofty patriotism and misty, death-oriented and nonsectarian religious fervor."[25] But rather than join their ranks and betray her craft, Marcia accepts meager newspaper writing jobs in which she describes the gowns worn at society balls or collects jokes for the humor columns—a bitter and paradoxical outcome for which she is paid three dollars a week. She also takes a job stitching socks, a female trade that would have paid her about the same wage.[26] Thus, while many sentimental authors announced that their tales issued from an unconscious and irresistible flow of female creativity (Harriet Beecher Stowe reported that God wrote *Uncle Tom's Cabin*),[27] Davis insists that writing is a professional activity—a skilled, competitive, deliberate, and underpaid job.

In this story of a destitute woman who fails at this job, Davis conflates the choices for women with the situation of American literature in her time. Sentimentalism, observes Ann Douglas Wood, "asserts that the values a society's activity denies are precisely the ones it cherishes."[28] Or claims to cherish: most authors of sentimental fiction left its paradoxical assertions of female subservience and superiority unresolved. For example, Marcia believes that her mother has "one of the finest minds in the world. . . . But . . . she has read nothing, knows nothing" (311). With her acute but uneducated sensibility and her unfulfilled instinct for beauty, Marcia's mother, whose children all died in infancy except Marcia, has "nothing to do, nothing to think of" and is going mad, taking opium to "quiet" herself. Again Davis uses the metaphor of silence as the repository of women's material as well as intellectual discontent.

In "Marcia" Davis continues to challenge the view that family will guarantee women a refuge from economic and worldly tensions. The implicit marital contract within domestic ideology has been betrayed by Marcia's father, the colonel, who thinks that women "are like mares—only useful to bring forth children" (311). But from her window in the big house Marcia's mother sees only the graves of her dead babies, a haunting landscape, a wasteland of her capitulation to appropriate female creativity. "Marcia" is Davis's most developed story of a mother-daughter relationship. In the figure of Mrs. Barr, Davis recuperates her own mother as a model for a daughter's intellectual inspiration. Mrs. Barr's relationship with Marcia exposes their shared inheritance of female ignorance and abuse and reveals the complicated projection involved in a daughter's choice of profession.

Marcia, like Jenny in "Earthen Pitchers" or Anne (in the story of the same name written in 1889), is punished for her worldly aspirations; in the end, she denies her literary ambitions and accepts a proposal of marriage from Mr. Biron, the abrasive overseer of her family's decaying plantation who has come north to claim her. The figure of Biron, however, exposes Davis's ambivalence about this resolution. An "ignorant, small-minded man" (313), Biron has come to Philadelphia "on business"—to propose marriage to Marcia, an economic transaction arranged by her father. As in "Berrytown," Davis again inserts references to slavery into a discussion of marriage. At a time of the collapse of Reconstruction and the ongoing popularity of *Uncle Tom's Cabin*, Davis's readers were likely to associate Biron, who comes to retrieve Marcia after her "mad flight" (314), with vicious slave overseers and hunters of fugitive slaves, characters who were familiar in fiction. When Marcia hears of Biron's arrival, she tries to steal some money in order to escape. Arrested for theft, she attempts to kill herself by swallowing poison. As she lies comatose in her jail cell, Biron undresses her, "turning down the poor bit of lace and red ribbon at her throat, his big hairy hand shaking" (315–16), a symbolic violation. After their marriage, he clothes her in as costly silks as her new "owner" can buy, a slavery metaphor reenforced by his abusive orders to the cab driver, "You, nigger" (316), uttering an epithet of contempt common since the 1820s. As Biron asserts his economic, masculine, and racial authority, Davis subverts the sentimental promise of marriage. Not only does Marcia, the aspiring realist writer, marry an ignorant and abusive man; she also marries her father's employee. In every way she has married "down"— an atypical ending.

Marcia's final punishment is to suffer literary silence. Unlike the robust statue of the korl woman in "Life in the Iron-Mills," hungry "for summat to make her live," Marcia is literally suffering from malnutrition, a condition that also represents her unfulfilled artistic and intellectual quest. The story, which opens with Marcia's desire for publication and visibility, ends with her request that the meek publisher burn her manuscripts, what Biron calls "rubbish." Indeed, in the end she asks to be silenced: "Do not leave a line, a word" (316). Thus Marcia makes the publisher ultimately responsible for her erasure—as in fact, he is.

In "Marcia" Davis traces the causes and assumptions that led to the long exclusion of women from the canon of American literature.[29] Because Marcia always slips a loose thread between her pages, only to find it there when her manuscripts are returned, she knows that they were unread, suggesting a basic preconceived bias against women authors. Nina Baym suggests that women's work is frequently not deemed "excellent" for reasons that are "connected with their gender although separable from it." For example, a "great" work of nineteenth-century literature was traditionally expected to display a dense texture of classical allusion at a time when formal classical education was restricted to men—a deprivation Marcia decries. Baym also argues that the critical goal of "Americanness" limited women's literary status. She cites Marius Bewley, for example, who believes that the American artist found "'no social surface responsive to his touch.'" Bewley concludes that because "the scene was crude, even beyond social satire; . . . the [local color] tradition as I have set it up . . . has no room for the so-called realists and naturalists." The tradition of male criticism, suggests Baym, supports Joel Porte's assessment in 1969 that the "rise and growth of fiction in this country is dominated by our authors' conscious adherence to a tradition of nonrealistic romance."[30] In their detailed and circumstantial portraits of American women's lives, stories such as "Marcia," or stories such as Marcia wrote, could not comfortably fit the pattern of the romantic quest for experience. As a projection of Davis, Marcia challenges the publishing industry's preconceptions about female literature and its enduring code that restricted the style and scope of women's writing to matters of the hearth. And she fails.

Although Marcia's sojourn in Philadelphia ends in literary defeat, sexual surrender, and even her rejection of the publisher's offer to send reading matter to Mississippi (foretelling a silent destiny like her mother's), her story represents a quiet insurrection on Davis's part. Davis exposes her own frustration with the role of domestic fiction in the literary marketplace. Marcia's physical malnutrition is a symbol of the state of American literary aesthetics as well as a tacit reproach to the masculine domination of the publishing industry; it also exposes the fantasies of masculine protection—of the culture and of the home. With her "ugly face," her "selfish" ambition, and her debilitating illness, Marcia can neither please nor serve men. The fact that Marcia and her mother do not survive in either the world of writing or the world of marriage suggests Davis's conflict about the prevailing feminine literary tradition and the ideology that constitutes it. This story addresses the misogyny of the publishing world. The emergence of a group of female writers who threatened to corner the market alarmed men such as Hawthorne, who felt his work would "have no chance of success while the public taste is occupied with [women's] trash."[31]

In "Marcia" Davis deconstructs the waning cult of domesticity and the tradition of sentimental fiction that inscribes it. In telling the story of Marcia's mother and her desperate need for education, Davis herself refused to bow to the literary marketplace. "Marcia," a metatext on the patriarchy of the publishing trade, documents the ongoing public hostility to women's education and intellectual work at a time of an unprecedented flowering of fiction written by and for women. "Marcia" is also an assertion of a woman's right to expression; it is a self-reflexive story about writing that profoundly questions the tradition to which it refuses to succumb.[32]

Whereas Catherine Maria Sedgewick observes, "Literary occupation is rather a pastime than a profession with me,"[33] Davis announces in "Marcia" that women's writing is very much a profession that involves making money and is not merely a pastime for inspiration, leisure, or the feminine duty to entertain others. In *Doing Literary Business,* Susan Coultrap-McQuinn explains how women succeeded as writers in the face of attitudes and behavior that could render them invisible. Unlike Marcia, observes Coultrap-McQuinn, women writers were quite outspoken on their own behalf. By virtue of their connections with one another and their popularity with audiences, they were well aware of their importance in the literary marketplace and used this knowledge effectively in their negotiations with the publishing and literary world.[34] Ironically, the form of the domestic novel itself also allowed women's participation in the literary marketplace—a bizarre tautology that found sentiment and feelings inappropriate in the competitive world of business but acceptable in the cultural representations of human relationships and the growth of moral character. Women's public utterance was acceptable because it was about private life, a restricted area of female expertise that authorized women to write. Thus despite the ideological message that women's realm was in the home, a message often popularized by female authors, the fact was that by this decade women had gone outside—into the wide, wide world of work, women's clubs, reform movements, utopian communities, and the professions. Davis, however, like her character Marcia, collapsed the era's discursive categories and engaged the public discourse in fiction.

Although Davis silences her literary doppelganger in "Marcia," she continues to be haunted by the image of the silenced woman writer, the artist manqué. "The Poetess of Clap City" (1875) is the story of Maria Heald, a gifted young woman who has been discouraged from writing by poverty, limited education, and social disapproval.[35] After a troubled marriage to a romantic alcoholic, the birth of several children, and a series of female jobs —running a boardinghouse, machine sewing by the yard, teaching in a primary school, and selling vegetables and butter—Maria meets Miss Aiken, a popular woman writer who encourages her to send off her one lifelong poem, a realistic and autobiographical portrait of the "fraction of the world which she had seen." While all the publishers reject this piece as "trash" and Maria dies a "voiceless singer" whose music is "still inside her" (615), Miss Aiken continues to pitch her writing to the literary market. She reports:

> [I] put my best work on that vollum, half my mental capital, compacted it down. The publisher . . . told me women were too diffuse; so I wasted stuff in that book which would have made a dozen magazine articles at ten dollars a page. These papers on our city charities which I'm furnishing to the "Sunday Age" pay me fifteen per cent. (614).

Miss Aiken, however, was doing much better than Davis, who received a mere $50 for "Life in the Iron-Mills" and $75 for "John Lamar" from the *Atlantic Monthly*.[36] Initially, Davis was both flattered at such a highbrow reception of her work and naive about the economics of publishing. When James Fields offered her an advance of $100 for the early version of *Margret Howth*, she declined, explaining,

> Money is enough of a "needful commodity" with me to make me accept with a complacent style whatever you think the articles are worth. But if I were writing with a hundred dollar bill before me in order to write on it "I have paid him" I am afraid the article would be broad and deep just $100 and no more.[37]

Throughout her relationship with the *Atlantic*, Davis tended to accept whatever Fields thought the "articles" were worth. Sharon Harris demonstrates that James Fields was significantly underpaying his friend. But Davis was not without initiative; even though she frequently reiterated her commitment to write solely for the *Atlantic*, soon after the publication of "Life in the Iron-Mills" she also began to write for *Peterson's Magazine*, a new ladies' journal based in Philadelphia and owned by friends of her husband, Clarke. Peterson paid Davis as much as $1,000 for a novel that would run for several months in the 1860s, a stipend many times the fee she would have received from James Fields.[38] According to Harris, in the early 1860s Davis still did not understand her publishing rights. She did not even know, for example, that *Margret Howth* had gone into a third printing until she read about it in a newspaper, and she remained confused about what she should receive from its sale. Although the total sales for the novel eventually exceeded 2,500 copies, Davis earned only $125 for the book version. Even in 1862, Harris asserts, "this was a ludicrous arrangement" because by 1857 the standard royalty was closer to Miss Aiken's 15 percent, occasionally going up to 25 percent, a figure that endured until the 1890s, even with the publishing uncertainties of the Civil War. Thus, Fields's payment to Davis of one-half of one percent royalty, new author though she was, was unheard of.[39]

Davis slowly became more sophisticated in her negotiations with publishers and more demanding in her dealings with Fields. By 1862, when *Peterson's* offered her $300 for a short story, she wrote to Fields that while it did her "no good" to write for *Peterson's*, "as times are I am not justified in refusing the higher price."[40] When Fields quickly replied, offering her $8 per page, one of the highest stipends paid by the *Atlantic* at the time,[41] Davis promised to write for him exclusively. Yet she continued to be a frequent and prolific contributor to *Peterson's*, an arrangement of which Fields must have been aware. By the late 1860s, references to "exclusives" are few in the Davis-Fields correspondence, and in 1866, she agreed to write a serial, *Waiting for the Verdict*, for F. P. and William Conant Church, who had recently launched *Galaxy Magazine*. For this long serial novel, Davis eventually earned $3,600, six times what she would have received from the *Atlantic* for a story of similar length.[42] Like most authors, Davis struggled with her relations with many of her publishers throughout her writing career, but as her reputation became secure, the fees she received appear more appropriate and her letters less abject. Toward the end of her career, even with publications with which she had long professional relationships such as the *Independent*, she would name her price before submitting an essay.[43]

"A Day with Doctor Sarah," written in 1878, continues Davis's exploration of what happens to a woman when she enters the public world.[44] This story, which anticipates the conflicting ideologies of the new woman and the Gibson girl by at least a decade, is not only Davis's most extensive portrait of a suffragist but also a sensitive study of the painful choices women make when they become involved in a political movement—in defining their priorities, their personal relationships, and their awareness that as women they are challenging powerful stereotypes about female identity. The story opens at a ladies' luncheon in Murray Hill, an upscale neighborhood in Manhattan, where, as the narrator observes, "An idea, naked and freshly born into the world, would have been as out of place if dragged into sight at Mrs. Epps's luncheon table as a man, or a greasy joint, or the Archangel Michael with his flaming sword" (317). But the (phallic) intruder is Dr. Sarah Coyt, a prominent reformer on behalf of women's rights, whose only weapon is her supply of ideas: "She kept a stock of them, as David did of pebbles, and was perpetually slinging them at the head of one Goliath of custom or another." Currently, Sarah is engaging in a "hand-to-hand fight" over women's suffrage (317).

Initially the guests think that their elegant hostess's decision to support women's suffrage is just another of Maria Epps's "freaks," a tolerable "fad" that has attracted "some very respectable people": "'She is always aiming at the *bizarre*. You remember she was the first to drive three ponies *à la Russe* in the Park'" (318). Others conclude that Maria's newfound political identity is just a ploy to gain a political appointment for her husband. Others hint at the new sexuality surrounding feminism and announce that many suffragists believe in free love.

Davis plays on this twist, however, with a homoerotic suggestion. As Mrs. Epps introduces Sarah, her friends "felt a shock as from an electric battery, and then they all roused into pleasurable excitement" (317), an image that frames the political in a technological and sexual metaphor. As Carroll Smith-Rosenberg observes, the debate over the new woman's sexual and political legitimacy was one of the few times in which women adopted male language for their own symbolic and political intent.[45] The guests' attraction is ideologically tempered because Sarah's pugnacious spirit is seen as masculine;[46] one of the women remarks that the newspapers view Sarah as "a kind of intellectual Heenan or Morrissey" (318)—two professional boxers who competed for the title of heavyweight champion in the late 1850s.[47] Sarah's passion, however, has been sublimated to her cause, conflating the erotic and nonerotic and thereby diminishing both. Sarah also describes her involvement in the women's movement in its largest female context. She tells the guests that aesthetic pleasures are aspects of her political work: "Nature and art give me a better insight into the needs of my sex" (318). Hearing this observation, the ladies suddenly feel that they are "no longer Maria Epps's chance guests, lazily sipping chocolate; they were human beings—to be, to do, and to suffer" (318).

In "A Day with Doctor Sarah," Davis ultimately satirizes the view that women's political activism is masculine, and, as such, emotionally deprived. At first, in her "aggressive purple dress," Sarah appears immodest, obsessive, and intolerant. She has arrogantly refused to let any other women participate in her forthcoming lobbying trip to Washington: "There's always an obstacle. This one must make her living by writing slipshod novels or lecturing, that one has a baby, another a dead lover to mope over" (320). To Sarah, the dense texture of other middle-class women's professional and emotional lives prevents them from focusing on the needs of other women, who, she sees, are in "as perilous a strait as was ever church or slave" (321). Thus, while Davis still represents the unmarried woman and professional woman as eccentric and socially superfluous, Sarah dismantles the ideology in which affection, romance, and marriage bracket the lives of middle-class women represented by Mrs. Epps's guests. Yet even in her character study of an obsessive female activist, Davis refers to the fact that other women reformers do marry, form close friendships, and lean on each other.

In "A Day with Dr. Sarah," female psychology is traced not to biology or instinct, but to a particularized history of patriarchy. Like Maria Muller, the physician in "Berrytown," Sarah also had to struggle to be allowed to become a doctor. It is worth recalling that as late as 1905, the first year for which numbers are available, women represented only 4 percent of American medical school graduates. But unlike the life Sarah has chosen for herself, many women physicians married. An 1881 survey found that half of the female medical students and 80 percent of practicing female physicians were married, and 90 percent found the practice of medicine had a "favorable" impact on their marriage.[48]

Consistent with these findings, Davis suggests that the real source of Sarah's misery is her political rather than professional drive. Twenty years before, Sarah had rejected a lover in order to marry a "male pioneer" in the reform movement. Now a widow, she is chastened when her old suitor, Matthew, a clergyman, appears at Mrs. Epps's luncheon with his crippled daughter. When Sarah sees the half-starved girl limp into the luncheon, she berates the gathering, "You render her—a nullity. Will nobody give that child a chair?" (322). Thus Davis assigns the suffragist vocabulary of political nonexistence to the situation of a child. But this time Sarah shelves her political role for her female *and medical* identity; she walks out in the middle of her speech on suffrage in order to assist the child who, Sarah realizes, might have been her own. As she holds the girl against her chest, Sarah's "sharp features" soften with "the remembrance of the dead-born baby which had never lain there. The breast had been full of milk then, but the dead little lips had never touched it, and the breast had shrivelled slowly and grown hard" (323). Sardonically referring to men's fears of women's sexual initiative, Davis describes how Matthew begins to quake as Sarah approaches him, panicked that she will refer to their old romance: "What if she should propose to him? There was nothing which these unsexed women would not do" (324). His alarm is also a parody of the era's conflation, stimulated to a great degree by male physicians, that an educated woman might develop masculine physiological and character traits.[49]

Soon Sarah leaves the luncheon to travel to Washington to undertake her lobbying campaign for women's suffrage. During the seventies and eighties, legislation affirming that "the right of citizens of the United States to vote shall not be denied or abridged by the United States or by any state on account of sex" was repeatedly introduced in Congress, which perforce focused the movement's attention on legislative hearings, press releases, and petitions. Sarah happens to be on the same train as Matthew, who is returning to his Maryland parish. A violent railway collision occurs. Despite the importance of her upcoming testimony before Congress, Sarah remains behind to rescue

Matthew and his daughter, both critically injured. As she recalls the political cause to which she has devoted her life, she assures the dying man that she will raise his children. Meanwhile, the congressional committee waits in vain for Dr. Sarah. One of the male activists, echoing Sarah's earlier comment, indignantly observes, "There is always an obstacle in the way with women. . . . But why must it always be a man or a baby?" (328). Embedded in the conventional ending of motherhood over movement, however, is Sarah's display of medical skill after the train disaster. Davis nowhere suggests that Sarah abandons her profession along with her politics. The ending not only recuperates Sarah's maternal nature—a response to male psychiatrists, doctors, and academics, and psychologists who diagnosed the new woman as hostile to motherhood and hence deviant[50]—but also suggests Davis's awareness, as a mother and a prominent author, of the practical stresses and competing emotional demands in the life of public women.

"A Day with Doctor Sarah" is set in the 1870s, just when the implications for female political identity of the Fourteenth and Fifteenth Amendments were becoming clear. At that time, two highly publicized legal cases claimed women's right to suffrage based on a "citizenship" argument derived from the Fourteenth Amendment. In 1891 in the antisuffrage journal the *Remonstrance*, Davis writes, "Should the right of suffrage be extended to women? I am very sure that I for one should sit by the fire on election day while my cook and laundress voted. I do not believe that I should be any more conscientious or faithful to my duty in this matter than are the majority of educated American men in our cities who now leave the control of the primary elections and the polls to men who are neither educated nor American."[51] Even so, in my view "A Day with Dr. Sarah" shows that Davis saw the issue of political identity to be of driving concern to women. As Maria Epps explains her conversion to suffrage to her luncheon guests, "A woman is . . . first of all, a citizen. She loves, marries, by accident, but she is a citizen by inalienable right" (322). The language of the Fourteenth Amendment made it clear that another amendment would be needed before women could vote, and for this, as Dr. Sarah attests, women would have to lobby Congress. This interpretation differs from that of Sharon Harris, who holds that while Davis advocated women's suffrage, she often "demeaned the 'New Woman.'"[52] Similarly, Tillie Olsen reproaches Davis for not attending the meeting at the

1876 Philadelphia Centennial Exposition, when the leaders of the women's movement "sat in" and took over the platform to read their Women's Declaration of Rights.[53] This was not a well-organized protest, however, but rather a surprise move on the part of Susan B. Anthony, of which Davis was surely unaware. Indeed, there is no record of Davis participating in any of the campaigns, petition drives, or lobbying efforts launched by any women's organization.[54] In a letter to Annie Fields, apparently written in 1876, she says, "The fact is when our sex get into corporate bodies I have an instinct that warns me off—haven't you? 'I am never less a woman than when I have been among women' as Seneca *didn't* say."[55] Given the current storm of women's activities and Davis's friendship with such female activists as Lucretia Mott, it is hard not to read her total silence on the campaign for women's rights as a significant one. Although Davis was concerned about abolition, temperance reform, divorce law, and prostitution, it appears that she never joined groups or walked in any marches on behalf of these causes.

"A Day with Doctor Sarah" also points to Davis's development as a realist. Her female characters from this last fertile period of social fiction, such as Sarah, Maria, and Marcia, mark Davis's break with the sentimental view that assigned to women biologically predetermined roles. The identities of Davis's female characters are woven into the moving fabric of postbellum political and economic changes—their roles as orators and writers are not foreordained subjectivities, but are shaped by their specific relations to their family, education, class, and race. Their destinies are not bound by a genre that inevitably concludes with economic and romantic rewards, but rather, her women's destinies are the outcome of their experience of social history. Davis's female characters of this period make choices from options that are socially available to them; these complicated choices, rather than a predetermined set of female attributes, reveal their personalities. The accretion of social details in Davis's fiction that began with the flitch, the dirty rain, and the industrial fog in "Life in the Iron-Mills" reaches a point in the 1870s where she can picture a dialectic between character and lived history that creates decisions—that is, plot—and that limits the sentimental commitment to inevitability itself.

In her topical stories of the 1870s, Davis identifies her own authorship with that of new womanhood, rooting her fiction in immediate political controversies of great concern to women. In so doing, she forged an early and unique type of social realism. In "Put Out of the Way" (1870), Davis exposed "civil commitment," or enforced institutionalization in insane asylums.[56] Two years earlier, Clarke Davis, who had left the practice of law to become managing editor of the *Philadelphia Inquirer*, had published *A Modern Lettre de Cachet* on the legal abuses and physical tortures endured by patients in Pennsylvania's mental institutions—one of his most famous pieces of investigative reporting. Although, as Clarke stated, a criminal cannot be imprisoned without a warrant, hearing, and trial, anyone could be committed to a lunatic asylum at the whim of a relative, physician, or enemy. No writ of habeas corpus protected a citizen from a "living grave" in a mental institution. As a test case, Clark tried to place a "patient" in Frankford Lunatic Asylum in Pennsylvania, where the director assured him that if he purchased a private room, the alleged patient need never be seen again by anyone but his doctor and private attendant. Clarke also described how a husband, seeking grounds for divorce, had his wife incarcerated at the Pennsylvania Hospital for the Insane, where physicians who never met her promised to testify to her insanity. He reported that patients' attempts to escape, complain, or resist became further "evidence" in these "manufactures of madness." Citing reports of the Pennsylvania Medical Association and a special governors' commission, Clarke described basement cells, inadequate food, and enforced nudity in contemporary asylums where patients had been chained to the floor for twenty years.

When Davis sought to fictionalize these materials, she closely followed the legal machinations traced by Clarke, but in focusing on the pain and isolation of insanity and in feminizing the male captive, she also implicates other social practices that confine women. "Put Out of the Way" is the story of how a young painter, Dick Wortley, is institutionalized by Colonel Leeds, the scheming guardian of a young heiress, Lotty Hubbard, in the hope that she will marry his son instead. To put Wortley "out of the way," Leeds easily bribes a doctor to sign commitment papers without ever examining him. After Wortley is secretly captured and institutionalized, he is allowed no contact with the outside world. The asylum administrators destroy his desperate letters to his family and his legal friends, and for years no one knows what has happened to him.

The compelling power of Davis's story resides not only in its cold accuracy—the legal frustrations, the brutality of the stone cells, the levels or grades to which the inmates are assigned according to their degree of compliance, the intimidating beatings, and the slow water tortures—episodes unlike anything else in Davis's writings in their violent detail. As in Gilman's "The Yellow Wallpaper" (1892) and in Sylvia Plath's *The Bell Jar* (1963) written eighty years later, the story's appeal also resides in Davis's stunning descriptions of the ambiguous psychology of the sane person in an insane environment and the hostility and fear with which normal people treat those whom they presume to be mentally ill. She follows Dick's deteriorating struggle to remain in control of his mind, despite his isolation, intellectual deprivation, and doses of chloroform; his "tortured soul within was seeking, at eyes and mouth, some means of escape" (35). After one particularly brutal beating, Dick returns to consciousness: "It was late in June before he was himself enough to know that the claw-like fingers, picking at the sheet were his own . . . he had learned reticence; he asked no questions, made no comments . . . and laughed quietly to himself" (35–36). Images of silence and confinement return us to Davis's vocabulary of female repression, while the references to the immobilizing pain of Dick's "brain fever," technically a form of meningitis but also a nineteenth-century catchall term for various experiences of depression, suggest the neurasthenia Rebecca suffered during her first pregnancy.

Despite harrowing escape attempts, Dick remains in the asylum until a young girl finds a desperate letter to a judge that he has thrown over the asylum wall. Although his efforts to flee are drawn from sentimental or crime fiction, most episodes in "Put Out of the Way" turn on contemporary legal references. For example, the burden of proof of sanity remains with Dick, who is trapped in an asylum without legal or financial resources, and Dick discovers that a suit for false imprisonment is notoriously difficult to win. As the asylum superintendent maintains, "I can arrest any man before me [with a slip of paper from any physician]. . . . I can call upon the police to aid me, use what secrecy I choose, and hold him imprisoned for what time *I* think proper" (117). Thus, Dick is reduced to a voiceless and powerless state—a female trope in Davis's work. His eventual release and his romantic reunion with Lotty is at odds with the apologia, which refers us to the unfinished business in the world.

In "Put Out of the Way," Davis forged an unusual political text. Not only are Dick and a fellow patient rescued by the actions of two young women, the girl who bravely mails Dick's letter over her father's objections, and Lotty, who boldly intervenes with a reluctant family to save an elderly patient confined for decades. The disjointed and incomplete ending also stimulates the reader to take action outside of the text and become part of an unusual joint crusade on the part of Rebecca and Clarke, who continued to pursue the issue in his editorial column in the *Philadelphia Inquirer.* Eventually, Clarke was appointed to a commission to revise the lunacy laws of Pennsylvania[57] and the next few years witnessed the enactment of legislation to protect the rights of the mentally ill.[58]

While Davis's topics were becoming increasingly political, her fiction from the mid-seventies on reveals her problems in narrating these concerns. She found it increasingly difficult to frame her views on women's confined lives and repressed identities in narratives that would engage an articulate woman in public action and expose the implications of female impoverishment and intellectual deprivation. Emplotment of male characters seems less a problem, as she refashioned contemporary fictional tropes—mistaken identity, the chase, the quest, the reformed rake—with political themes.

John Andross (1874), her most explicitly political novel, was Davis's last attempt at a lengthy narrative in which she tried to integrate politics and literary form.[59] The novel works on two levels—a tale of political scandal, crime, and corruption in the Whiskey and Tweed Rings, and a psychological study of the emotional life of frustrated women who, lacking education and deprived of direct access to power, live to manipulate political men—to the peril of both. Thus *John Andross* is a story of what happens when the world of politics is deprived of female sensibility and of what happens when female sensibility is deprived of power. Public institutions, she suggests, mirror the aggression, competition, and insecurity of the men who control them. At the same time, because women lack access to public life, they appeal to emotionality, sexuality, and indirection to enact their justifiable desire for influence and authority.

John Andross is a psychological study of a well-meaning but weak man caught in a web of political corruption. While Sharon Harris reads *John Andross* as an example of early naturalism,[60] I find that Davis situates her

character in a world of complex moral choices. John Andross is not a powerless victim of the malevolent, deterministic, and inexorable forces that drive
naturalist texts, but rather an ambitious but weak man who is easily tempted
by social pressures; as such, he anticipates such figures as Howells's Silas
Lapham, Chopin's Edna Pontellier, and Twain's Huck Finn. As Andross's
employer tells him, "It seems to me as if you stood on the edge of the pit.
There's no force that need compel you to go down it. There are no devils to
enter into a man now as in old times" (51). Andross responds, "You're mistaken. There are forces outside of a man nowadays—here, all about him—
just as strong to compel him to ill-doing as ever there were in the wilderness
or in hell" (51). Davis's astute, accurate, and detailed portrait of the "hold"
on Andross situates this text in the world of realism—a moment in cultural
consciousness between predestination and social inevitability, between essentialism and biological determinism. This is a world of social and hence
changeable evil that, as Andross observes, "buys and sells" the government,
the press, the pulpits, and the courts "at will."

Davis wrote *John Andross* in the early 1870s in the midst of the journalistic
expose of the Whiskey Ring, initially a conspiracy between federal revenue
officers and whiskey distillers to build campaign funds for liberal Republicans by defrauding the government of taxes on liquor. Launched during the
administration of President Andrew Johnson, the rings flourished under
President Ulysses S. Grant, whose personal friend and Collector of Internal
Revenue, General John McDonald, alone defrauded the government of two
and a half million dollars. To hide such missing funds, the rings bought the
silence of newspaper editors, judges, tax collectors, and local elected officials.
In May 1875, the rings were officially exposed by the secretary of the treasury,
who seized sixteen distilleries and indicted 350 distillers and government
officials. However, because these officials, including the president's private
secretary, were closely tied to the Republican Party, Grant was reluctant to
prosecute vigorously, and in the end, the guilty parties received minimal sentences and most were soon pardoned.

The serialized version of *John Andross* in *Hearth and Home* in 1874 appeared
soon after the conviction of "Boss" William Marcy Tweed (1823–1878), who
had plundered the revenues of the city of New York through fraudulent
building and construction projects. Journals with which Davis was affiliated

—*Harper's Weekly*, the *New York Times*, and the *New York Herald Tribune*—had been instrumental in publicizing these scams. Davis's description of the rings' operations—bribes for journalists, local elections "bought" for the ring by lobbyists from trade associations, piles of cash taped to barrels of whiskey—is accurate, focused, and detailed. Unlike Silas Lapham (with whom John Andross has been compared), William Dean Howells's corrupt businessman who suffers humiliation and possible destitution for a private and generous, if foolish, payoff, John Andross is the weak but willing victim of a corrupt conspiracy. Hence, Andross is a social victim, albeit one who is a bit too intrigued by Boston transcendentalism (78–79)—still an egregious sin in Davis's cosmos.

Initially sucked into the ring in order to pay off a family debt, Andross soon accepts a slot as the ring's candidate for the state senate in Harrisburg. While he tries to pursue a career as a reform-minded politician, his political debt comes back to haunt him, as the ring orders him to vote to protect the stock of a cover organization. Pressuring Andross is a frightened group of men whose careers also depend on the beneficence of the ring and who tempt him in his Faustian debate over how to vote. These include Laird, the suave head of the ring who brilliantly glues together emotional, financial, and political debts, an unwitting and disbelieving Civil War veteran, a disreputable newspaper reporter, and a corrupt judge.

One of Davis's last interesting female characters is Anna Maddox, a capricious, bright, and frustrated woman who, deprived of power, operates through flirtation, seduction, and childishness, and who asserts, "[I can only use] what power I have" (204). Anna is the only character to recognize the complex emotional, legal, and financial web that Laird has spun. Standing at the end of Davis's sentimental journey, Anna signifies the danger Davis sees in a woman who is deprived of access to meaningful speech and activity; her gestures toward female political engagement, independence, candid expression, and romantic choice can function only through moral corruption and financial bankruptcy.

Ultimately, the only constructive role for a female citizen in *John Andross* is that of Isabel Latimer, the colonel's steadfast daughter, whose contribution to the health of the republic is to take responsibility for a pastoral mountain home the family emblematically left behind and to remove her family from the inevitable corruption of public and urban life. In this story, the moral charge that impelled many women into political activism in the 1870s recedes back into the family through the dutiful daughter and forgiving wife. But this, as Davis has repeatedly described, is a place of stasis, constriction, and silence. For Davis, the powerful female voice is not to be raised in the polis for that is a site of masculine, corrupt, and deceitful discourse.

In HER FICTION of the sixties and seventies, Davis describes women's economic and intellectual poverty; she writes of the plight of female factory workers, seamstresses, and slaves; she pictures the temptations of liquor and opium and depicts the danger of alcoholic men and the despair of their abused wives and abandoned children. She illustrates women's need for access to divorce. Fascinated with the contradictions in women's lives, Davis also describes how maternity complicates women's independence, professional identity, and self-definition. Unlike many of her peers, she never suggests that an active role in public life endangers a woman's purity, although she frequently suggests that it endangers her gender identity. Frequently using the rhetoric of abolition, Davis indicates that full human emancipation, the abolition of people as property, is incomplete. Her observations on female political equality, few that they are, draw upon the liberal ideals and vocabulary of the antislavery movement. For the most part, she justifies women's emancipation in terms of their right to public equality—a legacy of the Enlightenment—and their right to self-fulfillment—a legacy of romanticism. While she rarely suggests that women have a special moral character that requires their participation in political reform, she finds that the polis would be well served by women's contribution.

Although Davis saw no inherent split between the domestic woman and the woman author, she did see a split between the domestic woman and the political woman. In her fictional portraits of female activists, Davis was interested in how pressures of a life of political activism shape a woman's character, determine how men perceive her and define how, within an economic system and social ideology structured around women's roles as wives and mothers, the political woman will perceive herself. Nonetheless, her stories on women and publishing make it clear that she did not view women's creativity as the private lyrical expression of female subjectivity. Her fictive artists—such as Hugh Wolfe and Marcia Barr—produce socially engaged and realistic art—as did she. Yet in her portraits of autonomous women and their domestic insurgence, acts of female protest are muted through a narrative tradition that resuscitates the marriage plot that Davis has just questioned. In picturing the new woman, Davis situates her within the historical debates surrounding women in the earlier years of the women's movement. In writing realistically of women's lives, she perforce redefines women's fiction, insisting on its challenge to the social and literary tradition that spawned her own work.

Notes

1. Introduction

1. RHD, "Marcia," *Harper's New Monthly Magazine* 53 (November 1876), in *A Rebecca Harding Davis Reader*, ed. Jean Pfaelzer (Pittsburgh: University of Pittsburgh Press, 1995), 310. Unless otherwise specified, citations from Davis's work are from the *Reader*.

2. See Jane Atterbridge Rose, "A Bibliography of Fiction and Non-Fiction by Rebecca Harding Davis," *American Literary Realism* 22:3 (spring 1990): 67–86. There is no bibliography for the early pieces Davis wrote for the Wheeling *Intelligencer* or her later essays and editorials for the *New York Herald Tribune*.

3. RHD, "Women in Literature," *Independent* 43 (7 May 1891), in *A Rebecca Harding Davis Reader*, 404.

4. Cited in Amy Kaplan, *The Social Construction of American Realism* (Chicago: University of Chicago Press, 1988), 9.

5. Ibid., 9.

6. Ibid., 7.

7. Charlotte Perkins Gilman, *The Yellow Wallpaper* (New York: Feminist Press, 1973), 10–11.

8. RHD to Annie Fields, 10 January 1863, in Richard Harding Davis Collection (# 6109), Clifton Waller Barrett Library, Manuscript Division, Special Collection Department, University of Virginia Library, hereafter "U.Va."

9. Jane Atterbridge Rose, *Rebecca Harding Davis* (New York: Twayne Publishers, 1993), xii, states that Davis destroyed most of her personal correspondence.

10. RHD to Annie Fields, 6 December 1862, U.Va.

11. Patricia J. Williams, *The Alchemy of Race and Rights* (Cambridge: Harvard University Press, 1991), 92.

12. Marianna Torgovnick, *Gone Primitive: Savage Intellects, Modern Lives* (Chicago: University of Chicago Press, 1990), 9.

13. Karen Sanchez-Eppler, "Bodily Bonds: The Intersecting Rhetorics of Feminism and Abolition," *Representations* 24 (1988): 31–32.

14. Suzanne Clark, *Sentimental Modernism: Women Writers and the Revolution of the Word* (Bloomington: Indiana University Press, 1991), 29.

15. See Theresa de Lauretis, *Feminist Studies/Critical Studies: Issues, Terms, and Contexts* (Bloomington: Indiana University Press, 1986), 1–18.

16. Biographical material can be found in Rebecca Harding Davis, *Bits of Gossip* (Boston: Houghton Mifflin, 1904); Gerald Langford, *The Richard Harding Davis Years: A Biography of Mother and Son* (New York: Holt, Rinehart and Winston, 1961); Charles Davis, ed., *Adventures and Letters of Richard Harding Davis* (New York: Charles Scribner's Sons, 1917); Sharon Harris, *Rebecca Harding Davis and American Realism* (Philadelphia: University of Pennsylvania Press, 1991); Arthur Lobow, *The Reporter Who Would Be King: Biography of Richard Harding Davis* (New York: Scribner's, 1992); Rose, *Rebecca Harding Davis;* Helen Woodward Sheaffer, "Rebecca Harding Davis, Pioneer Realist" (Ph.D. diss., University of Pennsylvania, 1947); William F. Grayburn, "The Major Fiction of Rebecca Harding Davis" (Ph.D. diss., Pennsylvania State University, 1965); and correspondence at U.Va. and Huntington Library, San Marino, Calif., hereafter "Huntington Library."

17. Langford, *The Richard Harding Davis Years,* 6.

18. Ibid., 4.

19. RHD, *Bits of Gossip,* 68–69.

20. Ibid., 1.

21. Ibid., 4.

22. RHD, "Boston in the Sixties," from *Bits of Gossip,* in *A Rebecca Harding Davis Reader,* 443.

23. Ibid., 444.

24. Sharon Harris, in *Rebecca Harding Davis and American Realism,* suggests that Davis wrote and edited in the *Intelligencer* before the publication of "Life in the Iron-Mills" (1861), which heretofore seemed to spring mysteriously from the pen of a young mountain woman.

25. Ibid., 24–26.

26. Ibid., 25; RHD to James Fields, 16 November 1861, U.Va.

27. RHD, to Annie Fields, Monday evening [probably late January 1863], U.Va.

28. RHD, "Boston in the Sixties," 445.

29. Ibid.

30. Ibid., 446.

31. Ibid., 449.

32. Ibid., 450.

33. See Joanne Dobson, "The Hidden Hand: Subversion of Cultural Ideology in Three Mid-Nineteenth Century American Women's Novels," *American Quarterly* 38:2

(1986): 223–42, on Susan Warner's *the Wide, Wide World* (1850), E. D. E. N. Southworth's *The Hidden Hand* (1859), and A. D. T. Whitney's *Hitherto: A Story of Yesterdays* (1869).

34. RHD, "The Newly Discovered Woman," *Independent* 45 (30 November 1893), in *A Rebecca Harding Davis Reader*, 405.

35. Ibid., 406.

36. RHD, "The Middle-Aged Woman," *Scribner's Monthly Magazine*, July 1875, in *A Rebecca Harding Davis Reader*, 374.

37. RHD, "The Black North," *Independent* 54:6 (6 February 1902), in *A Rebecca Harding Davis Reader*, 441.

38. RHD, "The Work Before Us," *Independent* 51 (19 January 1899), in *A Rebecca Harding Davis Reader*, 427.

39. Ibid.

40. RHD to Annie Fields, Sunday evening [probably early 1866], U.Va.

41. Nancy Armstrong, *Desire and Domestic Fiction* (New York: Oxford University Press, 1987), 24. This discussion of the social implications of sentimentalism is indebted to Armstrong.

42. See Elaine Showalter, "Dinah Murlock Craik and the Tactics of Sentiment: A Case Study in Victorian Female Authorship," *Feminist Studies* 2 (1975).

43. Claudia Tate, "Allegories of Black Female Desire; or Rereading Nineteenth-Century Sentimental Narratives of Black Female Authority," in *Changing Our Own Words*, ed. Cheryl A. Wall (New Brunswick, N.J.: Rutgers University Press, 1987), 103.

44. Dobson, "The Hidden Hand," 230.

45. Nancy Bentley, "White Slaves: The Mulatto Hero in Antebellum Fiction," *American Literature* 65:3 (September 1993): 512.

46. Philip Fisher, *Hard Facts: Setting and Form in the American Novel* (New York: Oxford University Press, 1985), 99.

47. RHD, "Life in the Iron-Mills," *Atlantic Monthly* 7 (April 1861), in *A Rebecca Harding Davis Reader*, 11.

48. Ibid., 4.

49. See Nancy Chodorow, "Gender, Relation and Difference in Psychoanalytic Perspective," in *The Future of Difference*, ed. Alice Jardine and Hester Eisenstein (Boston: G. K. Hall, 1980): 3–19.

50. Marianne Hirsch argues that the repression of the fictional mother "stands at the very basis of the marriage plot" and suggests that we need to include maternal absence, silence, and negativity in this analysis; she also considers the impact of eliminating the mother on the heroine's development and allegiances (*The Mother/Daughter Plot: Narrative, Psychoanalysis, Feminism* [Bloomington: Indiana University Press, 1989], 3, 46–50).

51. See Kaplan, *The Social Construction of American Realism*, 3; my analysis is indebted to Kaplan.

52. Ibid., 7.

53. RHD, "Life in the Iron-Mills," 3.

54. Annette Kolodny, *The Land Before Her: Fantasy and Experience of the American Frontiers, 1630–1860* (Chapel Hill: University of North Carolina Press, 1984), xii–xiv.

55. See Annette Kolodny, *The Lay of the Land: Metaphor as Experience and History in American Life and Letters* (Chapel Hill: University of North Carolina Press, 1975), 4.

56. See L. J. Jordanova, "Natural Facts: A Historical Perspective on Science and Sexuality," in *Nature, Culture and Gender*, ed. Carol P. MacCormack and Marilyn Strathern (Cambridge: Cambridge University Press, 1980), 44–61; Raymond Williams, *The City and the Country* (London: Chatto and Windus, 1973), 1–8.

2. *The Terrible Question of "Life in the Iron-Mills"*

1. RHD, "Life in the Iron-Mills," *Atlantic Monthly* 7:42 (April 1861), in *A Rebecca Harding Davis Reader*, 4. The original manuscript of "Life in the Iron-Mills" is filed in the papers of James Fields, Huntington Library, San Marino, California.

2. *Picker* refers both to the person and the machine for separating and cleaning the cotton fibers.

3. Cora Kaplan suggests that Mary Wollstonecraft's unfinished novel *Maria, or The Wrongs of Woman* foreshadowed "a century of symbolization in which the physical habitation of the inner city is used to denigrate the subjectivity of its population" ("'Like a Housemaid's Fancies': The Representation of Working-Class Women in Nineteenth-Century Writing," in *Grafts: Feminist Cultural Criticism*, ed. Susan Sheridan [London: Verso, 1988], 64).

4. See Lora Romero's discussion of the trope of female confinement in domestic architecture, female fashion, and young girls' play in the writings of Catherine Beecher in "Domesticity and Fiction," in *The Columbia History of the American Novel*, ed. Emory Elliott (New York: Columbia University Press, 1991), 120–21.

5. Alfred, Lord Tennyson, "In Memoriam A. H. H." (1833), sec. 12 l. 16; sec. 56, ll. 25, 27. Section 56 reads in full:

> O life, as futile, then, as frail!
> O for thy voice to soothe and bless!
> What hope of answer, or redress?
> Behind the veil, behind the veil.

Davis's quotation lacks the compensatory second line and the portentous closing line.

6. For a discussion of this trope in European romanticism, see Susan Kirkpatrick,

Las Romanticas: Women Writers and Subjectivity in Spain, 1835–1850 (Berkeley: University of California Press, 1989), 13.

7. Susan Harris argues that sentimental language encourages "auditors" to conceive of their experiences metaphorically in order to re-envision themselves as part of a set of universal patterns, hence sentimentalism places them in a universal context. "Ultimately what is created is a platonic image of the feminine that is intensely intertextual. . . . In fact, the intertextual portions of the individual novels, taken out of the contexts of the works and brought into conjunction with each other, create a dialogue of their own about the nature and status of women that is simultaneously historicized and universalized" ("'But is it any *good?*': Evaluating Nineteenth-Century American Women's Fiction," *American Literature* 63:1 [March 1991]: 56).

8. Ralph Waldo Emerson, "The American Scholar," quoted in Ronald E. Martin, *American Literature and the Destruction of Knowledge: Innovative Writing in the Age of Epistemology* (Durham: Duke University Press, 1991), 7. Martin observes, "Striving for disengagement from tradition and from the ideas, language, and rationality that culture interposed, the knower, according to Emerson's new-world myth, needed to establish personal experience as the basis of knowing. Only through immersion in the immediacy, the multifariousness, the spontaneity of firsthand experience could a person hope to know the world in its essential otherness" (7).

9. Suzanne Clark, *Sentimental Modernism: Women Writers and the Revolution of the Word* (Bloomington: Indiana University Press, 1991), 23.

10. Harris argues, by contrast, that the narrator's frame draws on the language of romanticism but contextually demands that the reader evaluate the story in decidedly realistic terms (*Rebecca Harding Davis and American Realism* [Philadelphia: University of Pennsylvania Press, 1991], 29).

11. Clark, *Sentimental Modernism*, 22.

12. In *Rebecca Harding Davis and American Realism*, Sharon Harris sees the narrator as residing in an upper tier, Hugh in an underworld, and Deb, as guide, translator, and mediator at an intermediary level. In my view, there is no evidence that Deb is of a separate class from Hugh, nor that she acts as a guide or translator. Both are of the industrial working class; both Hugh and Deb have geographic mobility, and both serve as projections of the narrator's fluid consciousness.

13. Robyn R. Warhol, "Toward a Theory of the Engaging Narrator: Earnest Interventions in Gaskell, Stowe, and Eliot," *PMLA* 101:5 (October 1986): 811–18.

14. For elaboration of these distinctions, see Martin, *American Literature and the Destruction of Knowledge*, xxii–xxiii.

15. Emerson, "The Poet," in *Essays and Lectures*, ed. Joel Porte (New York: Library of America, 1983), 491–92.

16. RHD to James Fields, 26 January 1861, U.Va.

17. Melville, "The Paradise of Bachelors and the Tartarus of Maids," *Harper's New Monthly Magazine*, April 1855, is generally credited with being the first portrait of industrial labor in mainstream American fiction.

18. In an editorial for *The Quaker City* on shoemakers, Lippard wrote, "Just look through the window of yonder room. . . . Do you notice the unnatural position in which they are forced to work—The breast bent, the stomach cramped . . . there they sit twelve hours per day. How long do you think the *human machinery* will last at this rate? . . . see those foreheads that indicate the presence of intellect of no mean character—and then ask your own heart whether these men were born to work, work, work, and to have no fair chance of development, moral, mental, or physical? . . . These men were born with as fine an intellect as yours" (in *George Lippard, Prophet of Protest: Writings of an American Radical, 1822–1854*, ed. David S. Reynolds [New York: Peter Lang, 1986], 47).

19. The night shift generally followed the introduction of the Bessemer process. Initially, mill owners wanted to make steel cheaply enough to produce large pieces, such as the artillery shell and the long gun barrel. Instead of refining pig iron by placing it directly on a pile of coal, Bessemer invented the process of keeping it molten in a vat and blowing cold air through it. The air, with the oxidized impurities attached to it, would come out the top. This process required maintaining huge vats of molten pig iron that took a great deal of time to heat up and cool down; to reduce labor and coal costs, management introduced the night shift.

20. Discussions of naturalism in "Life in the Iron-Mills" can be found in Harris, *Rebecca Harding Davis and American Realism;* Sandra Gilbert and Susan Gubar, eds., *The Norton Anthology of Literature by Women: The Tradition in English* (New York: Norton, 1985), 903; Jean Pfaelzer, "Rebecca Harding Davis: Domesticity, Social Order, and the Industrial Novel," *International Journal of Women's Studies* 4:3 (May 1981): 234–44.

21. David Hume, *A Treatise of Human Nature*, ed. L. A. Selby-Bigge (Oxford: Oxford University Press, 1965). Quoted in Thomas W. Laqueur, "Bodies, Details, and the Humanitarian Narrative," in *The New Cultural History*, ed. Lynn Hunt (Berkeley: University of California Press, 1989), 180.

22. Glenn Hendler, "The Limits of Sympathy: Louisa May Alcott and the Sentimental Novel," *American Literary History* 3:4 (winter 1991): 686, 695.

23. I borrow this phrase from Kirkpatrick, *Las Romanticas*, 291.

24. In her discussion of Mme. de Staël's *Corinne*, Kirkpatrick suggests that the tragic inevitability of the romantic female subject stems from the impossibility of reconciling female genius with the social views of femininity and the consequent distribution of elements of female subjectivity among a number of fictional characters (ibid., 139).

25. Amy Schrager Lang, "Class and the Strategies of Sympathy," in *The Culture of Sentiment: Race, Gender, and Sentimentality in Nineteenth-Century America*, ed. Shirley Samuels (New York: Oxford University Press, 1992), 130.

26. Philip Taylor, *The Distant Magnet: European Immigration to the U.S.A.* (New York: Harper and Row, 1971), 46, 86–87, 89.

27. Jane Tompkins thus calls sentimental fiction a "political enterprise" (*Sensational Designs: The Cultural Work of American Fiction 1790–1860* [New York: Oxford University Press, 1985], 126–27).

28. Elaine Showalter, "Dinah Murlock Craik and the Tactics of Sentiment: A Case Study in Victorian Female Authorship," *Feminist Studies* 2:2–3 (1975); Henry Nash Smith, "The Scribbling Woman and the Cosmic Success Story," *Critical Inquiry* (September 1974): 20.

29. Armstrong, *Desire and Domestic Fiction*, 20–21, 24.

30. See Julie Elison, *Delicate Subjects: Romanticism, Gender and the Ethics of Understanding* (Ithaca: Cornell University Press, 1990).

31. See Martin's discussion of the ambiguity of knowledge in romanticism in *American Literature and the Destruction of Knowledge*. In Emerson and Melville, for example, Martin argues that the "meaning of anything is strictly relative to the individual, transient state of its beholders. For Emerson in these relativistic frames of mind it would seem that there is no possibility whatever of direct knowledge or reality, however strong his urgings toward pure of unmediated experience." Thus in Emerson all symbols are "fluxional" (9–10).

32. Kirkpatrick, *Las Romanticas*, 11.

33. Ibid., 14.

34. Ellen Moers, *Literary Women* (Garden City, N.Y.: Doubleday, 1976).

35. Hendler, "The Limits of Sympathy," 696.

36. Harris, *Rebecca Harding Davis and American Realism*, 37.

37. Annette Kolodny, *The Land Before Her: Fantasy and Experience of the American Frontiers 1630–1860* (Chapel Hill: University of North Carolina Press, 1984), 6.

38. Harris, *Rebecca Harding Davis and American Realism*, 38–39.

39. Lang, *The Culture of Sentiment*, 138.

40. Ibid., 139.

41. See Tompkins, *Sensational Designs*, 127 ff.

42. Kirkpatrick, *Las Romanticas*, 123.

43. In "'But is it any *good?*'" Harris contends that women's fiction of the mid-nineteenth century represents less a struggle of self against society than a struggle of self against self. Both selves are presented metaphorically: "In Richard Rorty's terms, these texts embody a battle for definition that pits two linguistically contingent world views against one another. Neither the self struggling to come into being

nor the one (usually spoken by the narrator) socially determined has any intrinsically objective reality; rather the validity of each rests on the reader's capacity for processing it" (54–55).

3. The Common Story of Margret Howth

1. See RHD to James Fields, 11 April 1861, U.Va., which indicates that "The Deaf and Dumb" was the initial title for this story.

2. RHD to James Fields, 10 May 1861, Huntington Library.

3. Jean Fagan Yellin, "Afterword," in Rebecca Harding Davis, *Margret Howth: A Story of Today* (New York: Feminist Press, 1990), 271–302. RHD received $125 for the book form of her novel, a minimal royalty of about one-half of one percent (see chap. 9). See Sharon Harris, *Rebecca Harding Davis and American Realism* (Philadelphia: University of Pennsylvania Press, 1991), 82–33.

4. RHD to James Fields, 30 July 1861, U.Va.

5. Rebecca Harding Davis, *Margret Howth: A Story of To-day*, ed. Jean Fagan Yellin (New York: Feminist Press, 1990), 3. All further quotations are from this edition.

6. Fred Kaplan, *Sacred Tears: Sentimentality in Victorian Literature* (Princeton: Princeton University Press, 1987), 3.

7. Review of *Margret Howth*, *Peterson's Magazine* 41:4 (April 1862): 343–44.

8. Review of *Margret Howth*, *Continental Monthly* 1 (April 1862): 467.

9. Ibid.

10. Harris, *Rebecca Harding Davis and American Realism*, 63.

11. Yellin, "Afterword."

12. See Mary Poovey, "My Hideous Progeny: Mary Shelley and the Feminization of Romanticism," *PMLA* 95 (January 1980): 333–34, for a discussion of the politics of romantic eroticism, in particular.

13. RHD to James Fields, 9 August 1861, U.Va.

14. I am indebted to Benedict Anderson for this term. See in particular *Imagined Communities: Reflections on the Origin and Spread of Nationalism*, rev. ed. (New York: Verso, 1991), chap. 1.

15. Nina Baym, "Melodramas of Beset Manhood: How Theories of American Fiction Exclude Women Writers," *American Quarterly* 33 (1981): 132.

16. Poovey, "My Hideous Progeny," 334.

17. Jane Tompkins, *Sensational Designs: The Cultural Work of American Fiction, 1790–1860* (New York: Oxford University Press, 1985), xvii ff.

18. Susan Harris, "'But is it any *good*?': Evaluating Nineteenth-Century American Women's Fiction," *American Literature* 63:1 (March 1991): 60.

19. Ralph Waldo Emerson, "The American Scholar," in *Selected Essays, Lectures, and Poems of Ralph Waldo Emerson*, ed. Robert E. Spiller (New York: Washington Square Press, 1965), 73.

20. Davis is referring to the practice whereby draftees into the Union Army could hire a substitute or pay a commutation fee of $300, a privilege that produced the slogan "Rich man's war and poor man's fight." James McPherson, *Battle Cry of Freedom: The Civil War Era* (New York: Oxford University Press, 1988), 603.

21. RHD to James Fields, 11 April 1861, U.Va.

22. Emerson, "The American Scholar," 78.

23. Jane Tompkins observes, "'Sentimental' novels take place, metaphorically and literally, in the 'closet.' Their heroines rarely get beyond the confines of a private space—the kitchen, the parlor, the upstairs chamber—and most of what they do takes place inside the 'closet' of the heart" ("Afterword," in Susan Warner, *The Wide, Wide World* [New York: Feminist Press, 1987], 594).

24. See RHD to James Fields, 17 August [1861], U.Va.; RHD to James Fields, n.d., U.Va.; 16 January [1862], U.Va.; RHD to James Fields, n.d. [probably autumn 1862], U.Va. Harris notes that in the late 1860s Davis, encouraged by her husband Clarke, allowed her name to appear as "Mrs. R. H. Davis." Beginning in the 1870s, with her focus on women's issues, she changed her by-line to "Rebecca Harding Davis" (*Rebecca Harding Davis and American Realism*, 318, n. 38).

25. RHD to James Fields, 17 August [1861], U.Va.

26. Kaplan, *Sacred Tears*, 17–18.

27. Ibid., 16.

28. Leslie Rabine holds that while contemporary critics view essentialism as necessarily conservative, thereby making women complicitous with the ideology of the dominant class and race, the strategy of changing structural relations around an unchanging essence in fact offered the only means available to speak against the ideology of gender ("Essentialism and Its Contexts: St. Simonian and Post-Structuralist Feminisms," *Differences* 1:2 [1990]: 105–23).

29. Thomas Laqueur, "Bodies, Details, and the Humanitarian Narrative," in *New Cultural History*, ed. Lynn Hunt (Berkeley: University of California Press, 1989), 176–204.

30. See, for example, Margaret Fuller's dispatches to the *Tribune* of 7 and 13 May 1848, in Bell Gale Chevigny, *The Woman and the Myth: Margaret Fuller's Life and Writings* (Boston: Northeastern University Press, 1994), 449–53.

31. Nancy Schnog, "Inside the Sentimental: The Psychological Work of *The Wide, Wide World*," *Genders* 4 (spring 1989): 18.

32. Originally, Davis may have intended Holmes to display the influence of Fichte.

As she first considered revising the story, she wrote to Fields, "Would the character of Holmes be distasteful to your readers? I mean—the development in common vulgar life of the Fichtian philosophy and its effect upon a self made man, as I view it?" (RHD to James Fields, 10 May 1861, Huntington Library).

33. Nancy Cott, "Passionlessness: An Interpretation of Victorian Sexual Ideology, 1790–1850," *Signs* 4 (1978): 223.

34. Suzanne Clark, *Sentimental Modernism: Women Authors and the Revolution of the Word* (Bloomington: Indiana University Press, 1991), 21.

35. Julie Elison, *Delicate Subjects: Romanticism, Gender and the Ethics of Understanding* (Ithaca: Cornell University Press, 1990), 13–14.

36. Emerson, "The American Scholar," 68.

37. Emerson, "Nature," in *Selected Essays*, 179.

38. Ibid., 181.

39. Ibid., 211.

40. Ibid., 185.

41. Ibid., 189.

42. Ibid., 208.

43. Marianne Hirsch, "Spiritual *Bildung*: The Beautiful Soul as Paradigm," in *The Voyage In: Fictions of Female Development* (Hanover, N.H.: University Press of New England, 1983), 23–24.

44. Emerson, "The American Scholar," 73.

45. See Tompkins, "Afterword," 584–607.

46. RHD to James Fields, 17 August 1861, U.Va.

47. See RHD to James Fields, 26 November 1861, U.Va, about revising the serialized story for publication in book form.

4. The Savage Necessity of Abolition and the Civil War

1. William Dean Howells, "Review of *Miss Ravenal's Conversion from Secession to Loyalty* by J. W. De Forest," *Atlantic Monthly* 20 (July 1867): 121.

2. On the iconography of silence in the representation of the slave, see Jean Fagan Yellin, *Women and Sisters: The Antislavery Feminists in American Culture* (New Haven: Yale University Press, 1989), esp. "The Speechless Agony of the Fettered Slave."

3. "John Lamar," "David Gaunt," and "Blind Tom" were first published in the *Atlantic Monthly* in 1862, all in *A Rebecca Harding Davis Reader*.

4. Jane Tompkins, "The Other American Renaissance," in *The American Renaissance Reconsidered*, ed. Walter Benn Michaels and Donald E. Pease (Baltimore: Johns Hopkins University Press, 1985), 37.

5. In 1861 Davis wrote to James Fields, "I hope sincerely the disaster at Edwards Ferry did not touch you personally. God grant the war may never be to you in Boston what it is to us here" (RHD to James Fields, 31 October 1861, U.Va.). The realities of the war affected Davis's practical dealings with the *Atlantic*. By August 1861, fearing that General Lee would pass through the General Rosecranz's northern line and "scatter our Wheeling government," Davis asked Fields to direct all correspondence to her relatives' home in Washington, Pennsylvania. As she explained, "Just now 'New Virginia' and its capitol are in a state of panic and preparation not to be described" (RHD to James Fields, 17 August 1861, U.Va.). In September she wrote that she could not travel to Boston to meet him until the war was over, which she feared was a long way off (RHD to James Fields, September 1861, U.Va.). In December, the war touched her on a more mundane level and caused her considerable anxiety when the manuscript of "John Lamar," of which she had made no copy, was lost for several weeks in the mail.

6. The Harding family had servants, but I find no evidence indicating that they were slaves, although Tillie Olsen, among others, believes that this was possibile ("A Biographical Interpretation," in *Life in the Iron-Mills*, by Rebecca Harding Davis [New York: Feminist Press, 1972], 71). Davis's unpublished correspondence contains explicit statements of opposition to slaveholding.

7. RHD, "Two Methods With the Negro," *Independent* 2574 (31 March 1898), in *A Rebecca Harding Davis Reader*, 424.

8. RHD, "A Peculiar People," *Saturday Evening Post*, 10 January 1903, 20.

9. The new constitution of West Virginia freed all slaves born after 4 July 1863 and all others on their twenty-fifth birthday.

10. RHD, "A Peculiar People," 9.

11. RHD, "A Peculiar People," *Saturday Evening Post*, 17 January 1903.

12. In her abolitionist sympathies, Davis was probably closest in temperament to Lucretia Mott, whom she describes in "A Peculiar People." This late study of her personal recollections of well-known abolitionists also includes portraits of Francis Le Moyne, Sara Clarke, John C. Fremont, Horace Greeley, Wendell Phillips, Mrs. Frances Harper, Mary Grew, and Elizabeth Burleigh. On Lucretia Mott, see Blanche G. Hersh, "Am I Not a Woman and a Sister? Abolitionist Beginnings of Nineteenth-Century Feminism," in *Anti-Slavery Reconsidered: New Perspectives on the Abolitionists*, ed. Lewis Perry and Michael Fellman (Baton Rouge: Louisiana State University Press, 1979), 261–62.

13. RHD, "A Peculiar People," 20.

14. Ibid., 9.

15. In March 1863, Congress passed a conscription act. A Union draftee who

could not claim dependent relatives could pay a $300 commutation fee; of the 207,000 men who were drafted, 87,000 paid the fee and 74,000 furnished substitutes, a pool supplied by eighteen- and nineteen-year-olds and by immigrants who had not filed for citizenship. See James McPherson, *Battle Cry of Freedom: The Civil War Era* (New York: Oxford University Press, 1988), 601. On 27 July 1864, Davis wrote to Annie Fields, "Clarke was drafted and says very heroically that $300 is very little service for him to offer his country, which is all very well for patriots of his and your persuasion to say. I notice however that he is nursing the rheumatism . . . [in] one foot very assiduously ever since Saturday. Of course I can't guess for what" (U.Va.).

16. Daniel Aaron, *The Unwritten War: American Writers and the Civil War* (New York: Oxford University Press, 1973), xvii.

17. Ibid., xviii.

18. Hazel Carby, "Ideologies of Black Folk: The Historical Novel of Slavery," in *Slavery and the Literary Imagination,* ed. Deborah E. McDowell and Arnold Rampersad (Baltimore: Johns Hopkins Press, 1989), 125.

19. Quoted in Eric Sundquist, "Slavery, Revolution and the American Renaissance," in *The American Renaissance Reconsidered,* ed. Walter Benn Michaels and Donald E. Pease (Baltimore: Johns Hopkins University Press, 1985), 12.

20. Louis Masur, "The real war will never get in the books," in *Selections from Writers During the Civil War* (New York: Oxford University Press, 1993), 161.

21. Nathaniel Hawthorne to Francis Bennoch, Concord [July 1861], quoted in ibid., 164.

22. Nathaniel Hawthorne to Horatio Bridge, 13 February 1862, quoted in ibid., 167.

23. Quoted in Aaron, *The Unwritten War,* 25.

24. McPherson, *Battle Cry of Freedom,* 832.

25. Kathleen Diffley, *Where My Heart is Turning Ever: Civil War Stories and Constitutional Reform, 1861–1876* (Athens: University of Georgia Press, 1992), xii; Diffley found over three hundred stories in sixteen literary magazines during the Civil War that reveal how domestic rhetoric and narrative strategies tried to contain the disruption of the war, partricularly when they take up matters of race, political section, and gender. Also Masur, responding to Whitman's assertion that "the real war will never get in the books," collected selections from personal letters, diary entries, and journal articles that articulate a striking literary landscape of wartime writings by authors who, in Melville's phrase, could not escape the "skeletons of actual reality" (xxx).

26. Aaron, *The Unwritten War,* xviii.

27. Edgar Allan Poe, "Review," *Southern Literary Messenger* (April 1836). Like many others, I attribute this review to Poe. See Bernard Rosenthal, "Poe, Slavery, and the *Southern Literary Messenger*: A Reexamination," *Poe Studies* 7:2 (1974): 29–38.

28. Aaron, *The Unwritten War*, xviii.

29. Werner Sollars, "Of Mules and Men," *American Quarterly* 42 (1990): 181.

30. Carolyn Karcher, "Rape, Murder and Revenge in 'Slavery's Pleasant Homes':
Lydia Maria Child's Antislavery Fiction and the Limits of Genre," *Women's Studies
International Forum* 9:4 (1986): 323.

31. Frederick Douglass, "The Heroic Slave," in *The Life and Writings of Frederick
Douglass*, ed. Philip Foner (New York: International Publishers, 1950).

32. See also Lydia Maria Child, "The Black Saxons," set in colonial times, in
which a slaveowner witnesses a secret meeting of slaves who are debating whether or
not to murder their owners and join the British forces (*Fact and Fiction: A Collection of
Stories* [New York: C. S. Francis, 1847], 190–204).

33. Louisa May Alcott, "The Brothers," *Atlantic Monthly* 12 (November 1863) was
published elsewhere as "My Contraband," a title that signifies the slave as captured
property. See also Alcott's "An Hour," the story of a guilt-stricken master who
thwarts a slave revolt by immediately freeing his slaves. The story ends with the
slaves kissing his feet as they listen for the arrival of the Union troops (*Hospital
Sketches and Camp and Fireside Stories* [Boston: Roberts Brothers, 1869, 1892]).

34. Harriet E. Prescott, "Ray," *Atlantic Monthly* 13 (January 1864). See also
Prescott's "Down the River," *Atlantic Monthly* 16 (October 1865), in which a slave girl,
inadvertently trapped in the swamps with her young mistress, loyally returns to the
plantation to save the life of her mistress and only later runs away.

35. Carolyn Karcher, *The First Woman in the Republic: A Cultural Biography of Lydia Maria
Child* (Durham: Duke University Press, 1994), 330.

36. Eugene Genovese, *Roll, Jordan, Roll: The World the Slaves Made* (New York: Pantheon
Books, 1974), 615–19. See also Kenneth Stampp, *The Peculiar Institution: Slavery in the
Ante-Bellum South* (New York: Vintage Books, 1956), 131; and Herbert Aptheker,
American Negro Slave Revolts (New York: Columbia University Press, 1943).

37. RHD, "A Peculiar People," 20.

38. John Garraty, *The American Nation: History of the United States to 1877* (New York:
Harper and Row, 1971), 393.

39. RHD to James Fields, 30 December 1861, U.Va.

40. RHD, "Life in the Iron-Mills," *Atlantic Monthly* 7:42 (1861), in *A Rebecca Harding
Davis Reader*, 16.

41. William Chafe, "Sex and Race: The Analogy of Social Control," in *Racism and
Sexism: An Integrated Study*, ed. Paula S. Rothenberg (New York: St. Martin's Press,
1988), 334.

42. Davis discusses the division of Virginia in "A Peculiar People" and in *Bits of
Gossip* (Boston: Houghton Mifflin, 1904).

43. McPherson, *Battle Cry of Freedom*, 608.

44. Hazel Carby, "'On the Threshold of Woman's Era': Lynching, Empire, and Sexuality in Black Feminist Theory," in *Race, Writing, and Difference*, ed. Henry Louis Gates, Jr. (Chicago: University of Chicago Press, 1986), 315.

45. McPherson argues that the "twenty slave exemption code" not only sought to stem the problems of southern food production, plantation discipline, and runaway slaves. It also sought to "preserve a certain vision of womanhood. To leave white women alone on plantations to cope with large numbers of slaves was hardly compatible with his vision" (*Battle Cry of Freedom*, 611–12).

46. Carby, "Ideologies of Black Folk," 139.

47. See Rachel Blau DuPlessis, *Writing Beyond the Ending: Narrative Strategies of Twentieth-Century Women Writers* (Bloomington: Indiana University Press, 1985) for an analysis of the impact of feminist perspectives on narrative closures.

48. Elizabeth Fox-Genovese, *Within the Plantation Household: Black and White Women of the Old South* (Chapel Hill: University of North Carolina Press, 1988), 236.

49. See Herbert Gutman, *The Black Family in Slavery and Freedom* (New York: Pantheon Books, 1976), 293–96, for a discussion of how the relationship between mid-nineteenth-century class and sexual beliefs reinforced racial stereotypes.

50. Quoted in ibid., 295.

51. Ralph Ellison, *Shadow and Act* (New York: Random House, 1964), 97.

52. Gutman, *The Black Family in Slavery and Freedom*, 296.

53. Jean Fagan Yellin, *Women and Sisters: The Antislavery Feminists in American Culture* (New Haven: Yale University Press 1989), 45.

54. Mary Dearborn, *Pocahontas's Daughters: Gender and Ethnicity in American Culture* (New York: Oxford University Press, 1986), 133.

55. Sterling Brown, "A Century of Negro Portraiture in American Literature," *Massachusetts Review* 7 (1966), 78.

56. Sander Gilman, *Difference and Pathology: Stereotypes of Sexuality, Race and Madness* (Ithaca: Cornell University Press, 1985), 109.

57. Fox-Genovese, *Within the Plantation Household*, 34; see also George Fredrickson, *The Arrogance of Race: Historical Perspectives on Slavery, Racism and Social Inequality* (Middletown, Conn.: Wesleyan University Press, 1988), 241.

58. Fox-Genovese, *Within the Plantation Household*, 291; see also Fredrickson, *The Arrogance of Race*, 17.

59. William Lloyd Garrison, white abolitionist and publisher of the *Liberator* from 1831 to 1866, consistently argued for nonviolent resistance to slavery without, as Truman Nelson notes, curbing descriptions of slavery that made the paper "incendiary" ("Introduction," in *Documents of Upheaval: Selections from William Lloyd Garrison's The Liberator, 1831–1865* [New York: Hill and Wang, 1966], xiv).

60. Stephen Heath, "Difference," *Screen* 19 (1978): 53. I am grateful to Sander Gilman for this reference.

61. Mary Ryan, *The Empire of the Mother: American Writing About Domesticity* (New York: Harrington Park Press, 1982), 138.

62. Gillian Brown, "Getting in the Kitchen with Dinah: Domestic Politics in *Uncle Tom's Cabin*," *American Quarterly* 36 (1984): 510.

63. RHD to James Fields, 14 April 1862, U.Va.

64. RHD to James Fields, 30 December 1861, U.Va.

65. RHD, *Bits of Gossip*, 116–17.

66. RHD to Annie Fields, 22 August 1862, U.Va.

67. For a different interpretation, see Jane Atterbridge Rose, *Rebecca Harding Davis* (New York: Twayne Publishers, 1993), 11 who suggests that Davis was a "devout Christian." During the formative period of American realism, Rose argues, Davis aligned sentimentalism with critical realism through "a Christian critique of society."

68. Philip Fisher, *Hard Facts: Setting and Form in the American Novel* (New York: Oxford University Press, 1985), 99–114.

69. RHD to James Fields, 27 May 1862, U.Va.

70. Marianna Torgovnick, *Gone Primitive: Savage Intellects, Modern Lives* (Chicago: University of Chicago Press, 1990), 9.

71. I take the phrase from Henry Louis Gates, "Writing 'Race'" and the Difference It Makes," in *"Race," Writing, and Difference*, 5.

72. For a classic definition of the stereotype of the comic Negro, see Sterling Brown, "The Negro Character as Seen by White Authors," *Journal of Negro Education* 2 (1933): 179–203.

73. In addition to Davis's study, biographical information on Thomas Greene Bethune is based on Robert Goldenson, *Mysteries of the Mind: The Drama of Human Behavior* (Garden City, N.Y.: Doubleday, 1983); Edward Seguin, *Idiocy and Its Treatment by the Physical Method* (1866; reprint, New York: A. M. Kelley, 1971); Benjamin Brawley, *The Negro Genius: A New Appraisal of the Achievement of the American Negro in Literature and the Fine Arts* (New York: Biblo and Tannen, 1966), 131–33.

74. See Michael J. A. Howe, *Fragments of Genius: The Strange Feats of Idiots Savants* (New York: Routledge, 1989); D. A. Treffert, M.D., *Extraordinary People: Understanding "Idiot Savants"* (New York: Harper and Row, 1987); Goldenson, *Mysteries of the Mind*.

75. Brawley, *The Negro Genius*, 13.

76. On 2 January 1867 the Glasgow *Daily Herald* reported, "Mozart, when a mere child, was noted for the delicacy of his ear, and his ability to produce music on a first hearing; but Burney, in his *History of Music*, records no instance at all coming up to this Negro boy for his attainments in phonetics, and his power of retention and reproduction of sound" (cited in ibid., 130–31).

77. RHD to Annie Fields, 10 July 1862, U.Va.

78. On 12 July 1862, Davis wrote to James Fields, "I am quite interested in the 'Tom' question. This morning I received a present of a large full length likeness of him from a musician here. If I cannot find a chart of his 'bumps' I will have Fowles see the photograph and say what he thinks."

79. See Lora Romero, "Bio-Political Resistance in Domestic Ideology and *Uncle Tom's Cabin*," *American Literary History* (winter 1989): 726.

80. See Brown, "Getting in the Kitchen with Dinah," 503–23.

81. See William L. VanDeburg, *Slavery and Race in American Popular Culture* (Madison: University Wisconsin Press, 1984), esp. 17–41.

82. Werner Sollars, "Of Mules and Men," *American Quarterly* 42 (1990): 186.

83. Karen Sanchez-Eppler, "Bodily Bonds: The Intersecting Rhetorics of Feminism and Abolition," *Representations* 24 (1988): 31–32.

84. RHD to James Fields, n.d., U.Va.

85. Fisher, *Hard Facts*, 94.

86. Ibid., 99.

87. Davis's correspondence with Fields indicates that Charles Dickens read "Blind Tom" with great approval, but Davis was unable to use this praise to break into the English market (RHD to James Fields, 4 September 1862, U.Va.).

88. Tompkins, "The Other American Renaissance," 40.

5. *The Soul Starvation of the Domestic Woman*

1. Jane Tompkins, *Sensational Designs: The Cultural Work of American Fiction, 1790–1860* (New York: Oxford University Press, 1985), 124.

2. Astute analyses of relations between women in the mid-nineteenth century include Nancy Cott, *The Bonds of Womanhood: "Woman's Sphere" in New England, 1780–1835* (New Haven: Yale University Press, 1977); Carroll Smith-Rosenberg, "The Female World of Love and Ritual," *Signs* 1 (1975): 1–29; Mary Ryan, *The Empire of the Mother: American Writing About Domesticity, 1830–1860* (New York: Harrington Park Press, 1985).

3. RHD, *Bits of Gossip* (Boston: Houghton, Mifflin, 1904), 69.

4. Ibid., 68.

5. RHD to Annie Fields, 10 January 1863, U.Va.

6. RHD to Annie Fields, n.d., U.Va.

7. RHD, "The Promise of the Dawn: A Christmas Story," *Atlantic Monthly* 11 (January 1863).

8. Sources for the discussion of the history and ideology of prostitution in the mid-nineteenth century include Ruth Rosen, *The Lost Sisterhood: Prostitution in America*

1900–1918 (Baltimore: Johns Hopkins University Press, 1982); John D'Emilio and Estelle B. Freedman, *A History of Sexuality in America* (New York: Harper and Row, 1988); David J. Pivar, *Purity Crusade, Sexual Morality, and Social Control, 1868–1900* (Westport, Conn.: Greenwood Press, 1973).

9. Rosen, *The Lost Sisterhood,* xii.

10. D'Emilio and Freedman, *A History of Sexuality in America,* 52.

11. Caroline Healey Dall, *"Women's Right to Labor" or Low Wages and Hard Work* (1860; reprint, New York: Garland, 1987), 15.

12. William W. Sanger, *The History of Prostitution: Its Extent, Causes, and Effects Throughout the World* (1859; reprint, New York: Arno Press, 1972).

13. Ibid., 456.

14. G. M. Goshgarian, *To Kiss the Chastening Rod: Domestic Fiction and Sexual Ideology in the American Renaissance* (Ithaca: Cornell University Press, 1992), 59.

15. C. E. Rogers, *Secret Sins of Society* (Minneapolis: Union Publishing, 1881).

16. RHD to Annie Fields, 6 December 1862, U.Va.

17. D'Emilio and Freedman, *A History of Sexuality in America,* 153.

18. Ibid., 78.

19. Goshgarian, *To Kiss the Chastening Rod,* 59–60.

20. RHD wrote to Annie Fields, "I confess I never wrote anything so hard or repugnant to my feelings . . . which, when done, I was more indifferent to censure or praise. I *know* I was right. I was very sorry Mrs. Fremont did not think the effort one of feasible utility—but I have Christ on my side" (18 February 1863, U.Va.).

21. See Dee Garrison, "Immoral Fiction in the Late Victorian Library," *American Quarterly* 28 (1976): 72.

22. RHD, "The Second Life," *Peterson's Magazine* 44 (January–June 1863).

23. See Mary S. Hartman, *Victorian Murderesses: A True History of Thirteen Respectable French and English Women Accused of Unspeakable Crimes* (New York: Schocken Books, 1977).

24. RHD, "Paul Blecker," *Atlantic Monthly* 11 (May–June 1863).

25. Roderick Phillips, *Untying the Knot: A Short History of Divorce* (New York: Cambridge University Press, 1991), 171–73. Other sources used in this discussion are D'Emilio and Freedman, *A History of Sexuality in America;* Roderick Phillips, *Putting Asunder: A History of Divorce in Western Society* (New York: Cambridge University Press, 1988); Alfred Cahen, *Statistical Analysis of American Divorce* (New York: AMS Press, 1932); Nelson Manfred Blake, *The Road to Reno: A History of Divorce in the United States* (New York: Macmillan, 1962).

26. Phillips, *Untying the Knot,* 177–78.

27. Ibid., 150; Cahen, *Statistical Analysis of American Divorce,* 21.

28. RHD to James Fields, n.d., U.Va.

29. RHD to Annie Fields, Monday [1863], U.Va.

30. RHD to Annie Fields, Tuesday and Wednesday [1863]. U.Va.; RHD, "The Wife's Story," *Atlantic Monthly* 14 (July 1864), in *A Rebecca Harding Davis Reader.*

31. RHD to Annie Fields, 26 January 1863, U.Va.

32. See Joanne Dobson, "The Hidden Hand: Subversion of Cultural Ideology in Three Mid-Nineteenth-Century American Women's Novels," *American Quarterly* 38:2 (1986) on narrative strategies in Susan Warner's *The Wide, Wide World* (1850), E. D. E. N. Southworth's *The Hidden Hand* (1859), and A. D. T. Whitney's *Hitherto: A Story of Yesterdays* (1869).

33. Elaine Showalter, "Dinah Murlock Craik and the Tactics of Sentiment: A Case Study in Victorian Female Authorship," *Feminist Studies* 2 (1975); Helen Waite Papashvily, *All the Happy Endings* (New York: Harper, 1956), xvii.

34. Dobson, "The Hidden Hand," 226.

35. Ibid., 230.

36. Ibid., 234.

37. See Sharon Harris, *Rebecca Harding Davis and American Realism* (Philadelphia: University of Pennsylvania Press, 1991), 111–12.

38. Glenn Hendler, "The Limits of Sympathy: Louisa May Alcott and the Sentimental Novel," *American Literary History* 3:4 (1991): 694.

39. See Carroll Smith-Rosenberg and Charles Rosenberg, "The Female Animal: Medical and Biological Views of Woman and Her Role in Nineteenth-Century America," *Journal of American History*, September 1973, 332–56.

40. See the different interpretation in Margaret M. Culley, "Vain Dreams: The Dream Convention in Some Nineteenth-Century American Women's Fiction," *Frontiers: A Journal of Women Studies* 1 (winter 1976): 94, 101.

41. See Hendler, "The Limits of Sympathy," 695–97, on Louisa May Alcott's *An Old Fashioned Girl.*

42. RHD, "The Harmonists," *Atlantic Monthly* 17 (May 1866), in *A Rebecca Harding Davis Reader.*

43. See Carol Kolmerten, *Women: The Ideology of Gender in the American Owenite Communities* (Bloomington: Indiana University Press, 1990), esp. 90–100.

44. Some portions of this discussion of "The Harmonists" and "Transcendental Wild Oats" appeared originally in Jean Pfaelzer, "The Sentimental Promise and the Utopian Myth: Rebecca Harding Davis's 'The Harmonists'" and Louisa May Alcott's 'Transcendental Wild Oats,'" *ATQ* n.s. 3 (March 1989).

45. Jean Pfaelzer, *The Utopian Novel in America, 1886–1896: The Politics of Form* (Pittsburgh: University of Pittsburgh Press, 1984), 18.

46. Jane Tompkins, *Sensational Designs: The Cultural Work of American Fiction, 1790–1860* (New York: Oxford University Press, 1985), 135.

47. RHD, "Lois Platner," *Peterson's Magazine* 371–79 (November 1869).

48. See Lawrence Foster, *Religion and Sexuality: The Shakers, the Mormons, and the Oneida Community* (Urbana: University of Illinois Press, 1984); Don Blair, *The New Harmony Story* (New Harmony, Ind., n.d.); Kolmerten, *Women: The Ideology of Gender in the American Owenite Communities.*

49. See Marianne Hirsch, *The Mother/Daughter Plot: Narrative, Psychoanalysis, Feminism* (Bloomington: Indiana University Press, 1989), esp. 46–50.

50. Sandra Gilbert and Susan Gubar, *The Madwoman in the Attic: The Woman Writer and the Nineteenth-Century Literary Imagination* (New Haven: Yale University Press, 1979), 174.

51. Adrienne Rich, *On Lies, Secrets and Silence: Selected Prose, 1966–1978* (New York: Norton, 1979), 91.

52. See Nancy Chodorow, "Gender, Relation and Difference in Psychoanalytic Perspective," in *The Future of Difference*, ed. Alice Jardine and Hester Eisenstein (Boston: G.K. Hall, 1980), 3–19.

53. Jessica Benjamin, "A Desire of One's Own: Psychoanalytic Feminism and Intersubjective Space," in *Feminist Studies/Critical Studies*, ed. Teresa de Lauretis (Bloomington: Indiana University Press, 1986), 80.

54. Drucilla Cornell and Adam Thurschwell, "Feminism, Negativity, Intersubjectivity," in *Feminism as Critique: On the Politics of Gender*, ed. Seyla Benhabib and Drucilla Cornell (Minneapolis: University of Minnesota Press, 1987), 157. However, Jane Flax argues in "The Family in Contemporary Feminist Thought," in *The Family in Political Thought*, ed. Jean Bethke Elshtain (Amherst: University of Massachusetts Press, 1982), 223 that, by considering intersubjectivity within utopian formations, we can contextualize the process of gender formation and consider its implications in the distribution of power and access to activity. This gendered view of child rearing implicates the psychodynamics of the postindustrial family in the persistence of patriarchy and positions the inversions in personal life of modern feminist utopias.

55. But "genuine difference" is "inseparable from a notion of relationality" (Cornell and Thurschwell, *Feminism as Critique*, 161).

56. RHD, "The Story of Christine," *Peterson's Magazine* 50 (September 1866), in *A Rebecca Harding Davis Reader.*

57. In *Republica v. Gaoler* (1794) the Pennsylvania Supreme Court upheld the right of masters to manumit and then immediately indenture their slaves. Cited in Sharon Salinger, *"To Serve Well and Faithfully": Labor and Indentured Servants in Pennsylvania, 1682–1800* (New York: Cambridge University Press, 1987), 146.

58. See John van der Zee in *Bound Over: Indentured Servitude and American Conscience* (New York: Simon and Schuster, 1985), 31; see also Sharon Salinger, *"To Serve Well and Faithfully"*; Cheesman Abiah Herrick, *White Servitude in Pennsylvania: Indentured and Redemption Labor in Colony and Commonwealth* (1926; reprint, Freeport, N.Y.: Books for Libraries Press, 1970).

59. RHD, "In the Market," *Peterson's Magazine* 53 (January 1868), in *A Rebecca Harding Davis Reader*.

60. Lydia Maria Child, *Letters*, in Rosen, *The Lost Sisterhood*, 8.

6. Race, Reconstruction, and the Discourse of Sentiment

1. *Waiting for the Verdict* (1867; reprint, Upper Saddle River, N.J.: Gregg Press, 1968); the novel was serialized in *Galaxy Magazine* in 1867. Further references are to this edition.

2. David Brion Davis, *Antebellum American Culture: An Interpretive Anthology* (Lexington, Mass.: Heath, 1979), 273–314.

3. Ellen DuBois warns, "It is a common error among historians of American feminists to attribute American women's consciousness about oppression of their sex to the antislavery movement" ("Women's Rights and Abolition: The Nature of the Connection," in *Antislavery Reconsidered: New Perspectives on the Abolitionists*, ed. Lewis Perry and Michael Fellman [Baton Rouge: Louisiana State University Press, 1979], 238).

4. The Ku Klux Klan was organized as a secret social club in Pulaski, Tennessee, in 1865 or 1866. Targeting freedmen in particular, Klan violence reached a peak in 1868 and was the subject of congressional investigations by 1871. See Martha Hodes, "The Sexualization of Reconstruction Politics," in *American Sexual Politics: Sex, Gender, and Race since the Civil War*, ed. John C. Fout and Maura S. Tantillo (Chicago: University of Chicago Press, 1993), 59–74.

5. Nancy Bentley comments that "the domestic novel *is* finally a respecter of persons" but is "structured by different rules of representation for women and men, for black and white" ("White Slaves: The Mulatto Hero in Antebellum Fiction," *American Literature* 65:3 [September 1993]: 502).

6. Typical is Davis's description of John C. Fremont as "the incarnation of the chivalric and noble side of Abolitionism [who] made Freedom a religion. I don't know that he had any especial liking for the negro—very few Abolitionists, by the way, had that" ("A Peculiar People," *Saturday Evening Post*, 17 January 1903, 8).

7. Karen Sanchez-Eppler, "Bodily Bonds: The Intersecting Rhetorics of Feminism and Abolition," *Representations* 24 (1988): 30. See also Blanche Hersh, "Am I Not a Woman and a Sister?" in *Antislavery Reconsidered: New Perspectives on the Abolitionists*, ed.

Lewis Perry and Michael Fellman (Baton Rouge: Louisiana State University Press, 1979), 252–86.

8. See Jules Zanger, "The 'Tragic Octoroon' in Pre–Civil War Fiction," *American Quarterly* 18 (1966): 63–70.

9. See Jean Fagan Yellin, *Women and Sisters: The Antislavery Feminists in American Culture* (New Haven: Yale University Press, 1989), 50. Abolitionist-feminist women speakers were accused of violating prohibitions both against sexual activity outside marriage and interracial sex. Mary N. B. Smith, for example, explained to well-known abolitionist speaker Abbe Kelley that she was "'*branded* with such names as, *Elect, Lady, Comodore,* and willing to sleep with the *niggers* children to marry them etc. and etc.'" (ibid., 47, 289–90).

10. See Carolyn Karcher, *The First Woman in the Republic: A Cultural Biography of Lydia Maria Child* (Durham, N.C.: Duke University Press, 1994), 528. In comparing Davis and Child, Karcher concludes that "Davis's phobia of interracial marriage can be ascribed to her southern background."

11. Mary Dearborn, *Pocahantas's Daughters: Gender and Ethnicity in American Culture* (New York: Oxford University Press, 1986), 143.

12. Judith Berzon points out that the American definition of race was unlike that of Jamaica or Santo Domingo, where white minorities defined mulattoes as a third race (*Neither White nor Black: The Mulatto Character in American Fiction* [New York: New York University Press, 1978], 8).

13. Sanchez-Eppler argues that in sentimental novels antislavery feminists represented the slave in order to obliquely depict their own fears and desires; hence the racial and the sexual come to displace one another as they obliterate the particularity of black and female experience ("Bodily Bonds," 40–51).

14. Novels with miscegenation as a theme include the following: Elizabeth Stoddard, *Two Men* (New York: Bunce and Huntington, 1865); Lydia Maria Child, *A Romance of the Republic* (Boston: Ticknor and Fields, 1867); Anna E. Dickinson, *What Answer?* (Boston: Ticknor and Fields, 1868); Henry Churton [Albion Tourgee], *Toinette: A Novel* (New York: J. B. Ford, 1874).

15. Dearborn, *Pocahantas's Daughters,* 150.

16. See Blyden Jackson, "A Golden Mean for the Negro Novel," *College Language Association Journal* 3:2 (1959): 84–85.

17. See Marianna Torgovnick, *Gone Primitive: Savage Intellects, Modern Lives* (Chicago: University of Chicago Press, 1990), 8–34, on the role of the "primitive" in modern anthropological studies, see Karcher, *The First Woman in the Republic,* 331; and Dearborn, *Pocahantas's Daughters,* 140, who argue that literary mulattoes in texts by white authors express white narcissism.

18. See Karcher, *The First Woman in the Republic*, 324; Anna Dickinson's *What Answer* (1868) pictures a successful interracial marriage.

19. RHD, "Two Points of View," *Independent*, 9 September 1897, in *A Rebecca Harding Davis Reader*, 420–21.

20. Berzon also observes that after revelation the mulatto can fight against "the objectification of his being—the tendency to see himself as an 'object' created out of others' consciousness rather than as a subject emanating his essence, as assertion of will in an indifferent universe. . . . [Because] assertion of will requires responsibility, it is only through the acceptance of responsibility that freedom is won" (*Neither White nor Black*, 130).

21. William Wells Brown, *Clotel: or, The President's Daughter; A Narrative of Slave Life in the United States* (London: Partridge and Oakey, 1853).

22. Werner Sollars, *Beyond Ethnicity: Consent and Descent in American Culture* (New York: Oxford University Press, 1986), 41.

23. Claudia Tate, "Allegories of Black Female Desire; or, Rereading Nineteenth-Century Sentimental Narratives of Black Female Authority," in *Changing Our Own Words*, ed. Cheryl Wall (New Brunswick, N.J.: Rutgers University Press, 1987), 102.

24. Hazel Carby, "Ideologies of Black Folk: The Historical Novel of Slavery," in *Slavery and the Literary Imagination*, ed. Deborah McDowell and Arnold Rampersad (Baltimore: Johns Hopkins, 1989), 133.

25. Henry James, "Waiting for the Verdict," *Nation*, 21 November 1867, 410–11.

26. Ibid.

27. Henry James, from *Notes of a Son and Brother*, cited in Daniel Aaron, *The Unwritten War: American Writers and the Civil War* (New York: Oxford University Press, 1973), 106.

28. John De Forest, "The Great American Novel," *Nation*, 9 January 1868, 28.

29. See Joan D. Hedrick, *Harriet Beecher Stowe: A Life* (New York: Oxford University Press, 1994), 348–54.

30. James Playsted Wood, *Magazines in the United States* (New York: Ronald Press, 1971), 188; see also John Tebbell and Mary Ellen Zuckerman, *The Magazine in America 1741–1990* (New York: Oxford University Press, 1991), 89, 120–23.

31. "The Intermarriage Bugbear," *Nation*, 12 December 1867, 481–82, emphasis added. Articles and editorials in the *Nation* were unsigned during these years.

32. Sharon Harris observes that this time Davis was "no longer the newcomer who had allowed *Howth* to be battered by editorial demands; . . . she intended to do battle with the *Galaxy* editors who . . . seemed intent upon destroying it" (*Rebecca Harding Davis and American Realism* [Philadelphia: Pennsylvania University Press, 1991], 132). See RHD to F. P. Church, 4 June 1866, William Conant Church Papers, New

York Public Library; RHD to William and F. P. Church, 1 November [1866] and 4 June [1867], Church Papers, cited in ibid., 325.

33. RHD to William and F. P. Church, 30 November [1866], cited in ibid., 132.

34. Nina Silber observes that intersectional romances were rare in the postbellum years (*The Romance of Reunion: Northerners and the South 1865–1900* [Chapel Hill: University of North Carolina Press, 1993], 40).

35. Herbert Gutman, *The Black Family in Slavery and Freedom: 1750–1935* (New York: Pantheon, 1976) argues that there was more cohesiveness in the slave family than plantation owners acknowledged.

36. RHD, "What About the Northern Negro?" *Independent* 41 (24 January 1889), 1.

37. Ibid.

38. Sanchez-Eppler, "Bodily Bonds," 102.

39. Jane Tompkins, *Sensational Designs: The Cultural Work of American Fiction* (New York: Oxford University Press, 1985), 122–46.

40. Caroline Healey Dall, *Standard* [probably 25 January 1868]. This chapter is indebted to Karcher's discovery of the Dall-Forten debate on *Waiting for the Verdict* (*The First Woman in the Republic*, 528, 737).

41. Charlotte L. Forten, "Waiting for the Verdict," *The Standard*, 22 February 1868, 3.

42. Lydia Maria Child to Charlotte Forten, 6 March 1868, cited in Karcher, *The First Woman in the Republic*, 737.

43. Bertram Wyatt-Brown argues that abolitionists appealed to a transcendental and romantic ideology that purported to have a classless perspective in "Proslavery and Antislavery Intellectuals: Class Concepts and Polemical Struggle in *Antislavery Reconsidered: New Perspectives on the Abolitionists*, ed. Lewis Perry and Michael Fellman (Baton Rouge: Louisiana State University Press, 1979), 310–11.

44. Mary Ryan argues, by contrast, that domesticity "constrain[s] the imagination and perceive[s] the world within the bounds of woman's sphere" (*The Empire of the Mother: American Writing About Domesticity, 1830–1860* [New York: Harrington Park Press, 1982], 120).

45. In these novels, Susan Gillman suggests, the black mother "provides a domestic space for the competing claims for racial self-definition" ("The Mulatto, Tragic or Triumphant: The Nineteenth-Century American Race Melodrama," in *The Culture of Sentiment*, ed. Shirley Samuels [New York: Oxford University Press, 1992], 222).

46. *Godey's Lady's Book and Magazine* 76 (January 1868), 98, briefly reviewed *Waiting for the Verdict*: "A story of more than ordinary interest, written in a clear, forcible style, such as, were it not for the name on the title-page, would lead to its being ascribed to a masculine pen."

47. "A Peculiar People," *Saturday Evening Post*, 10 January 1903, 9.

48. Yellin, *Women and Sisters*, 3.

49. RHD, "A Peculiar People," 9.

50. Quoted in Yellin, *Women and Sisters*, 51.

51. RHD, "A Peculiar People," 9.

52. Ryan, *The Empire of the Mother*, 133.

53. James Kinney, *Amalgamation!: Race, Sex, and Rhetoric in the Nineteenth-Century American Novel* (Westport, Conn.: Greenwood Press, 1985), 104–05.

7. Nature, Nurture, and Nationalism

1. See Richard Brodhead, *Cultures of Letters: Scenes of Reading and Writing in Nineteenth-Century America* (Chicago: University of Chicago Press, 1993), 119–20.

2. See Richard Slotkin, *The Fatal Environment: The Myth of the Frontier in the Age of Industrialization, 1800–1890* (New York: Atheneum, 1985), 117, 284–85; Frederick Merk, *History of the Westward Movement* (New York: Alfred A. Knopf, 1978), 236.

3. James Fenimore Cooper, "American and European Scenery Compared," in *Home Book of the Picturesque* (New York: G. P. Putnam, 1851), 52.

4. Ibid., 56–57.

5. Ibid., 58.

6. Washington Irving, *A Tour of the Prairies*, quoted in Roderick Nash, *Wilderness and the American Mind* (New Haven: Yale University Press, 1982), 73.

7. RHD, "A Faded Leaf of History," *Atlantic Monthly* 31 (January 1873), in *A Rebecca Harding Davis Reader*. (Davis adopts the spelling "Dickenson" from either the 1700, 1701, or 1720 editions of *God's Protecting Providence*.)

8. Evangeline Walker Andrews, introduction to *Jonathan Dickinson's Journal or God's Protecting Providence* (1699; reprint, New Haven: Yale University Press, 1945), 18. Quotations from Dickinson are from this edition, which strictly follows the text of the 1699 first edition. Richard VanderBeets states that there were twenty-one editions, including translations into Dutch and German ("The Indian Captivity Narrative as Ritual," *American Literature* 43 [January 1972]: 548).

9. The Ais Indians, called "Jece" by Dickinson, were the largest and most powerful tribe along Florida's southeast coast from the time of the earliest Spanish settlements until the eighteenth century, when the remaining Ais may have emigrated to Cuba. All efforts to convert them apparently failed, and the Ais seem to disappear from historical records after 1703. See John R. Swanton, *The Indian Tribes of North America*, bulletin 145 (Washington, D.C.: Smithsonian Institution Bureau of American Ethnology, 1952), 121–22.

10. Robert F. Berkhofer, *The White Man's Indian: Images of the American Indian from Columbus to the Present* (New York: Knopf, 1978), 95–106.

11. Berkhofer reports that the post–Civil War policy of the federal government was to have Native Americans enter the polis as individuals rather than as tribes (ibid., 155).

12. Slotkin, *The Fatal Environment*, 304.

13. Berkhofer, *The White Man's Indian*, 167.

14. Wilcomb Washburn, *The Indian in America* (New York: Harper and Row, 1975), 201; see also Angie Debo, *A History of the Indians of the United States* (Norman: University of Oklahoma Press, 1970), 151.

15. *The Harvard Encyclopedia of American Ethnic Groups* (Cambridge: Harvard University Press, 1980) 59, 69; *The World Book Encyclopedia* (Chicago: World Book, 1991), 191.

16. Lora Romero observes, in discussing the "legibility" of paternal power, "Although *the* book is usually associated with the reign of the father, in the antebellum period *books* seem to be associated with the reign of the mother." Figures like Thoreau, she argues, are anxious about both the multiplicity of female texts and women's assumption of educational duties formerly administered by the father ("Vanishing Americans: Gender, Empire, and New Historicism," in *The Culture of Sentiment: Race, Gender, and Sentimentality in Nineteenth-Century America*, ed. Shirley Samuels [New York: Oxford University Press, 1992], 122).

17. See Amy Kaplan, "Romancing the Empire: The Embodiment of American Masculinity in the Popular Historical Novel of the 1890s," *American Literary History* 2 (1990): 676.

18. Slotkin, *The Fatal Environment*, 102–03.

19. Michel De Certeau, *The Writing of History*, trans. Tom Conley (New York: Columbia University Press, 1988), xxv–xxvi.

20. Louis Montrose, "The Work of Gender in the Discourse of Discovery," *Representations* 33 (winter 1991): 5.

21. VanDerBeets, "The Indian Captivity Narrative as Ritual," 550–51.

22. Kathryn Zabelle Derounian-Stodola and James Arthur Levernier, *The Indian Captivity Narrative, 1550–1900* (New York: Twayne, 1993), 126–27.

23. Drucilla Cornell and Adam Thurschwell observe that this sort of explanation traces social and institutional forms of power to individual psychological motivations ("Feminism, Negativity, and Intersubjectivity," in *Feminism as Critique: On the Politics of Gender*, ed. Seyla Benhabib and Drucilla Cornell [Minneapolis: University of Minnesota Press, 1987], 157). However, Jane Flax reminds us that the family comprises three types of social relations: production, reproduction, and psychodynamics ("The Family in Contemporary Feminist Thought," in *The Family in Political*

Thought, ed. Jean Bethke Elshtain [Amherst: University of Massachusetts Press, 1982], 223).

24. Romero, "Vanishing Americans," 119.

25. Kaplan, "Romancing the Empire," 664.

26. Ibid., 674.

27. Annette Kolodny, *The Land Before Her: Fantasy and Experience of the American Frontiers, 1630–1860* (Chapel Hill: University of North Carolina Press, 1984), xii–xiv.

28. Ibid., 7.

29. See, for example, Carroll Smith-Rosenberg, "Subject Female: Authorizing American Identity," *American Literary History* (1993), 482.

30. David Miller, *Dark Eden: The Swamp in American Culture* (New York: Cambridge University Press, 1989), 10.

31. Ibid., 8.

32. Miller observes that the "good" mother who bestows sustenance turns into the "terrible" mother who threatens annihilation if the hero tries to establish his independence by going beyond the "objective reality" of nature (ibid., 103). Yet this trope applies only to male characters' relationship to nature.

33. Slotkin, *The Fatal Environment*, 63.

34. Barbara Novak, *Nature and Culture: American Landscape and Painting: 1825–1875* (New York: Oxford University Press, 1980), 17.

35. Smith-Rosenberg notes that many nineteenth-century white women who contested "with white men for a liberal humanist subjectivity [also] joined with them in espousing Europe's imperial venture, and in so doing, denied subjectivity to women of color" ("Subject Female," 486).

36. Henry David Thoreau, *The Maine Woods* (New York: Harper and Row, 1987), 93–95.

37. Alexis de Tocqueville, *Journey to America*, trans. George Lawrence, ed. J. P. Mayer (Garden City, N.Y.: Doubleday, 1971), 354.

38. William H. Truettner, "Prelude to Expansion: Repainting the Past," in *The West As America: Reinterpreting Images of the Frontier, 1820–1920*, ed. Truettner (Washington D.C.: Smithsonian Institution Press, 1991), 73.

39. Richard VanDerBeets, "A Surfeit of Style: The Indian Captivity Narrative as Penny Dreadful," *Research Studies* 39 (December 1971), 305.

40. See June Namias, *White Captives: Gender and Ethnicity on the American Frontier* (Chapel Hill: University of North Carolina Press, 1993), 67.

41. Ibid., 15.

42. Derounian-Stodola and Levernier, *The Indian Captivity Narrative*, 2.

43. See Namias, *White Captives*, 97–122; Lonnie J. White, "White Women Cap-

tives of Southern Plains Indians, 1866–1875," *Journal of the West* 8 (July 1969): 327–54; Stanley B. Kimball, "The Captivity Narrative on Mormon Trails, 1846–65," *Dialogue* 18 (winter 1984): 82–88; Derounian-Stodola and Levernier, *The Indian Captivity Narrative*, 127.

44. Derounian-Stodola and Levernier, *The Indian Captivity Narrative*, 3–5.

45. Gayatri Spivak, "Displacement and the Discourse of Woman," in *Displacement: Derrida and After*, ed. Mark Krupnick (Bloomington: Indiana University Press, 1983), 169.

46. Smith-Rosenberg, "Subject Female," 486.

8. The Politics of Nature

1. Angela Miller, "Everywhere and Nowhere: The Making of the National Landscape," *American Literary History* 4 (summer 1992): 213.

2. Ibid.

3. RHD, "The Yares of Black Mountain," *Lippincott's Magazine* 16 (July 1875), in *A Rebecca Harding Davis Reader*.

4. On Thoreau, see Max Oelschlaeger, *The Idea of Wilderness: From Prehistory to the Age of Ecology* (New Haven: Yale University Press, 1991), 149–52.

5. Robert Bredeson, "Landscape Description in Nineteenth-Century American Travel Literature," *American Quarterly* 20 (spring 1968): 89.

6. RHD, "By-Paths in the Mountains," *Harper's New Monthly* 61 (July–September 1880): 167–85, 353–69, 532–47; "Here and There in the Old South," *Harper's New Monthly* 75 (July–November 1887): 235–46, 431–43, 593–606, 747–60, 914–25.

7. John Sears, *Sacred Places: American Tourist Attractions in the Nineteenth Century* (New York: Oxford University Press, 1989), 122, 124–27.

8. Ibid., 54.

9. Angela Miller, in *The Empire of the Eye: Landscape Representation and American Cultural Politics 1825–1875* (Ithaca: Cornell University Press, 1993), 243–88, by contrast, sees luminosity in paintings by male artists as an automatic sign for feminine fluidity.

10. Howard Mumford Jones, *O Strange New World: American Culture in the Formative Years* (1964; reprint, Westport, Conn.: Greenwood Press, 1982), 361–62.

11. On the sublime, see in particular *Dark Eden: The Swamp in Nineteenth-Century American Culture* (New York: Cambridge University Press, 1989); and "The Iconology of Wrecked or Stranded Boats in Mid to Late Nineteenth-Century American Culture," in *American Iconology: New Approaches to Nineteenth-Century Art and Literature* (New Haven: Yale University Press, 1993), 186–208, esp. 186–87.

12. David Miller, *Dark Eden*, 16.

13. Angela Miller, *Empire*, 244–49.

14. Jones, *O Strange New World*, 351.

15. Sandra Zagarell, "Narrative of Community: The Identification of a Genre," *Signs* 13 (spring 1988): 500.

16. Harold Bloom, "The Internalization of the Quest Romance" in *Romanticism and Consciousness: Essays in Criticism*, ed. Harold Bloom (New York: W. W. Norton, 1970), 6.

17. Ibid., 9.

18. Annette Kolodny, "Narrative of Community," in *The Land Before Her: Fantasy and Experience of the American Frontiers 1630–1860* (Chapel Hill: University of North Carolina Press, 1984).

19. See Annette Kolodny, *The Lay of the Land: Metaphor as Experience and History in American Life and Letters* (Chapel Hill: University of North Carolina Press, 1975), 4.

20. See ibid., 6, 22.

21. Kolodny locates such alien figures in the tales of E. D. E. N. Southworth and Maria Cummins in *The Land Before Her*, 202.

22. Ralph Waldo Emerson, *Selected Writings of Ralph Waldo Emerson*, ed. William H. Gilman (New York: New American Library, 1965), 217.

23. Oelschlaeger, *The Idea of Wilderness*, 93.

24. Ibid., 69.

25. RHD, "Life in the Iron-Mills," *Atlantic Monthly* 7 (April 1861), in *A Rebecca Harding Davis Reader*, 3.

26. Henry David Thoreau, "The Natural History of Massachusetts," *The Writings of Henry David Thoreau* (Boston: Houghton Mifflin, 1906), 5:131.

27. Carol MacCormack observes, "When women are defined as 'natural' a high prestige or moral 'goodness' is attached to men's domination over women, analogous to the 'goodness' of human domination of natural energy sources or the libidinal energy of individuals" ("Nature, Culture, and Gender: A Critique," in *Nature, Culture and Gender*, ed. Carol MacCormack and Marilyn Strathern [Cambridge: Cambridge University Press, 1980], 6).

28. L. J. Jordanova, "Natural Facts: A Historical Perspective on Science and Sexuality," in *Nature, Culture and Gender*, ed. Carol MacCormack and Marilyn Strathern (Cambridge: Cambridge University Press, 1980), 42.

29. See ibid., 44–61; Raymond Williams, *The City and the Country* (London: Chatto and Windus, 1973), 1–8.

30. Warner Berthoff, summarizing mainstream views of local color, quoted in Louis J. Renza, *"A White Heron" and the Question of Minor Literature* (Madison: University of Wisconsin Press, 1984), 44–45.

31. From the *Nation*, 27 September 1919, cited in Caroline Gebhard ("The Spinster

in the House of American Criticism," *Tulsa Studies in Women's Literature* 10 [spring 1991]: 79). Gebhard surveys the critical attack on local color literature as trivial, senile, and sterile narratives written by unmarried women. Originating with the wave of masculinist nationalism around the turn of the twentieth century, this charge (according to Gebhard) appears to have been first popularized by George Santayana in "The Genteel Tradition in American Philosophy" (1911), through reviews in the *Nation*, Henry Adams, Van Wyck Brooks, V. L. Parrington, to Ann Douglas's *The Feminization of American Culture* (New York: Knopf, 1977).

32. George Santayana, "The Academic Environment," *Character and Opinion in the United States* (New York: Charles Scribner's Sons, 1920), 44.

33. Cited in Gebhard, "The Spinster in the House of American Criticism," 83.

34. Kolodny, *The Land Before Her*, 6.

35. Ibid., 7.

36. Ann Douglas [Wood], "The Literature of Impoverishment: The Women Local Colorists in America, 1865–1914," *Women's Studies* 1 (1972): 14.

37. See Josephine Donovan, *New England Local Color Literature: A Woman's Tradition* (New York: Frederick Ungar, 1983).

38. Roger Stein, *The View and the Vision: Landscape Painting in Nineteenth-Century America* (Seattle: University of Washington Press, 1968), 8–9.

39. Simone de Beauvoir, *The Second Sex* (New York: Knopf, 1953), 710–11; see also Annis Pratt, "Women and Nature in Modern Fiction," *Contemporary Literature* 13 (autumn 1972): 477–90.

40. Gail David, *Female Heroism in the Pastoral* (New York: Garland Publishing, 1991), xvii–xviii.

41. Zagarell, "Narrative of Community," 499.

42. Sears, *Sacred Places*, 52; Angela Miller, "Everywhere and Nowhere," 214.

43. Miller, "Everywhere and Nowhere," 224.

9. To Be, to Do, and to Suffer

1. Jane Atterbridge Rose states that during 1875–1889 Davis pursued "less ambitious projects that would not compromise her role as wife and mother" (*Rebecca Harding Davis* [New York: Twayne, 1993], 103).

2. Ann Ardis, *New Women, New Novels: Feminism and Early Modernism* (New Brunswick, N.J.: Rutgers University Press, 1990), 12.

3. Ibid., 13.

4. Quoted in Suzanne Clark, *Sentimental Modernism: Women Writers and the Revolution of the Word* (Bloomington: Indiana University Press, 1991), 28–29.

5. Ibid., 29.

6. Ibid.

7. Sara M. Evans, *Born for Liberty: A History of Women in America* (New York: Free Press, 1989), 123.

8. Andrea Moore Kerr, *Lucy Stone: Speaking Out for Equality* (New Brunswick, N.J.: Rutgers University Press, 1992), esp. chap. 8.

9. Elizabeth Cady Stanton, *Eighty Years and More*, cited in Mabel C. Connelly, *The American Victorian Woman* (New York: Greenwood Press, 1986), 85.

10. Evans, *Born for Liberty*, 137.

11. See ibid.; Linda Kerber and Jane Sherron De Hart, *Women's America: Refocusing the Past* (New York: Oxford University Press, 1995); Eleanor Flexner, *Century of Struggle: The Women's Rights Movement in the United States* (New York: Atheneum, 1974); Melvyn Dubofsky, *Industrialism and the American Worker 1865–1920* (New York: Thomas Y. Crowell, 1975); Robert Weibe, *The Search for Order 1877–1920* (New York: Hill and Wang, 1967); Philip Foner, *History of the Labor Movement in the United States* (New York: International Publishing, 1947); Robert O. Boyer and Herbert M. Morais, *Labor's Untold Story* (New York: United Electrical, Radio, and Machine Workers of America, 1955).

12. Evans, *Born for Liberty*, 143.

13. RHD, "Men's Rights," *Putnam's Magazine*, n.s. 3 (February 1869), in *A Rebecca Harding Davis Reader*, 344.

14. RHD, "Clement Moore's Vocation," *Peterson's Magazine* 57 (January 1870): 54.

15. RHD, "Two Women," *Galaxy* 9 (June 1870): 804.

16. RHD, "Earthen Pitchers," *Scribner's Magazine* 7 (November 1873–April 1874), in *A Rebecca Harding Davis Reader*.

17. Susan Kirkpatrick, *Women Writers and Subjectivity in Spain, 1835–1850* (Berkeley: University of California Press, 1989), 60–61.

18. RHD, "Berrytown," *Lippincott's Magazine* 11 (April–June 1873), later published as *Kitty's Choice* (Philadelphia: Lippincott, 1873).

19. Carol Lopate, *Women in Medicine* (Baltimore: Johns Hopkins University Press, 1968), 4.

20. Harris, *Rebecca Harding Davis and American Realism*, 152.

21. Ibid., 195.

22. RHD, "Dolly," *Scribner's Magazine* 9 (November 1874), in *A Rebecca Harding Davis Reader*, 288.

23. RHD, "Marcia," *Harper's New Monthly Magazine* 53 (November 1876), in *A Rebecca Harding Davis Reader*.

24. Ann Wood, "The 'Scribbling Women' and Fanny Fern: Why Women Wrote," *American Quarterly* 23 (1971): 7.

25. Ibid.

26. See Rosalyn Baxandall, Linda Gordon and Susan Riverby, eds., *America's Working Women: A Documentary History—1690 to the Present* (New York: Vintage Books, 1976).

27. Quoted in Wood, "The 'Scribbling Women,'" 8.

28. Ann Douglas [Wood], *The Feminization of American Culture* (New York: Knopf, 1977), 12.

29. Nina Baym, "Melodramas of Best Manhood: How Theories of American Fiction Exclude Women Authors," *American Quarterly* 33 (1981): 123.

30. Quoted in ibid., 126–27.

31. Hawthorne's letter to his publisher, Ticknor, quoted in Wood, "The 'Scribbling Women,'" 9; see also Caroline Ticknor, *Hawthorne and His Publisher* (Boston: Houghton Mifflin, 1913), 141.

32. By 1882, as Davis retreated into a period of not writing fiction, she described another woman who gave up her career for marriage in love in "A Rainy Day," one of her last portraits of a woman writer. Mrs. Lloyd, a minor journalist living in Philadelphia, endures the fame she enjoys in her distant Delaware village—perhaps a gentle parody on Davis's own connection to Wheeling. Many cousins send her poems and novels with the expectation she will get them published; some wonder when she will start to lecture on women's rights or go on the stage; others "innocently" ask, "'Who takes care of the house, and the children, poor little things?'" (49). During the Centennial Exposition of 1876, she is visited by a young cousin who, "starved in mind" by canning, pickling, sewing, and sausage making, has run away from her family farm, where there is no chance "for a woman with brains," and has come to the city to make her living as a poet. Instead of publishers, however, the cousin meets and marries a large jolly lumberman from Michigan who announces that he means to do the thinking for his wife and with great relief, she exchanges poetry for porridge. RHD, "A Rainy Day," *Peterson's Magazine* 81 (January 1882).

33. Cited in Susan Coultrap-McQuinn, *Doing Literary Business: American Women Writers in the Nineteenth Century* (Chapel Hill: University of North Carolina Press, 1990), 14.

34. See ibid., 1–26.

35. RHD, "The Poetess of Clapp City," *Scribner's Monthly* 9 (March 1875).

36. It is easiest to document the early fees RHD received for her writings for she often including an acknowledgement for the receipt of a check in a postscript in her letters to James or Annie Fields. On her later economic negotiations with publishers, see Harris, *Rebecca Harding Davis and American Realism*.

37. RHD to James Fields, 13 March 1861, U.Va.

38. Harris, *Rebecca Harding Davis and American Realism*, 73.

39. Ibid., 82. See also William Charvat, *The Profession of Authorship in America, 1800–1867*, ed. Matthew Bruccoli (Columbus: Ohio State University Press, 1968).

40. RHD to James Fields, November 3, 1862, U.Va.

41. Harris, *Rebecca Harding Davis and American Realism*, 99.

42. Gerald Langford, *The Richard Harding Davis Years: A Biography of a Mother and Son* (New York: Holt, Rinehart and Winston, 1961), 49; Harris, *Rebecca Harding Davis and American Realism*, 131.

43. Harris, *Rebecca Harding Davis and American Realism*, 257. The economics of writing continued to be a haunting theme for Davis. "Doctor Pajot" (1877) is a tale of an academic who has impoverished his family while he writes the exhaustive "History of Civilization in All Ages," only to be rescued by his wife, who publishes a profitable series of textbooks made up of the applied lessons in mathematics and geography she wrote for her children. RHD, "Doctor Pajot," *Appleton's Journal*, n.s. 2 (June 1877).

44. RHD, "A Day with Dr. Sarah," *Harper's New Monthly Magazine* 57 (September 1878), in *A Rebecca Harding Davis Reader*.

45. Carroll Smith-Rosenberg, *Disorderly Conduct: Visions of Gender in Victorian America* (New York: Oxford University Press, 1985), 246.

46. Ibid., 258.

47. John "Benicia boy" Heenan (1833–1873) and John Morrissey (n.d.) were professional boxers who competed for the title of American heavyweight champion in the late 1850s.

48. In 1881 Dean Rachel Bodley of the Women's Medical College of Pennsylvania, one of the few schools to train women physicians, surveyed the school's graduates. Of 166 respondents, 129 were married, and only 5 left the practice after marriage. Nearly half were married when they studied medicine. Because the issue of the influence of practicing medicine on women's roles as wives and mothers prompted the greatest criticism, Dean Bodley happily announced that of the 52 married women who responded to this question, 45 found the influence "favorable"; 6 responded "not entirely favorable"; and only 1 "unfavorable" (Lopate, *Women in Medicine*, 10–11).

49. Smith-Rosenberg, *Disorderly Conduct*, 261.

50. Ibid., 265.

51. *The Remonstrance* (Boston, Mass.: Massachusetts Association Opposed to the Further Extension of Suffrage to Women, 1891), 2.

52. Harris, *Rebecca Harding Davis and American Realism*, 5.

53. Tillie Olsen, "A Biographical Interpretation," *Life in the Iron Mills* (New York: Feminist Press, 1972), 146–47.

54. In 1891 the *Remonstrance* collected statements from well-known women authors, including Rose Terry Cooke, Gail Hamilton, and Davis, who wrote, "Should the right of suffrage be extended to women? I am very sure that I for one should sit by the fire on election day while my cook and laundress voted. I do not believe that I should be any more conscientious or faithful to my duty in this matter than are the majority of educated American men in our cities who now leave the control of the primary elections and the polls to men who are neither educated nor American" (2). This comment, which appeared fifteen years after the stories discussed in this chapter, has been cited as an instance of Davis's antisuffrage position. It is unlike the comment of Rose Terry Cooke, "Nothing would induce me to go to the polls and vote. For the reason that I do not think it is a woman's place or within a woman's capacity to do so. I fully agree with St. Paul in his estimate of a woman's power and duties" (2). Davis's troubling comment, however, also suggests a condemnation of middle-class apathy and implies that the laundress and the cook would indeed participate in the public process.

55. RHD to Annie Fields, 6 November [n.d.], U.Va.

56. RHD, "Put Out of the Way," *Peterson's Magazine* 57 (May–June 1870).

57. Langford, *The Richard Harding Davis Years*, 53.

58. Gerald Grob, *Mental Institutions in America: Social Policy to 1875* (New York: Free Press, 1973); see also Harris, *Rebecca Harding Davis and American Realism*, 160. Between 1868 and 1873, the Pennsylvania Hospital for the Insane remained on the defensive when a series of writs of habeas corpus freed several patients who had been involuntarily confined.

59. RHD, *John Andross* (New York: Orange Judd, 1874).

60. Harris, *Rebecca Harding Davis and American Realism*, 18.

Index

Chodorow, Nancy, 134

Christianity, 49, 50, 66, 71–72, 95–99, 110, 113–16, 152, 171, 173, 181, 255n67; Davis's opinion of, 66, 83; hypocrisy of, 113–14

Church, F. P., 157, 227

Church, Frederic, 193, 203–04

Church, William, 157, 227

Civilization: as feminine, 165–66, 192; inevitability of, 186; as masculine, 197, 200; utopian, 216–19

Civil Rights Act, 141

Civil War, 10, 20, 55–56, 189, 194–95; Davis's stories about, 76–106, 251n15; and draft, 251–52n15; effects of, 165, 170; in *Margret Howth*, 61; in *Waiting for the Verdict*, 140–64

Clark, Suzanne, 6, 30, 207

Class, 9–10, 61, 86, 105, 195, 198; and feminized males, 39–40, 42; in "Life in the Iron-Mills," 29, 36, 38–39, 41–43; of mulattoes, 147–48; and race, 86; working, 41–42, 46

"Clement Moore's Vocation," 207, 211

Commitment, 151, 198, 238–39; and identity, 126–27, 196, 215–16; vs. solipsism, 47, 52

Commonality, 91, 98–99; of blacks and whites, 142–43, 147

Community, 151, 196; family as, 127, 133; in *Margret Howth*, 57, 70, 73, 75; Rappite, 127–33; utopian, 62–64, 67–68, 134–35, 216–19; of women, 59–60, 73, 174–75, 195, 198, 201–02; women's understanding of, 81, 83, 159

Confinement, 51, 145, 217–18; in mental institutions, 233–35; slavery as, 83–84, 144–45; of women, 26, 28, 62–63, 94

Continental Monthly, 57–58

Cooke, Rose Terry, 201, 221, 273n54

Cooper, James Fenimore, 165–66, 186, 190

Corruption, in *John Andross*, 235–37

Cott, Nancy, 43

Coultrap-McQuinn, Susan, 225–26

Crane, Stephen, 34–35, 111

Creativity, 43, 100; and gender, 211–14; limitations of, 50–53; in *Margret Howth*, 63, 72; women's, 17–18, 123–27, 216, 221–26, 238–39

Cummins, Maria, 29

Dall, Caroline Healey, 111, 160

Dallas Galbraith, 13, 199, 207

Darwin, Charles, 101–02, 148

"David Gaunt," 12, 15, 20, 76, 93–99, 199

Davis, Charles Belmont (son), 16

Davis, L. Clarke (husband), 10–11, 78, 116, 211; report of on mental institutions, 233, 235

Davis, Nora (daughter), 15–16, 219

Davis, Rebecca Harding, works by: "Anne," 122, 223; "At Bay," 122; "Berrytown," 17–18, 207, 216–19; *Bits of Gossip*, 5, 97, 109; "Black North, The," 14; "Blind Tom," 12, 14, 17–18, 19, 76–77, 99–105, 161, 255n76; "By-Paths in the Mountains," 14, 191; "Clement Moore's Vocation," 207, 211; "David Gaunt," 12, 15, 20, 76, 93–99, 199; "Day with Dr. Sarah, A," 122, 207, 228–32; "Doctor Pajot," 272n43; "Dolly," 17–18, 122, 220–21; "Earthen Pitchers," 22, 122, 199, 212–16, 223; "A Faded Leaf of History," 13, 22, 167–88; "God Does Not Forget," 122; "The Harmonists," 17–18, 20, 122, 127–33; "Here and There in the Old South," 191; "House on the Beach," 199; "In the Gray Cabins of New England," 14; "In the Market," 122, 137–38, 205; *John Andross*, 207, 235–38; "John Lamar," 12, 14, 19, 76, 84–92, 105, 161; "Life in the Iron-Mills," 10–11, 20, 24–53, 198; "Lois Platner," 122, 131; "Lord Kitchener's Methods," 15; "Marcia," 1, 122, 221–26; *Margret Howth*, 12, 20, 25, 54–75, 125, 128, 135, 145, 162, 227; "The Mean Face of War," 15; "Men's Rights," 209–11; "The Middle-Aged Woman," 14; "The Newly Discovered Woman," 14; "Out of the Sea," 12–13, 199; "Paul Blecker," 12, 117–21, 123, 131, 205; "A Peculiar People," 162–63; "The Poetess of Clap City," 226; "The Promise of the Dawn," 12, 110–17; "Put Out of the Way," 233–35; "A Rainy Day," 272n32; "A Second Life," 117, 205; "Some Testimony in the Case," 14; "The Story of a Song," 122; "The Story of Christine," 17, 122, 135–37; "Two Methods with the Negro," 14; "Two Points of View," 14; "Two Women," 207, 211–12; "What About the Northern Negro?," 158; "The Wife's Story," 11, 17, 20, 122, 124–27, 135; "Women in Literature," 3, 241n3

Davis, Richard Harding (son), 4, 5, 11, 16

"Day with Dr. Sarah, A," 122, 207, 228–32

Dearborn, Mary, 147

Death, 50–51, 62, 74

De Forest, John, 155

Deformity, 38–39, 70–71, 99–105

Depression, Davis's, 4, 11, 121

Dickens, Charles, 256n87

Dickinson, Jonathan, 167–88
Diffley, Kathleen, 252n25
Disease, 136–37, 150
Divorce, 117–21. *See also* "Paul Blecker"
Dobson, Joanne, 122–23
"Doctor Pajot," 272n43
"Dolly," 17–18, 122, 220–21
Domesticity, 91; in Civil War stories, 105–06; and community, 81, 83; Davis's opposition to, 220–21; effects of, 107–39, 210–12; and the home, 99, 162, 195, 205; as image of home, 33, 39, 66–67; lack of refuge in, 84, 174; of the wilderness, 179–84; as women's sphere, 83–84, 219. *See also* Public vs. private lives; Sentimentalism
Donnelly, Ignatius, 42
Douglas, Ann (Wood), 59, 200, 222
Douglass, Frederick, 80–81, 154, 208
Dreiser, Theodore, 35, 42
Du Bois, W. E. B., 14–15

"Earthen Pitchers," 22, 122, 199, 212–16, 223
Economics: effect of on utopia, 129–30; and slavery, 154, 163–64; and women, 120–21, 123, 137–38, 205, 209–10
Edgeworth, Maria, 9
Editorials, Davis's, 10, 13
Education: Davis's, 9–10; for women, 209, 222, 225, 230
Eliot, George, 30, 48
Elison, Julie, 40, 71
Ellis, Edward, 184
Ellison, Ralph, 89
Emerson, Ralph Waldo, 11–12, 20, 30–31, 40, 44, 59–60, 65, 109; on nature, 71–72, 197, 204
Environment: pollution of, 27–28; role of, 144, 148, 164, 198
Eroticism, 89–90, 96, 113, 192, 228–29
Essays, 10, 13
Essentialism, 31, 81, 160, 200
Ethnicity, 99, 152
Eugenics, 34, 70, 101, 148, 151–53, 157

"Faded Leaf of History, A," 13, 22, 167–88
Family, 17, 95, 103, 133; image of, 3, 33, 39, 66–67; to regulate men's passions, 88–90; satisfaction for women in, 124, 139, 157–58, 224–25; in *Waiting for the Verdict*, 142, 150
Fathers: in Davis's stories, 7, 66–67, 86, 95, 146–47; as figure in utopian communities, 135
Feminist realism, 21
Fichte, Johann Gottlieb, 10, 67, 249–50n32

Fields, Annie, 4, 11, 95, 109–10, 114–15, 121–22, 129
Fields, James, 4, 10, 11, 21, 42, 59–61, 74–75, 83, 92, 109, 121, 226–27; influence of on Davis's writing, 31–32, 54–55, 58, 60–61
Fire, 34, 46
Fisher, Philip, 18–19, 96, 104
Food, 33, 175. *See also* Hunger
"Foreigner, The" (Jewitt), 191
Forten, Charlotte, 160–61
Fourier, Charles, 67
Fox-Genovese, Elizabeth, 89–90
Freeman, Mary E. Wilkins, 21, 201
Free will, 83
Fruitlands, 217. *See also* "Transcendental Wild Oats"
Fuller, Margaret, 10, 66, 125–26

Galaxy Magazine, 227; *Waiting for the Verdict* in, 140, 145, 148, 157, 227
Garrison, Dee, 116
Garrison, William Lloyd, 254n59
Gaskell, Elizabeth, 30
Gebhard, Caroline, 200, 269n31
Gender, 36, 198; and culture, 212–14; differences, 20–21, 81–83, 94–95, 110–16, 199–200; and race, 177–79, 186; relations, 199–200; roles, 135, 211–12, 232; and romanticism, 40–41, 51; spheres, 128–29, 133–34, 206, 216–19, 225, 238; tensions, 59–60, 65–66
Gilman, Charlotte Perkins, 3–4, 7, 11, 63, 105, 121, 128, 209–10, 234
Gilman, Sander, 89–90
"God Does Not Forget," 122
Godey's Lady's Magazine, 43
Godkin, E. L., 156
God's Protecting Providence . . . (Dickinson), 167–71
Goethe, Johann von, 10, 39
Goshgarian, G. M., 115
Gutman, Herbert, 89

Hampton Industrial School, 15
Harding, Rachel Leet Wilson (mother), 7–10, 109
Harding, Richard (father), 7–8
Harding, Wilson (brother), 9–10, 67
"Harmonists, The," 17–18, 20, 122, 127–33
Harmony, 56–57, 180–81
Harper, Frances, 78
Harpers New Monthly Magazine, 2, 203
Harris, Sharon, 34, 46, 58, 219–20, 227, 231, 235, 245n12, 262n32
Harris, Susan, 245n7, 247–48nn43, 248n18

Travel narratives, Davis's, 13–14, 191
Truettner, William, 183
Truth, Sojourner, 208
"Two Methods with the Negro," 14
"Two Points of View," 14
"Two Women," 207, 211–12
Typology of ethnicity, 152

Uncle Tom's Cabin (Stowe), 30, 32, 50, 91, 101, 143, 146, 160, 223
Underground Railroad, 77, 82, 144–45
Utopian communities: in "Berrytown," 216–19; role of women in, 13, 63–64, 67–68, 127–35

Venereal disease, of prostitutes, 110–13
Vernacular language, in Davis's writing, 21
Violence: in captivity narratives, 184–85; in "Put Out of the Way," 233–34
Vision, symbolism of, 41, 44, 49

Waiting for the Verdict, 14, 19, 137, 140–64, 210, 227, 263n46
War, opposition to, 15. *See also* "David Gaunt"; "Mean Face of War, The"; Pacifism
Warner, Susan, 29, 66, 70, 108, 122
Washington, Booker T., 14, 163–64
Weed, Charles Leander, 191
Welsh, stereotypes of, 36–37. *See also* Nativism
West, Benjamin, 184
West Virginia, creation of, 77
Wharton, Edith, 69
"What About the Northern Negro?," 158
Wheeling, West Virginia, 8–9, 77–78, 111–12. *See also* "Life in the Iron-Mills"
Wheeling Intelligencer, 5, 10, 109
Whipple, Charles, 89
Whiskey Ring, 235–38
White Slave, The (Hildreth), 146

Wide, Wide World (Warner), 29, 66, 70, 122
"Wife's Story, The," 11, 17, 20, 122, 124–27, 135
Williams, Patricia, 5
Wilson, Edmund, 76
Wilson, Harriet, 80, 207
Wollstonecraft, Mary, 6, 106–07, 110
Women, 12, 65–66, 95, 97, 201; ambivalence about, 7, 216; in captivity narratives, 184–88; and community, 37, 81, 83, 130–32, 134, 159, 174–75; and cross-dressing, 211, 213–14; Davis's relationships with, 109–10; endurance by, 51–52, 117, 184; as incomplete, 165–66; in indentured servitude, 135–37; and industrialism, 32–33, 208–09; and nature, 22–23, 179–82, 199–202; objectification of, 137–38, 178, 209–10, 237; as physicians, 229–31, 272n48; power of, 35–36, 177, 214; reformers, 102, 162–63; single, 38–39, 107, 118, 212. *See also* Bodies; Identity; Marriage; Motherhood; Public vs. private lives
Women and Economics (Gilman), 210
"Women in Literature," 3, 241n3
Women's rights movement, 118, 207, 212, 228–32; and Davis, 231–32, 239. *See also* Suffrage
Woolson, Constance Fenimore, 21
Work (L. M. Alcott), 127
"Work Before Us, The," 15
Work life, 33–34; of women, 206–39

"Yares of Black Mountain, The," 13, 22, 132, 189–204
Yellin, Jean Fagan, 55, 58, 163, 250n2, 261n9
"Yellow Wallpaper, The" (Gilman), 105, 121
Youth's Companion, 221

Zagarell, Sandra, 195
Zola, Émile, 34